HOW WOKE WON

THE ELITIST MOVEMENT THAT THREATENS
DEMOCRACY, TOLERANCE AND REASON

HOW WOKE WON

THE ELITIST MOVEMENT THAT THREATENS
DEMOCRACY, TOLERANCE AND REASON

JOANNA WILLIAMS

A catalogue record for this book is available from the British Library. Library of Congress Cataloguing-in-Publication data have been applied for.

ISBNs:
Paperback: 978-1-739841324
Ebook: 978-1-739841331

A *spiked* publication in partnership with John Wilkes Publishing

sp!ked

spiked-online.com

Requests to publish work from this book should be sent to the author.

Cover design: Alex Dale
Typesetting: Beyond Media Communications Limited
Printed and bound by CPI Group (UK) Limited, Croydon, CRO 4YY

About the author

Joanna Williams is a columnist at *spiked* and a frequent contributor to a range of publications including *The Times*, the *Spectator* and the *Telegraph*. After over a decade in academia, she left to set up her own think tank, Cieo, which provides a platform for research and debates that universities dare not touch. *How Woke Won* is Joanna's fourth book. Her previous work has explored academic freedom, feminism and higher education.

Photography: Rahil Ahmad

Praise for *How Woke Won*

'Joanna Williams has consistently and courageously spoken out against the woke fundamentalists attempting to reshape our society according to their own narrow and unrepresentative worldview. This book provides a searing assessment of how the West succumbed to such a pernicious ideology. It deserves the widest attention.'
– Paul Embery, author of *Despised*

'Joanna Williams has written a highly readable and gripping anatomy of the woke phenomenon which is poisoning our intellectual, social and political life. As she shows, it has gained a grip over many public institutions, from primary schools to universities, the civil service and cultural institutions. She tells the story of how this has happened, and explains why: because this ideology empowers the elite that runs a large part of our lives, and wants to run more. It's a worrying story of intimidation and moral blackmail. But she holds out the hope that woke's victory need not be permanent. In this brave and lucid book, she has done us a great service.'
– Robert Tombs, emeritus professor of French history, University of Cambridge, and author of *The English and Their History*

'Joanna Williams is one of Britain's sharpest and most eloquent writers on the "woke" phenomenon. In *How Woke Won*, she fearlessly and forensically exposes how the woke culture war has exploded into our schools, workplaces, media and politics – and why we need to fight back against this very real threat to our values and our freedoms.'
– Julia Hartley-Brewer, journalist and talkRADIO presenter

'How has it come to pass that gender ideology and critical race theory have become the dominant moral orthodoxies? *How Woke Won* is a thoughtful, lucid read that provides answers. If you've ever wondered why our cultural elites have been hoodwinked by something so conspicuously ideological that sows division among ordinary people, wonder no more. The answer lies within.'

– Peter Boghossian, author of *How to Have Impossible Conversations*

'Too often when people talk about the woke capture of our elite institutions they do so with an air of resignation, as if our only hope of reversing this process is to embark on a long march in the opposite direction. Not Joanna Williams. In this book, she argues convincingly that this authoritarian cult isn't as powerful as it seems and if the champions of liberal values band together it can be defeated.'

– Toby Young, founder and director of the Free Speech Union

'Williams has produced an awesome study that really digs deep into the woke phenomenon. After reading this book you will be left in no doubt about the corrosive and divisive impact of wokism on public life.'

– Frank Furedi, author and emeritus professor of sociology, University of Kent

'*How Woke Won* is an urgent reminder of how deep the trenches in the culture war are. It is an important pushback in the direction of genuinely progressive politics. Williams dissects woke thinking and in doing so puts ordinary people first. An incisive, brave and galvanising compendium on the culture war.'

– Laura Dodsworth, author of *A State of Fear*

'This is a thoughtful, well-measured and powerfully argued book on the phenomenon of "woke", exploring what it is and how it came to capture our institutions so completely that to even question its prevalence can be a career-threatening move.'
– Iain Dale, author and LBC radio presenter

'*How Woke Won* challenges the damaging, one-dimensional narrative that divides the world into victims and oppressors. As Joanna shows, being black doesn't make me a victim. Few people have hatred within them, making the terms of the current debate – as dictated by the new establishment – divisive and alienating. This book exposes the tactics and contradictions of an elitist minority trying to demonise the rest of us.'
– Dominique Samuels, political commentator, broadcaster and writer

'This brilliantly written and compelling book is as important as it is distressing. This is a must-read for anyone who values freedom and worries about the direction of Western society. I couldn't put it down. Grab a copy before it gets cancelled.'
– Mark Dolan, GB News presenter and stand-up comedian

'This book is the essential guide for our era of confusion and incoherence as moral revolutionaries tear down statues, institutions and widely held values. With clear thinking and gripping storytelling, Williams explains how a minority of the elites in Britain and America were able to intimidate the rest of the elites into silence or complicity, imposing a "revolution from above" that is anti-democratic and cruel. Anyone who wants to restore sanity, beauty or simple humanity to our public life should read *How Woke Won*.'
– Jonathan Haidt, Thomas Cooley professor of ethical leadership, New York University Stern School of Business, author of *The Righteous Mind*, co-author of *The Coddling of the American Mind*

Acknowledgements

Many people have helped make this book happen. Viv Regan, *spiked*'s managing editor, has encouraged me more than she can ever know. Not only did she conjure up a brilliant publishing company for me to work with, but she also gave me great feedback on my messy first drafts and kept me going when the task ahead seemed too onerous. Tom Slater has been the best editor any author could hope to work with. His commitment to the broader political project that lies behind this work, as well as his incredible eye for detail, helped shape the arguments, pinpoint examples and make the text coherent. His editorship of *spiked* inspires me on a daily basis. To all the team at *spiked* – thank you.

Likewise, I am grateful to Rob Lyons for his work on the mammoth task of sub-editing and fact-checking. I'm also thankful to Ben Cobley, Brendan O'Neill and Ellie Lee who generously provided commentary on early versions of this book. They all helped me work out what I wanted to say and why it needed saying. All the errors, of course, are mine alone.

David Green is the director of Civitas and the author of *We're (Nearly) All Victims Now!*. That book influenced my thinking in relation to victimhood culture and the pernicious influence of identity politics. I have enjoyed discussing these ideas with David and I will always be glad that he not only convinced me to write about race, gender and hate-crime laws for Civitas, but also then allowed me to draw extensively upon that work in this volume. Graham Child provided the initial impetus for me to trace the origins of woke and its influence on higher education.

Finally, this book is dedicated to Jim Butcher, my husband for the past 25 years. Without your continued support, encouragement and inspiration, none of this would have been possible.

Contents

Introduction – Woke Everywhere

Woke has conquered the West. From schools and universities to multi-national corporations, social media, journalism, and even the police and military, woke values dominate every aspect of our lives.

On Joe Biden's first day as US president he signed an Executive Order permitting boys who identify as girls to compete on female sports teams and enter female changing rooms. Statues of former presidents Abraham Lincoln and Theodore Roosevelt have been torn down by protesters amid claims the statues were racially demeaning.[1] Prince Harry, sixth in line to the British throne, regularly chastises the world's media for their alleged misogyny and racism. His wife, Meghan, loves to tell of how, as a child, she wrote to a washing-up liquid manufacturer to complain about sexist stereotyping in adverts.[2] In the UK, neither prime minister Boris Johnson nor Labour leader Sir Keir Starmer can say that only women have a cervix.[3]

Companies like Ben & Jerry's, Nike and L'Oréal have backed the Black Lives Matter movement. Premier League football players still routinely take the knee before matches kick off. Britain's most exclusive fee-paying schools have introduced gender-neutral school uniforms, while the famous St Paul's Girls' School in London has gone one better and abolished the title of 'head girl', following concerns that it was 'too binary'.[4] Two high-profile female journalists, Bari Weiss and Suzanne

Moore, publicly resigned from their posts in 2020 at the *New York Times* and the *Guardian* respectively, claiming they were bullied by colleagues for not expressing the correct views. The civil service, along with many other major employers, routinely offers training sessions informing staff that sex is on a spectrum.

Woke activists are obsessed with race and gender identity to the exclusion of almost all other issues. Woke describes a moral sensibility that insists upon putting people into identity boxes and then arranging the boxes into hierarchies of privilege and oppression, with some groups in need of 'uplifting' while others must beg atonement. To be woke is to speak of the importance of inclusion, diversity and equity, even if you are fabulously wealthy and have a lifestyle few can even imagine. Just like a previous era's 'political correctness', woke privileges performative displays and linguistic correctness above material change.

Woke values have been taken on board by the most powerful and influential sections of society and they have come to dominate our most important institutions. But defining woke is not straightforward. Woke may be ubiquitous, but it is also elusive. Few people describe themselves as woke. Few campaigners rally behind calls for people to be more woke. There are no political parties promising voters 'more woke'. Those who are most woke often deny they are any such thing. One reason they get away with this deception is because the meaning of woke has changed over time. Although it was originally used by progressives as a term of approval, woke has since come to describe hectoring, moral grandstanding and the anti-democratic imposition of rules and practices by a cultural elite that is remote from the concerns of most citizens.

Words and phrases like 'diversity', 'equity', 'inclusivity', 'gender neutral' and 'white privilege' signal the presence of woke values. Yet even here we have a problem. Some woke buzzwords, such as equality, have been stretched far beyond their original meaning, while others, like diversity and inclusivity, have become hollow vessels. But these words do point to a coming together of identity politics and victim culture that underpins the woke outlook. Woke might be difficult to pin down, but it is a useful concept. It allows us to describe the outlook that currently dominates our social, cultural and political lives.

Those who question woke values are considered 'problematic'. Those who transgress must be silenced. The sense of moral authority that comes from acting on behalf of groups thought to be oppressed legitimises vicious campaigns to drive people out of public life. Cancel culture describes woke's censorious approach to dissenters. Harry Potter author JK Rowling is a key target of the cancellers. For defending women's right to access single-sex spaces, she reports having received 'so many death threats I could paper the house with them'.[5] Bookshops, publishers and the stars of the Harry Potter film franchise have all sought to distance themselves from her. Professor Kathleen Stock faced a similar campaign of targeted abuse at the University of Sussex, all for expressing her belief that being a woman isn't simply an identity but a biological fact. Activists made her position at Sussex untenable.[6] It's not just women, either. Comedian Dave Chappelle has attracted the ire of trans activists, who picketed Netflix to urge it to withdraw his comedy specials.

Calling out celebrities who express views that rub up against woke orthodoxies is a favourite pastime of woke activists. Actress Lea Michele was recently taken to task by *Glee* co-star Samantha Ware for allegedly participating in 'traumatic microaggressions that made me question a career in Hollywood'. Michele lost an endorsement deal as a result.[7] Pop star Sia was called out for directing a film featuring a character with autism, but casting an actor without autism to play the part.[8] Former Little Mix star Jesy Nelson was accused of 'blackfishing' for using too much fake tan and 'appropriating' the style of black performers.[9]

Cancel culture is not about criticism and the exercise of free speech. It is not a call for debate, but a demand that transgressors be removed from social media and public life more broadly. This ruthless, censorious approach to anything that offends woke sensibilities extends to the past, with calls to remove statues and replace street names. It extends into all areas of culture, as episodes of once-popular television programmes or children's books are expunged from the public record. Yet when critics push back against this divisive and authoritarian regime, they are told there is nothing going on other than a valiant battle for social justice.

Woke has won. And yet the most vocal proponents of woke values deny that it even exists. The woke elite accuses critics of 'starting a culture war', despite the fact that those raising questions about changed policies and practices are often commenting after the event, on actions that have already been set in motion – it is their values that are being called into question. The gaslighting continues with claims that because so few people describe themselves as woke, and many have no idea what the word actually means, it does not really exist in any meaningful sense. Woke, the cultural elite tells us, is just a made-up, right-wing conspiracy theory. What they really mean is 'shut up'. Look the other way while we remove statues and clear books from library shelves without your permission. Don't ask questions when we teach your children that there are hundreds of different genders. Keep quiet about the person with a penis in the women's changing room.

In July 2021, the UK's Fabian Society became the latest in a long list of think tanks, university research centres and polling companies to claim that the notion of a culture war is based on 'confected outrage', with 'non-rows... amplified by opportunistic politicians and click-bait journalism'. A Fabian Society pamphlet warned that such controversies will push aside progress on 'unemployment, low pay, violence, poor housing, racism, discrimination against disabled people and the oppression of women and LGBT people', all because 'progressive movements and political parties' would become 'distracted, divided, demoralised and defeated by those pursuing a strategy around the so-called "culture wars"'.[10] While it is certainly true that most people are more concerned about making ends meet than they are the fate of statues, this does not mean they are happy for their values and traditions to be denigrated.

Denying the existence of a culture war makes challenging its impact all the more difficult – and the cultural elite knows this. Author Patrick Wright speaks on behalf of his class when he argues that 'the myth of a silenced English majority betrayed by a liberal metropolitan elite goes back decades'.[11] The assumption seems to be that eye-rolling combined with muttering 'same old, same old' will make the anti-woke masses disappear.

Arguing that the culture war is a right-wing plot to win votes has become a boilerplate response from woke's advocates. The UK's National Trust has perfected this approach perhaps more than any other organisation. Having been criticised for removing artefacts from display and highlighting historic properties' connections to slavery and colonialism, the National Trust has complained that it is facing an ideological campaign from a group it claims is trying to sow division.[12] Its own actions of late were, of course, entirely ideologically neutral and socially unifying.

This denialism speaks to two chinks in the armour of woke that should offer hope for a more democratic and positive future. Firstly, the existence of woke is denied on the basis that it is not a centrally coordinated plot, masterminded by an underground cadre of social-justice warriors. And this is true. There is no grand woke conspiracy, and suggesting there is one grants the cultural elite far more power than it actually possesses. Secondly, the denial of woke reveals the fundamental lack of confidence that woke's advocates have in the values they espouse. If the cultural elite was truly secure in its beliefs, it would not need to deny them all the time. Indeed, it would welcome public scrutiny, safe in the knowledge that its arguments would win out. Instead, woke activists continually fight shy of democracy.

The argument of this book is that even though today's cultural elite rejects the woke label, woke thinking has come to be accepted as common sense by the very same cultural elite. It is not difficult to understand why. Claiming to act on behalf of the oppressed allows wealthy people to morally justify their own privileged position. It permits them to rationalise the continued social inequalities from which they benefit. What's more, woke helps maintain elite rule by dividing the masses into more easily manageable groups.

Espousing a range of woke opinions allows a cultural elite to signal its own virtue and identify fellow travellers. Woke emboldens a cultural elite that lacks the legitimacy of mass appeal by providing it with a sense of purpose, giving directionless institutions a mission and justifying more direct forms of intervention into citizens' lives. Woke is how the professional-managerial class maintains its position.

Woke hijacks progressive rhetoric. But far from helping in the fight against discrimination, woke now provides the basis for contemporary forms of discrimination. Woke breathes new life into old forms of prejudice. Today, it is most likely to be trendy woke educators – not just teachers in schools and universities, but also workplace trainers and social-media activists – who order us to judge people by the colour of their skin, and tell us that women must give way to males who identify as women. There are many democratic, anti-racist and pro-equal-rights arguments for pushing back against woke. And we urgently need to push back if we want a genuinely progressive politics that puts ordinary people first.

This book begins by exploring the evolution of the word woke and tracing the development of a woke cultural elite. We then look more closely at schools and universities – institutions that have become intimately bound up in the project of socialising children and young adults, and which play a key role in transmitting woke values, as well as recruiting and training apprentice members of the cultural elite.

We go on to consider how the rise of woke values in policing and business serves the interests of the cultural elite. From here, we drill down into woke thinking on race and gender to explore where the cultural elite's ideas have emerged from and why they are so divisive. We end with a look at identity politics and the fetishisation of victimhood, two trends that underpin woke thought. In considering how best to push back against woke, I point to the one thing its proponents cannot abide: democratic scrutiny. Time and again, when woke ideas are put to the people in the form of surveys, referendums or elections, they are resoundingly rejected. My hope is that this book will help a few more people to understand and reject woke in favour of a more democratic and genuinely egalitarian future.

Endnotes

[1] 'Put these Biden fools in jail now': Furious Trump demands FBI find those responsible for pulling down statues of Abraham Lincoln and Teddy Roosevelt in Portland, *Daily Mail*, 12 October 2020

[2] Duke and Duchess of Sussex announce partnership with Procter & Gamble – a company she once called sexist, Sky News, 12 May 2021

[3] PM criticised for dodging cervix question, Politics.co.uk, 6 October 2021

[4] £26,000-a-year St Paul's Girls' School will no longer use the term 'head girl' because of its 'binary connotations', *Daily Mail*, 19 June 2021

[5] JK Rowling vows not to be silenced by trans activists after 'enough death threats to paper the house', *Sun*, 22 November 2021

[6] Kathleen Stock says she quit university post over 'medieval' ostracism, *Guardian*, 3 November 2021

[7] Lea Michele dropped from Hello Fresh deal over Samantha Ware allegations: 'We don't condone racism', *Independent*, 3 June 2020

[8] Sia says sorry to autism community for controversial film *Music*, BBC News, 4 February 2021

[9] What is blackfishing and why has Jesy Nelson been accused of it?, *Independent*, 14 October 2021

[10] *Counter Culture: How to resist the culture wars and build 21st century solidarity*, Fabian Society, July 2021

[11] 'The woke' are just the latest faux enemies of Englishness conjured up by the right, Patrick Wright, *Guardian*, 30 September 2021

[12] National Trust warns of threat from 'ideological campaign' waged against it, *Guardian*, 13 October 2021

1   A Brief History of Woke

The word 'woke' captures something in our political and cultural zeit-geist. It might be ubiquitous, but there's little consensus about what woke actually means. Even those who agree with woke values in general can't quite decide whether or not woke is a good thing to be. One day, being woke is so important that people are given instruction on 'be-coming woke in the wake of "Me Too"'[1] or are provided with 'The woke black person's guide to talking about oppression with family'.[2] Teachers are offered advice on 'keeping your classroom woke'[3] and the *Guardian* gives readers dating tips on how to find 'Mr Woke'.[4] Being woke is pro-gressive and fun!

But when critics pick up on this self-descriptor of choice, everything changes. US congresswoman Alexandria Ocasio-Cortez complains: '"Woke" is a term pundits are now using as a derogatory euphemism for civil rights and justice.'[5] 'Woke was kidnapped and has died', mourns author Rebecca Solnit. 'Woke's youth was among young black people but its illness and decline came after it was kidnapped by old white conservatives', she explains.[6]

Even as the complaints roll in, woke holds progressives in its grip. Charlie Higson, author of the Young Bond novels, swoons over Bond star Daniel Craig for his portrayal of a spy who is less Lothario and more woke. Craig's 007 is 'tender, cries and gets into the shower in his tuxedo to comfort a woman', gushes Higson.[7] Australian children's music group the Wiggles are praised for 'going woke' in their bid to 'better represent today's Australia', across age, race and culture, 'enabling children worldwide to see themselves reflected on the screen'.[8] A top headteacher bemoans the fact that calling young people 'woke' is offensive and might sap their appetite for activism.[9]

What all this boils down to is that those who are thoroughly imbued with woke ideas believe 'woke' is good if they say it, but bad if their critics say it. Those who are labelled woke deny being anything of the sort, but almost everyone can readily identify a set of woke concerns and values. And so despite few people claiming to be woke, woke values dominate our institutions. In this chapter, we will trace the ever-changing meanings of woke and consider why woke's leading proponents reject the label others attach to them.[10]

What is 'woke'?

To be 'woke' is to be awake; literally, not asleep. The Old English roots of 'awake' lie in both 'arise' and 'revive', and this has long prompted metaphorical usage. Spring awakens nature, passion can be awakened, and people become awake to new knowledge. Back in the early decades of the 20th century, this figurative meaning began to be applied to politics. Specifically, it came to mean politically awake and alert to racial discrimination and social injustice.

In 1923, a book which collected the aphorisms and ideas of Jamaican-born philosopher, black nationalist and political activist Marcus Garvey included the rallying cry 'Wake up Ethiopia! Wake up Africa!' as a 'call to global black citizens to become more socially and politically conscious', according to one article on the history of 'wokeness'.[11] This was taken up by black communities in the US.

In 1938, the phrase 'stay woke' was used by blues musician

Huddie Ledbetter, better known as Lead Belly, in a spoken afterword to the song 'Scottsboro Boys'. This was a protest song describing an incident from 1931 in which nine black teenagers from Scottsboro, Arkansas were accused of raping two white women. Lead Belly says: 'So I advise everybody, be a little careful when they go along through there – best stay woke, keep their eyes open.'[12] This spoke not just to the existence of racial injustice, but also to a more specific need among black people at that time: to stay alert to threats and dangers from white people in general and from the state in particular. 'Stay woke' reminded black people that they needed to be vigilant against the threat of racist violence.

By the mid-20th century in America, 'woke' was still used almost exclusively by members of the African-American population, but two meanings ran in parallel: be vigilant for potential threats from powerful whites and also be 'aware' or 'well informed' about political injustices in general. Both meanings were used in black dialect and were brought to the attention of the wider American public with a 1962 *New York Times* article by African-American novelist William Melvin Kelley. In 'If you're woke, you dig it', Kelley described the appropriation of black slang by white beatniks.[13] Decades later, 'woke' itself came to be appropriated by white hipsters, at the very same time that exposing and condemning the appropriation of black culture came to be a woke action.

Three years after Kelley's article was published, Martin Luther King, addressing crowds at the end of the 1965 civil-rights march from Selma to Montgomery, recalled an older meaning of 'woke' when he described the origins of racial segregation as emerging from opposition to the Populist Party of the 1890s. According to King, the white elite sought to challenge nascent populism because 'the leaders of this movement began awakening the poor white masses and the former negro slaves to the fact that they were being fleeced by the emerging Bourbon interests'.[14] *Garvey Lives!*, a 1972 play by Barry Beckham, features a character who says he'll 'stay woke' thanks to the work of Marcus Garvey: 'I been sleeping all my life. And now that Mr Garvey done woke me up, I'm gon' stay woke. And I'm gon' help him wake up other black folk.'[15]

Woke in the 21st century

Several decades passed before 'woke' exploded into popular usage. In 2005, singer Georgia Anne Muldrow wrote a song called 'Master Teacher' that featured the refrain 'I'd stay woke'. It was written for an album called *Black Fuzz*, by Sa-Ra Creative Partners, although neither the song nor the album was ever actually released. However, Muldrow's track was picked up by another singer, Erykah Badu, who released an updated version in 2008 on her album *New Amerykah Part One (4th World War)*.[16]

In 2014, protests broke out in Ferguson, Missouri following the police killing of Michael Brown. Activists rallied around the slogan Black Lives Matter. The phrase 'stay woke', popularised by Badu, quickly became associated with the Black Lives Matter movement through the sharing of the hashtag #StayWoke online. This was a call back to the 1930s warning to black people to stay alert to the threat of racist police brutality, but it rapidly expanded to encompass the broader sense of being aware of all forms of social injustice.

2016 was the year that being woke – and, importantly, letting people know that you are woke – became fashionable. Online magazines carried lists of the 'young and woke' featuring 'celebrities who lead by example'.[17] They profiled '15 Sexy Celebs Who Get Even Hotter Once You Realise How Woke They Are'[18] and gave us 'The Ultimate Guide to Woke Celebrity Bros'.[19] Praise was heaped upon public figures who made a display of being anti-racist, feminist, queer or gender nonconforming. Twitter CEO Jack Dorsey took to the stage at a major conference in June

2016 wearing a t-shirt emblazoned with '#StayWoke'. Back then, to be woke was cool and aspirational.

By the following year, 'woke' had become so mainstream that the *Oxford English Dictionary* listed it as one of its new words of note.[20] The definition reads: 'Originally: well-informed, up-to-date. Now chiefly: alert to racial or social discrimination and injustice.'[21] The online Urban Dictionary of street slang had defined 'woke' two years earlier as 'being aware... knowing what's going on in the community (related to racism and social injustice)'.[22]

Anti-woke

As foreshadowed by Kelley back in 1962, the word 'woke' has emerged into mainstream white culture. This has led some to decry the fact that, 'like anything created by black people', the word has been 'appropriated by the masses'.[23] As Dorsey's t-shirt demonstrated, by 2016 'woke' had become popularised, commercialised and even memeified. Perhaps unsurprisingly, by 2018, as woke entered everyday speech, the association of woke with superficial displays of moral superiority had also become firmly entrenched in the public imagination.

In turn, this backlash against woke prompted its own response. First came denial. 'Woke' was hastily dropped by the very same celebrities and commentators who had rushed to identify with the word just months earlier. By 2018, Urban Dictionary had a new definition: 'The act of being very pretentious about how much you care about a social issue.'[24] Some went so far as to suggest that woke had only ever been used by the right as an insult directed at all things progressive. Writing in the *Guardian* in 2019, Afua Hirsch claimed that anyone using the word is 'likely to be a right-wing culture warrior angry at a phenomenon that lives mainly in their imagination.'[25] Today's woke activists like to call out 'gaslighting' – that is, lying to make people doubt their own sanity. But gaslighting is not, it seems, something they are averse to practising themselves. After denial came reinvention. Those who persisted in mocking woke were directed to the word's more neutral definition of 'awareness' and accused of being insensitive to racist, sexist and transphobic discrimination. To add to the insult, another *Guardian* writer, Steve Rose, accused critics of woke of seeking 'victim status' for themselves, 'rather than acknowledging that more deserving others hold that status'.[26]

Attempts to reclaim the word 'woke' by so-called progressives have been largely unsuccessful and woke is today primarily used critically. As Evan Smith, also in the *Guardian*, writes: 'Rarely a week passes without a right-wing commentator warning about the rise of "cancel culture" or decrying the "woke agenda"'.[27] But these critics-of-the-critics miss the point. Opposing woke does not automatically make people right-wing. Opposing woke does not mean promoting racism, sexism, homophobia or other forms of bigotry and discrimination. Those pushing back against the rise of woke today are most often echoing views that were, not that long ago, considered radically progressive. They are concerned about a divisive shift in left-wing politics that risks pitching groups against each other according to race, gender and sexuality. Many of woke's critics are concerned about a growing hostility to the liberal principles of free speech, tolerance, civil rights and democracy. They are concerned about the inflationary rhetoric that brands those not completely on board with woke thinking 'homophobes', 'transphobes' or 'fascists'. As comedian and author Andrew Doyle explains, 'critics of "wokeness" are trying to resist bigotry rather than uphold it'.[28]

But while the cultural elite has rejected the label of woke, the values associated with being woke are more influential than ever. They have moved from the fringes of political life to the mainstream and now influence the actions of public institutions, national governments and private businesses. In the process, the meaning of these values has morphed and stretched. Some, such as 'diversity', have always been vacuous concepts, while others, such as inclusion, have been so expanded beyond their original application as to be rendered hollow.

The values promoted by woke are today most associated with an emergent elite that is socially and geographically mobile, highly educated and social-media savvy. Woke may not be this elite's self-descriptor of choice, but woke ideas underpin establishment decision-making and corporate mission statements. 'Woke' refers to the side in the culture war that denies it is waging a culture war, yet which repeatedly fires the opening salvos.

From radical to mainstream

The elastic definition of woke has allowed it to shift from aspirational to insulting and back again, while its key values have quietly gained ground. Woke campaigns often thrive by saying one thing but meaning another. No right-minded person doubts that black lives matter. However, many strenuously disagree with the specific political goals of Black Lives Matter (BLM), the political campaign group. BLM's success hinges on the organisation and the sentiment of the slogan becoming blurred. Rhetorical slippage between the general and the particular is exploited. This has created a fair bit of confusion. When Boris Johnson was asked by an interviewer if he thought Joe Biden was 'woke', Johnson felt the need to say that 'there's nothing wrong with being woke'. This is despite the fact that, on other occasions, his Conservative government has presented itself as critical of woke values.[29] When the penalty for challenging movements such as Black Lives Matter may be career-ending accusations of racism, it is understandable that people nod through the elisions.

The word 'woke' is similarly slippery. Activists may announce that being woke simply means being alert to social injustice. But, in practice, woke has come to mean far more than just awareness. It means adopting a particular outlook, but one that is also constantly changing. Author Shon Faye caveats *The Transgender Issue* with the acknowledgement that 'my terminology may seem dated in a few years' time'.[30] It is easy to cast this obsession with language as simply performative or harking back to an earlier era of political correctness. But woke is much worse than that. As we will explore in more detail in Chapter 10, woke is fundamentally at odds with older principles of civil rights and human rights. The implementation of woke ideas almost always has authoritarian consequences.

In many respects, Black Lives Matter perfectly epitomises woke. It is not enough for people to be aware of racial injustice – 'silence is violence', comes the retort. Nor is it enough for people not to be racist – they must, in the words of Ibram X Kendi, be actively anti-racist.[31] This means conforming to a quite specific set of views that fall under the rough heading of critical race theory. This means seeing people as racialised beings who passively enact deeply rooted unconscious biases. It means viewing society as systemically and irredeemably racist, an inevitable result of deeply entrenched white privilege, demonstrated through the microaggressions white people constantly inflict upon black folk. What's more, it means expressing these sentiments using a specific vocabulary, familiar only to true anti-racists: 'people of colour', 'Latinx', 'BIPOC'. One must police the language and behaviour of others, calling out not just those who are racist, but also those who hold the wrong form of opposition to racism. (We consider woke anti-racism more fully in Chapter Eight.)

To be woke, then, is less about identifying with a label and more about holding a particular set of values and adopting a particular stance – one that appears radically egalitarian but often runs entirely counter to previous movements for equality. To be woke is to see gender as multiple and fluid and to employ a complex vocabulary that begins with transgender and cisgender and branches out into nonbinary, agender, pangender, genderqueer, demigirl, and so on. Yet to be woke is also to believe that demonstrating masculine behaviour makes someone a man (whatever their sex), while to be a woman is to look and to act feminine.

Woke values aim to promote social justice through the foregrounding of identity politics. This entails categorising people according to immutable characteristics such as race or sex, before dividing and ranking them according to assumed hierarchies of oppression. A therapeutic ethos presents emotional safety and financial precarity as intrinsically linked; it assumes that people who are either traumatised or subjected to discrimination cannot compete as equals in the workplace. Shon Faye writes: 'To be trans is an experience bound up with economic struggle.'[32] In this way, Faye and other woke activists redefine social class. There is a world of difference between someone with connections, wealth and education falling upon hard times and the structural, generational and geographical disadvantages that working-class people routinely encounter.

All too often, the sense of virtue that comes from claiming to act on behalf of the disadvantaged and oppressed legitimises a refusal to countenance dissent – and a ruthlessness at dealing with those seemingly in opposition to the woke mission. Those deemed 'enemies' are readily written off. Philosopher and gender theorist Judith Butler argues that 'anti-gender movements are not just reactionary but fascist trends'.[33] Left-wing commentator Owen Jones says that 'the aftershocks of the 2008 financial crash had… many impacts. One was the global growth of the far right, who typically blamed Muslims, migrants, refugees and other oppressed and marginalised minorities for growing social trauma.'[34] Such hyperbole not only trivialises fascism and insults ordinary voters – it also legitimises an authoritarianism that belies the mantra #BeKind. As Professor Kathleen Stock discovered to her cost, when the backlash against her gender-critical views made her position at the University of Sussex untenable, censorship, cancelling, harassment, abuse and even death threats are all apparently justified if they are carried out in order to stem a perceived 'fascist' threat.[35]

Social-media platforms have undoubtedly played a part in accelerating the spread and attraction of woke ideas. Left-wing academics and activists have long expressed concern that the algorithms employed by YouTube and Facebook direct people to content they are already predisposed to agree with, and may even direct users towards ever-more extreme content in a bid to keep them on a particular site. In the aftermath of Donald Trump's 2016 presidential victory, there was also concern that Facebook and Twitter allowed people to create communities of the likeminded: social-media bubbles that confirmed participants' views and allowed more extreme opinions to flourish unchecked. But if these criticisms hold true of right-wing voters, they are also true of left-wing activists. Woke ideas flourish when virtue can be displayed at the click of a mouse. Woke one-upmanship leads to 'purity spirals', defined as 'vicious cycles of accusation and judgement' that lead to individuals deemed 'problematic' being targeted.[36] The impact of this on individuals can be devastating. But perhaps of more concern is the impact on debate: free speech is chilled and intellectual conformity is enforced when people fear saying what they truly think.

Twitter, in particular, has given birth to a lazy form of journalism that revolves around rehashing social-media commentary and presenting it up for public consumption in the form of articles. This practice means that the views of Twitter users are overrepresented in national debates and their ideas take on the appearance of a consensus. But Twitter users are not representative of the population. One academic study has suggested that 'Twitter and Facebook users differ substantially from the general population on many politically relevant dimensions including vote choice, turnout, age, gender, education and region'. It adds that 'Twitter users [are] a minority of every age group'.[37]

Woke values now extend far into established social and cultural institutions. This has happened not because of the strength of woke ideas, but because institutions have long since abandoned their founding principles. Schools, universities, museums and the media are no longer driven by an imperative to impart knowledge, to pursue truth, to preserve the past or to cultivate beauty. These important values were problematised and rejected a long time ago. Woke ideas have, far more recently, provided those in charge of national institutions with a new sense of purpose.

The importance of language

Language plays an important role in demarcating the woke from the non-woke. Knowing to say 'people of colour' rather than 'coloured people', 'transgender' rather than 'transsexual', 'Latinx' rather than 'Hispanic', and 'sex assigned at birth' rather than simply 'male' or 'female', serves to differentiate people who are woke from those who are not. This acts much the same way that saying lavatory or toilet, napkin or serviette, sofa or settee, signified social class in decades past. As we will explore more fully in Chapter Four, a key role of schools and universities today is inducting students into this woke language and its associated ideas, either through immersion or through formal training, in the form of mandatory anti-racism workshops or consent classes. In turn, young graduates carry this outlook with them into the workplace. The more woke language and principles are adopted by a social and cultural elite, the more they are assumed to be mainstream, and the more those who use outdated terminology stand out.

The obsessive focus on language leaves advocates of woke politics open to the accusation that their project is superficial and performative, rather than concerned with bringing about material changes to the quality of people's lives. For example, rather than campaigning for all parents to have access to free childcare for young children, woke activists focus on encouraging teachers to use gender-neutral language in nursery schools. It is easy to mock this as a bizarre attempt to bring political correctness to even the very youngest children at the expense of more important economic matters. But this misses the fundamentally corrosive impact of woke ideas. Attempts at imposing woke values upon children risk setting the generations at odds with each other as parents, and especially grandparents, may experience this as a direct attack upon their own way of life. In this way, woke educators – whether they realise it or not – end up challenging traditional family values in their bid to socialise children into what they assume to be a superior set of values. The woke project, then, is not a distraction from cost-of-living concerns, but another form of attack on the working class.

Woke politics

The woke outlook is fundamentally elitist. At its heart lies an assumption that some are too ignorant and others too vulnerable to be allowed to control their own lives and shape their nation. Woke reveals itself to be anti-democratic and censorious when policies aimed at curtailing debate are enacted, either by private social-media companies or national governments. When GB News – an alternative television-news station – launched in the UK in 2021, woke culture warriors immediately began a campaign to get advertisers to withdraw from the channel. They saw the prospect of anti-woke discussion as so dangerous that it had to be nipped in the bud.

This resort to censorship stems in part from insecurity. Woke ideas, in all their forms, are rejected by the bulk of the population. Whether it is falling viewing figures for woke awards ceremonies or the rejection of overtly woke political candidates in elections, time and again, when given the choice, the public reject woke. More and more people in politics are beginning to notice. Democratic political consultant James Carville has criticised the language used by leading Democrats in the US:

> You ever get the sense that people in faculty lounges in fancy colleges use a different language than ordinary people? They come up with a word like 'Latinx' that no one else uses. Or they use a phrase like 'communities of colour'. I don't know anyone who speaks like that. I don't know anyone who lives in a 'community of colour'. I know lots of white and black and brown people and they all live in... neighbourhoods.[38]

Carville makes an important point about woke language: it is convoluted, indecipherable and alienating. This reflects the woke assumption that people are either oppressors or oppressed, victims or perpetrators, and that liberating people from this predicament requires us to alter the very building blocks of language and thought.

Following the electoral collapse of the UK Labour Party in the Hartlepool by-election in 2021, Labour MP Khalid Mahmood quit Keir Starmer's frontbench, arguing that the party had lost touch with working-class voters and become more concerned with the interests of 'woke social-media warriors':

> They mean well, of course, but their politics – obsessed with identity, division and even tech utopianism – have more in common with those of Californian high society than the kind of people who voted in Hartlepool yesterday. The loudest voices in the Labour movement over the past year in particular have focused more on pulling down Churchill's statue than they have on helping people pull themselves up in the world.[39]

Here Mahmood goes beyond the usual criticism of woke as simply performative. He taps into a deeper vein of criticism that the Conservative Party, under Boris Johnson, has also begun to mine. There is a growing sense that people in more disadvantaged, less influential communities are angry at being treated as if they are in need of re-education and having their culture, heritage and values continually subjected to criticism.

Even though some in the political arena are becoming increasingly aware of woke's unpopularity, it will take more than a few voices speaking up to loosen woke's grip. Woke thinking has become the central driving force behind many state and private-sector institutions. As we explore in the next few chapters, the cultural elite – made up of those who produce books, films, art and fashion, report and comment on the news, and run universities – is thoroughly woke. This means that national governments only have limited scope to push back against this elite agenda.

Few self-identify as woke. No political party stands on a self-declared woke manifesto. Yet, over the course of several decades, a particular set of values has become embedded within our institutions, government and businesses. This movement resists a label and has few self-identified advocates. Still, its proponents are easy enough to spot. They insist on purity. They cast out those who might be sympathetic to their cause but are not au fait with the latest woke vocabulary, at the very same time as they refuse to engage in debate. Woke's advocates are critical of older arguments for equality. And, by focusing on identity, they overlook material concerns and see working-class people as requiring re-education. Woke is intolerant of national pride and is particularly scathing of national heritage and tradition. It is also anti-democratic – woke activists try to impose change from the top down, while denying that woke even exists.

The word 'woke' names one side of the culture war. And having named it, we can identify, expose and criticise it. That is the aim of the rest of this book.

Endnotes

[1] Becoming woke in the wake of 'Me Too'; everyday sexism, Adrienne Seal, Spirit Tree Consulting, 12 November 2019

[2] The Woke Black Person's Guide to Talking About Oppression with Family, Maisha Z Johnson, *Everyday Feminism*, 21 February 2016

[3] Keeping your classroom woke, Metro.us, 4 December 2017

[4] My search for Mr Woke: a dating diary, Kimberly McIntosh, *Guardian*, 11 August 2018

[5] Alexandria Ocasio-Cortez, Twitter, 8 November 2021

[6] We need to discuss the word 'woke', various authors, *Guardian*, 9 November 2021

[7] Daniel Craig 'is a woke 007' says Young James Bond author – 'Ian Fleming not total dinosaur', *Express*, 21 September 2021

[8] The Wiggles going 'woke' is a win-win: more role models for us, a bigger market for them, Kiran Gupta, *Guardian*, 25 August 2021

[9] Don't call young people 'woke', says leading head teacher, BBC News, 22 November 2021

[10] This chapter draws on an essay previously published by Cieo on 11 May 2021, entitled 'How woke conquered the world and why this is a problem'. It is reproduced here with permission

[11] A history of 'wokeness', Aja Romano, *Vox*, 9 October 2020

[12] A history of 'wokeness', Aja Romano, *Vox*, 9 October 2020

[13] If You're Woke You Dig It; No mickey mouse can be expected to follow today's Negro idiom without a hip assist, William Melvin Kelley, *New York Times*, 20 May 1962

[14] Our God is Marching On!, Martin Luther King Jr Research and Education Institute, 25 March 1965

[15] What does 'woke' mean? Origins of the term, and how the meaning has changed, Benjamin Butterworth, *i*, 26 June 2021

[16] The Origin of Woke: How Erykah Badu and Georgia Anne Muldrow sparked the 'Stay Woke' era, Elijah C Watson, Okayplayer, 27 February 2018

[17] Young and Woke under 30: 12 celebrity women who lead by example, Christina Coleman, *Essence*, updated 26 October 2020

[18] 15 Sexy Celebs Who Get Even Hotter Once You Realise How Woke They Are, Marquaysa Battle, *Elite Daily*, 7 April 2017

[19] The Ultimate Guide to Woke Celebrity Bros, Zing Tsjeng, *Vice*, 4 May 2016

[20] New words notes, June 2017, *Oxford English Dictionary*

[21] The Oxford English Dictionary Just Added 'Woke'. It's Older Than You Might Think, *Time*, 25 June 2017

[22] What does 'woke' mean? Origins of the term, and how the meaning has changed, Benjamin Butterworth, *i*, 26 June 2021

[23] The Origin of Woke: How Erykah Badu and Georgia Anne Muldrow sparked the 'Stay Woke' era, Elijah C Watson, Okayplayer, 27 February 2018

[24] Suggested by Vensamos, Urban Dictionary, 16 May 2018

[25] The struggle for equality is real. The 'woke police' are a myth, Afua Hirsch, *Guardian*, 26 September 2019

[26] How the word 'woke' was weaponised by the right, Steve Rose, *Guardian*, 21 January 2020

[27] The Conservatives have been waging their 'war on woke' for decades, Evan Smith, *Guardian*, 21 April 2021

[28] The trouble with 'woke', Andrew Doyle, *spiked*, 11 February 2021

[29] Is Joe Biden 'woke'? Meaning of the term after Boris Johnson says there's 'nothing wrong with it', Alex Finnis, *i*, 21 January 2021

[30] *The Transgender Issue: An Argument for Justice*, Shon Faye, Penguin (2021)

[31] *How to Be an Antiracist*, Ibram X Kendi, Bodley Head (2019)

[32] *The Transgender Issue: An Argument for Justice*, Shon Faye, Penguin (2021)

[33] Why is the idea of 'gender' provoking backlash the world over?, Judith Butler, *Guardian*, 23 October 2021

[34] *This Land: The Struggle for the Left*, Owen Jones, Penguin (2020)

[35] Kathleen Stock says she quit university post over 'medieval' ostracism, *Guardian*, 3 November 2021

[36] The Purity Spiral, BBC Radio 4, 11 February 2020

[37] Twitter and Facebook are Not Representative of the General Population: Political Attitudes and Demographics of Social Media Users, Jonathan Mellon and Christopher Prosser, *SSRN Electronic Journal*, January 2016

[38] 'Wokeness is a problem and we all know it', Sean Illing, *Vox*, 27 April 2021

[39] Labour MP Khalid Mahmood quits Keir Starmer's frontbench, warning party taken over by 'woke social-media warriors', *Independent*, 7 May 2021

2 Culture Wars

Culture, in all its forms, is contested. But talk of cancel culture, culture wars and cultural appropriation points to the disputes over values and battles for identity that play out not just in relation to film, music, art and literature, but also in mundane aspects of our lives: the everyday decisions we make about what to eat, how to dress, where to go on holiday or how to bring up our children. When these decisions get swept up in public debates about how we should live, they stop being purely personal matters and become political statements. They become part of a battle for competing values.

The term 'culture war' was popularised by American sociologist James Davison Hunter. In his 1991 book, *Culture Wars: The Struggle to Define America,* Hunter writes about battles over the family, art, education, law and politics. He points to the emergence of two distinct groups, which he labels the progressives and the orthodox. He argues that, for progressives, political authority stems from a morality that is fluid and context-dependent, whereas for the orthodox moral authority remains absolute, despite changing social and economic circumstances.[1]

The significance of Hunter's insight lies less in the labels he comes up with and more in his understanding that political struggles can play out as cultural struggles, in which there is 'a heightened awareness of culture itself and those who seek to shape it'.[2] In this way, the term 'culture war' comes to encapsulate a sense of conflict between two irreconcilable views on what is 'fundamentally right and wrong about the world we live in'. For our purposes, these 'irreconcilable worldviews' are best understood not as character traits, but as distinct political outlooks that have, over time, come to be associated with social-class positions. What has become known as the culture war is the playing out of the elite's assumption that its values are superior and should be adopted by the rest of society. In this chapter, we look at what is meant by culture and what happens when it gets caught up in a weight of disputes it was never intended to carry.

What is culture?

Culture is notoriously difficult to define. Raymond Williams, the British cultural critic, famously described 'culture' as being 'one of the two or three most complicated words in the English language'.[3] In his 1976 book, *Keywords*, Williams pointed out that the word 'culture' comes from 'cultivation' in relation to animals or crops. He noted that from the 18th century onwards culture began to be associated with people and the cultivation of morality. In this way, culture came to be understood as a process (cultivating) as well as particular outcomes or products. This dual meaning still exists today. Works of art, music or literature are cultural products, but culture also refers to the social, economic, moral and political circumstances that create the conditions in which particular artefacts are produced and in which we all live.

Since the 18th century, two further shifts in the meaning of the word 'culture' have occurred. We distinguish between 'high' culture and 'low' or 'mass' culture, with opera, classical music and works of literature pitched against pop music, television game shows and popular fiction. Until a few decades ago, high culture was more firmly associated with the tastes of the upper class. More recently, this has fundamentally shifted and today's elite not only distances itself from high culture, but also denigrates these artistic achievements as elitist and exclusive, tainted by their association with dead white males. Today's elite cannot rely on culture alone, but must find other, more subtle means of distinguishing itself from the rest of society.

Alongside this separation between high and mass culture, people also began talking of cultures, in the plural, and challenged the idea that a nation has one collective, unifying culture. Williams referred to the 'specific and variable cultures of social and economic groups within a nation'. Today, we talk of 'black culture' and 'working-class culture'. Linked to this is the way we now use the word 'community' to identify not those who live in the same neighbourhood, but those who share an identity – for example, 'the gay community' or 'the transgender community'. This comes with the suggestion that every community has its own culture that others must respect.

Williams suggested that, by the 20th century, culture had come to be defined in three broad ways:

- *a general process of intellectual, spiritual and aesthetic development;*
- *a particular way of life, whether of a people, a period, a group or humanity in general;*
- *the works and practices of intellectual and especially artistic activity.*[4]

When we talk about culture in this book, we are using all three of these definitions. As we will explore in this chapter, woke ideas shape 'works and practices of intellectual and especially artistic activity', but they also shape our attitudes towards daily life. When we view trends developing over time, we come to see them as reflecting the social and political context from which they emerged. As Williams suggested, this broader context is not distinct from culture, but rather is a fundamental part of it: culture also describes a 'particular way of life, whether of a people, a period, a group or humanity in general'.

Woke is a useful way of making sense of the culture that surrounds us today. Whether individuals agree with them or not, woke ideas have permeated every part of our society, shaping what we get to watch on television, at the theatre and at the cinema, as well as the adverts we see, the news we read, the way we interact with our friends on social media and with our colleagues at work. As this book explores, woke thinking now shapes the education of our children, the universities that train graduates for the workplace, the justice system that polices our behaviour and the businesses we shop at.

In all these different areas of our daily lives, we now swim in a woke culture. Those who share woke values are people who think that a person's gendered or racialised identity is the most important thing about them, who think diversity is an end in itself, who think the past is a source of shame, who think words can wound and should be carefully regulated. Then there are those who continue to see merit in an older set of values. Those who think social class is more likely to determine life chances than skin colour, who think being a woman means having a female body and is not a state of mind, who think equality before the law is fairer than special treatment for some, and who think free speech is more important than politically correct speech. Members of this latter group find themselves increasingly alienated from today's society.

The racialisation of culture

From *Hamilton* to *The Personal History of David Copperfield*, from *Harlots* to *Bridgerton*, films, plays and TV shows have embraced colour-blind casting in recent years. It no longer surprises us to see black actors cast as white characters or historical figures. When you truly lose yourself in a story or spectacle, trivial details like an actor's skin colour become irrelevant. Rosalind Eleazar, star of *Copperfield*, agrees. 'Most films, TV shows or plays are about things like the human condition and suffering. If that is the base level, then why on earth are we so reticent to cast people that have a different skin colour?', she said to the *Guardian* in 2020. Adaptations like *Copperfield*, Eleazar explained, can employ colour-blind casting because 'it is a story about the privileged and the poor and the wealth between them. And, most importantly, it's fictional.'[5] Imagination and empathy are at the heart of both fiction and acting. We forget the identity of the skilled actor or author and focus instead on the character being portrayed.

But woke culture is complicated. For a start, colour-blind casting is permitted in one direction only. Black and Asian actors must not be barred from any role, no matter how historically inaccurate this may render a production. Yet white actors can never be cast as people of colour or of mixed heritage – even when they might otherwise be considered the best actor for the part. In 2017, Scarlett Johansson found herself at the heart of a controversy over her role in *Ghost in the Shell*, a film adapted from a Japanese comic series and animated film. Johansson played Motoko Kusanagi, a woman turned cyborg, but critics argued this part should have gone to a Japanese actress.[6] Such policing of racial boundaries is not new. Decades earlier, a Broadway production of *Miss Saigon* was subject to protests over white actor Jonathan Pryce being cast as a half-Vietnamese / half-French character.[7] The argument is that given there are fewer opportunities for minority actors, the minority roles that are available should be their preserve.

Arts journalist Diep Tran argues that this form of colour-blind casting 'negates the very real structural hindrances that block actors of colour from the same opportunities as white actors – like low pay in the theatre industry, a lack of roles that are ethnically specific that actors of colour can play, and unconscious bias on the part of white theatres and casting directors'.[8] Negating 'structural hindrances' might seem like a good way to make the acting profession more diverse. But activists want colour-blind casting dropped in favour of 'colour-conscious casting'. Rather than roles being allocated to the most talented actors, irrespective of skin colour, producers and directors must foreground race when allocating roles and use casting to challenge stereotypes and prompt debates about racism. This moves drama away from the intentions of its authors. Rather than exploring 'the human condition', culture comes to revolve around just one issue: racism.

The obsessive focus on race means drama can never simply be enjoyed. Lin-Manuel Miranda went from being praised for his colour-blind musical, *Hamilton,* to being criticised for 'blackwashing' the story of America's Founding Fathers. The 2021 film adaptation of his first Broadway musical, *In the Heights*, was accused of 'colourism' for casting light-skinned rather than dark-skinned 'Afro Latinx' lead actors.[9] The BBC serialisation of Sally Rooney's novel, *Normal People*, may have been wildly popular, but it was criticised for using colour-blind casting and having black or Asian actors play complex antiheroes. Critics seem to think that actors of colour should be allowed to play any role they like, as long as the character demonstrates positive attributes and their portrayal generates productive conversations about race. White actors, meanwhile, must stick to playing white characters and baddies. This racial policing patronises people of colour and degrades drama as an art form. We are taught to see actors as, first and foremost, representatives of their racial groups.

Stay in your lane

Similar questions have been asked in relation to gender. In 2018, Scarlett Johansson found herself at the heart of another controversy. She had been cast for the lead role in *Rub & Tug*, a film based on the true story of a transgender massage-parlour entrepreneur who clashed with the Philadelphia mob. Johansson was criticised by transgender activists and actors for taking a role that, they suggested, should have gone to a transgender man. They argued that having cisgender people play transgender characters took limited opportunities away from minority communities. Johansson pulled out of the film and the entire project was postponed, though at the time of writing it seems to be in redevelopment as a TV series.[10] Campaigners have also objected to non-disabled actors playing disabled characters and straight actors playing gay characters.

But if actors can only ever portray people who are just like them, then they are not acting at all – they are simply representing their identity group. Drama stops being about storytelling and becomes instead an opportunity to recognise and affirm different identity groups. There is an insistence in all this that no one can speak on behalf of anyone else.

January 2020 marked the publication of *American Dirt*, a much-anticipated novel about a Mexican woman fleeing from a vengeful cartel boss. It had attracted considerable publicity as well as a sizeable advance for author Jeanine Cummins. The gripping thriller sought to highlight the traumatic experiences of immigrants to the US. This on-message page-turner seemingly ticked all the woke boxes, and early reviews compared it to John Steinbeck's *The Grapes of Wrath*.

But there was a problem. Cummins' one Puerto Rican grandparent did not qualify her as Latina, and so she was condemned for claiming ownership of experiences she had no right to possess. Author Julissa Arce proclaimed: 'As a Mexican immigrant, who was undocumented, I can say with authority that this book is a harmful, stereotypical, damaging representation of our experiences.'[11] The publisher brought Cummins' promotional tour to a swift end, citing concerns for her safety.

The death of fiction

Speaking at the Brisbane Writers Festival in 2016, novelist Lionel Shriver criticised fashionable ideologies which, she suggested, challenge our capacity to write fiction at all. 'The kind of fiction we are "allowed" to write', Shriver argued, 'is in danger of becoming so hedged, so circumscribed, so tippy-toe, that we'd indeed be better off not writing the anodyne drivel to begin with'.[12] In critics' rush to condemn, she argued, they fail to grasp that fiction is, by definition, a product of the imagination. So it was with Cummins. She had not enslaved or abused Mexican people or stolen someone else's intellectual efforts. She simply used her imagination to conjure up fictional characters. Talented authors seduce readers into suspending disbelief, and readers do so knowingly and willingly.

Yassmin Abdel-Magied, a young Sudanese-Australian journalist, was in the audience at Shriver's Brisbane speech and was so offended by what she heard that she walked out. 'It became about *mocking* those who ask people to seek permission to use their stories. It became a *celebration* of the *unfettered exploitation* of the experiences of others, under the guise of fiction', she later explained.[13] Here Abdel-Magied expresses the woke assumption that certain experiences are the property of particular identity groups, and that authors from privileged groups who seek to write about these experiences – even if they attempt to do so with empathy, honesty and integrity – are exploiting the oppressed for their own gain: 'The reality is that those from marginalised groups, even today, do not get the luxury of defining their own place in a norm that is profoundly white, straight and, often, patriarchal.'

This takes us a long way indeed from Roman playwright Terence's declaration that 'nothing that is human is alien to me'. Rather than walking a mile in someone else's shoes, we are expected to confine ourselves to that which is narrowly demarcated as our own terrain.

This restrictive approach to literature is profoundly anti-human. Great authors and playwrights have stood the test of time because of their capacity to portray what is universal in the human condition. But critics like Abdel-Magied deny there is any such thing. Rather than a shared humanity, we have only identity groups. Rather than individual experiences and struggles, we have only the perpetual battle between those caricatured as oppressors and oppressed. Woke critics hold fiction to a standard it was never designed to reach. People are complex and flawed; talented writers capture this ambiguity. Characters who are simply idealised representations of their identity, captured in politically unambiguous scenarios, make for dull stories.

It's not just contemporary authors who need to worry about woke condemnation or cancellation. When it was first published in 1960, *To Kill a Mockingbird* was lauded for its message of tolerance and racial equality, but now Harper Lee's award-winning novel, alongside other English-lesson favourites, is in the firing line. The head of English at a school in Scotland recently labelled *To Kill a Mockingbird* and John Steinbeck's *Of Mice and Men* 'problematical', because they both feature a white hero and use outdated language. *To Kill a Mockingbird* was singled out for using a 'white saviour motif'. [14] But this unfairly judges the past by the standards of the present. Harper Lee portrays not just the attitudes and values of the time she was writing about, but also the practical realities. We might wish it were otherwise, but in 1930s America middle-class white men were far more likely than black farmhands to become lawyers.

Teachers on a mission to impart particular views to the next generation have no time for ambiguity. Beautiful language is sacrificed to political correctness, and worthiness gets in the way of a good story. Any text that reflects the values of an earlier era is rendered hopelessly problematic. For this reason, many of the books that appear on children's recommended reading lists today were published in the past five years.

The result is that literature loses its capacity to forge bonds between the generations, and children become alienated from the history of their own societies. As Frank Furedi suggests in *100 Years of Identity Crisis*, this distancing from the past is often considered necessary to shield children from outdated values and allow professionals to promote an approved morality.[15] But it fuels alienation. This process has been going on for a very long time – the attacks on literature today reflect as much as prompt that sense of alienation.

Cultural appropriation

The woke directive to 'stay in your lane' extends beyond literature and into popular music, fashion and even food. The most trivial issues can now become the focus of protracted debate. Tequila-slamming students wearing sombreros have been subjected to scrutiny in recent years. A 2017 *Vice* article by Ruby Pivet chastised women who wear hoop earrings. 'Hoop earrings are my culture, not your trend', the headline read. Pivet urged teenage girls tempted to wear hoop earrings to 'think twice'. 'Hoops are worn by minorities as symbols of resistance, and strength', she wrote. Apparently, hoop earrings are the property of women of colour, and white girls who wear them are guilty of stealing the identity of oppressed groups who fought against 'colonial structures'. 'It's almost like you are the colonists', Pivet concluded.[16] This kind of discourse is an attempt to capture the essence of identity in trivial details. It speaks to an insecurity about our sense of self, our place in the world, and our claims to authority.

In *Who Owns Culture?: Appropriation and Authenticity in American Law*, Susan Scafidi considers the legal case for and against cultural appropriation. She describes cultural appropriation as taking intellectual property, traditional knowledge, cultural expressions or artefacts from someone else's culture without permission. This can include unauthorised use of another culture's dance, dress, music, language, folklore, cuisine, traditional medicine or religious symbols.[17] But who has the authority to grant permission for use of a particular cultural artefact? The charge of cultural appropriation is built on bad faith. Young women who follow fashion and want to look nice are hardly demonstrating ill will towards those they emulate. Indeed, it is precisely because a style is viewed as attractive that it is popularised. Throughout human history, trends in clothing, music, architecture and art have been admired, emulated, reinterpreted and, often, reappropriated in a different form by their originators. This is the beauty of cultural diversity. It illustrates humanity's boundless potential for creativity.

The charge of cultural appropriation seeks to end such cultural fluidity by fixing artefacts as the exclusive property of one particular group. This has the effect of entrenching racial categories. To see the problem with this, we need only turn the tables: no one should feel comfortable proclaiming that Shakespeare or motor cars or violin concertos are the exclusive property of white men. Those crying 'cultural appropriation' argue that when the cultural property of minority groups is exploited, everyone profits but them. When women of colour wear hoop earrings, for example, they are apparently looked down on, while white women are feted for doing the very same thing. Perhaps such claims speak to continuing racial inequalities. But these are unlikely to be solved by entrenching racial categories and attacking teenage girls for their fashion choices.

Diversity is excellence

The woke insistence that we stay in our cultural lane sits alongside a demand to celebrate diversity. University mission statements and the recruitment policies of multinational corporations proclaim the goal of being diverse. What they mean by this is including people from visibly different identity groups as an end in itself. Meanwhile, disparities between identity groups are held up as de facto evidence of discrimination.

Classical music has long been criticised for being too male and pale. Author and journalist Heather Mac Donald has explored the impact of 'specious charges of racism' on America's orchestras, opera companies and conductors. Mac Donald does not deny that racial disparities exist in the number of musicians performing in top orchestras, but she suggests there may be explanations for these differentials that go beyond racism. As one music director tells her: 'There are not enough black and other minority musicians studying at music schools or conservatories, let alone in the audition pool.'[18] This is not to say that there is no problem here, only that it is not one of racist orchestra leaders.

Campaigners are so certain that racism is the only explanation for racial disparities that they do not look any deeper into potential causes. Instead, they come up with 'solutions' that are destined either to fail or to change the very nature of the institution in question. For example, when concerns were raised about the underrepresentation of women in classical music, orchestras were urged to conduct 'blind auditions' with musicians performing behind a screen. Now that the focus has switched to race, there are calls to stop blind auditions so that positive discrimination can be used to recruit black musicians. This is an admission that positive discrimination involves lowering standards. Others go further and argue that classical music itself is steeped in white racial identity and so puts off black musicians. Classical works, therefore, must be dropped, or at the very least cut back on, to make way for other genres. The fact that abandoning the Western canon changes the very nature of the classical orchestra is not considered important. Mac Donald notes: 'This music is not about you or me. It is about something grander than our narrow, petty selves. But narcissism, the signal characteristic of our time, is shrinking our cultural inheritance to a nullity.'[19]

Just as with campaigns to decolonise the school or university curriculum, which will be discussed in subsequent chapters, those agitating for change in the cultural sphere insist that their aim is merely to expand reading lists or repertoires. But this is disingenuous. With limited time for teaching or performing, difficult decisions must be made. The problem here is not that some works will inevitably fall by the wayside, but the basis on which texts or scores are included or discarded. Rather than a repertoire being determined on merit alone, it ends up being determined by the identity of the composers, with skin colour and sex to the fore. At best, this approach leads to relativism, whereby nothing is considered inherently more worthy of studying or performing than anything else. At worst, it sounds the death knell for art entirely, as everything is reduced to an expression of identity to be judged through an intersectional framework. All criticism becomes *ad hominem*. Artists and authors can never transcend the confines of their identity. The cause of this cultural vandalism is not the strength of woke arguments but the cultural elite's lack of confidence in the ability of drama, literature and classical music to offer people anything of intrinsic value. Having failed to make a case for their art forms on their own terms, writers, directors and conductors crumble when they come under attack.

Cancel culture

Cancel culture refers to attempts at silencing political opponents rather than engaging with their arguments. This tactic is increasingly employed by activists from all sides of the political spectrum. But those who challenge woke thinking are a particular target of the cancellers. The first step in cancellation usually involves the sinner being 'called out' for something they have said or done. Simple criticism morphs into a full-blown attempt at cancellation when someone with a large social-media following gets involved. The attraction for those quick to lead or join a public shaming is that they can feel as if they are part of a bigger movement, one that is emboldened by moral righteousness. When compared to standing on a picket line or organising a protest, firing off a tweet is not just easy – it can also attract far more attention, particularly if amplified by traditional media outlets in search of a quick story.

Social-media platforms are not just where you call people out, either. They are also where you mine for evidence to support a cancellation campaign. In 2017, writer Freddie deBoer coined the term 'offence archaeologists' to describe those who dedicate time and effort to trawling through a target's social-media posts in order to discover something offensive.[20] Sadly, this practice has become increasingly widespread, and neither context nor youthful idiocy provides any defence against it. English cricketer Ollie Robinson was 18 and 19 when he sent tweets making crude racial and sexual jokes that, years later, led to him being suspended from international cricket for eight matches.[21] Ross Peltier, a former rugby player, was dropped by the Green Party as a by-election candidate after decade-old offensive tweets came to light.[22] Middlesbrough footballer Marc Bola was just 14 when he sent the allegedly homophobic tweet that led to him being charged by the Football Association (FA) with 'aggravated misconduct' when he was 23.[23] In each of these cases, there is no recognition that young people say and do idiotic things, but also that they grow up, learn and change. Cancel culture is ruthless and unforgiving.

Perhaps the most famous target of cancel culture is author JK Rowling. As previously noted, Rowling has upset transgender activists by reminding the world that people who menstruate are women and by supporting Maya Forstater, a gender-critical feminist who lost her job because of her views. Drawing on her experiences of domestic abuse and sexual assault, Rowling defends women-only spaces. What's notable is the lack of sympathy afforded to Rowling. Her views may be shared by many, but from the moment she was labelled a TERF (trans-exclusionary radical feminist) no threats or insults were off-limits, including graphic rape and death threats. In the eyes of transgender activists and their supporters, Rowling is a modern-day heretic who must be publicly shamed. The alleged righteousness of the mob's cause apparently makes misogyny acceptable.

The flagging up of past sins is followed by the demand that the sinner be sacked, shamed or otherwise removed from public life. The aim is to send a message to others about what is and isn't acceptable to say in polite society and, in the process, confirm the moral superiority of the people doing the calling out. In universities, this takes the form of No Platforming – that is, using petitions and protests to get a speaker's invitation rescinded. Initially, those driving cancellations relied on a similar strategy. They encouraged their social-media followers to join in with attacks on those perceived to have stepped out of line. But some recent cancellations have not required the involvement of a mob at all. Just one complaint was enough to spark the FA investigation into Marc Bola.

In 2021, the Royal Academy removed work by textile artist Jess de Wahls from its gift shop, following just eight complaints alleging that de Wahls is transphobic. De Wahls is a feminist and her work is a bold celebration of women and their bodies. One exhibition she held was titled *Big Swinging Ovaries*.[24] But de Wahls' crime lay less in her artwork than in her thoughts. Back in 2019, she wrote a gender-critical blog post and has been hounded for it ever since. Today's artists – especially, it seems, women – must not transgress against trans ideology if they want a place in our cultural institutions. Following a pushback from de Wahls and her supporters, the Royal Academy was forced to u-turn and apologise.[25] But such instances are rare. It seems that putting female artists or young black footballers out of work is a small price to pay to appease a tiny number of complainants. In every case of cancellation, the compulsion to acquiesce overrides all other factors, exposing the hollowness and cowardice of those running our institutions. Cancellations are becoming increasingly pre-emptive. Rather than waiting for a mob to form, those in positions of power act to dispel offenders at the merest hint of controversy. And rather than waiting to be called out, people self-censor and do not put their thoughts into the public domain in the first place. What we're left with is a conformist culture in which the means of compulsion have been rendered invisible.

Journalist Bari Weiss left her position at the *New York Times* three years after she was hired as a writer and editor for the opinion section 'with the goal of bringing in voices that would not otherwise appear in [its] pages'. Weiss aimed to expand the range of views offered to readers who had been shocked by Donald Trump's presidential victory. Once in post, she found her colleagues had little appetite for disagreement. Weiss points to the pernicious influence of social media in driving ideological conformity, noting that some columns now appear to be aimed at winning approval for the author on Twitter. 'Twitter is not on the masthead of the *New York Times*. But Twitter has become its ultimate editor', she argues.[26]

The phenomenon Weiss alludes to extends beyond America. The BBC's head of standards, David Jordan, recently warned staff of the dangers of becoming addicted to 'toxic' Twitter. He expressed concern that a desire for programme snippets to 'go viral' was overriding impartiality and accuracy.[27] When BBC output includes podcast clips berating white women for being 'Karens',[28] and clips of smug contestants on Radio 4 panel shows poking fun at the supposed ignorance of Brexit voters, it is clear that a Reithian commitment to public-service broadcasting has been replaced by hectoring and in-jokes among politically aligned friends.

Pursuing validation on Twitter is like walking a tightrope while drunk. Misspeak and you will be hounded until you repent. In her resignation letter, Weiss explains that her 'forays into Wrongthink' made her 'the subject of constant bullying by colleagues'. However, only so much blame for this dire situation can be left at the door of social media. As we will explore in later chapters, a perception of human vulnerability and a cult of emotional safety have undermined free speech. This process took hold in universities long before it did on social media. Universities have long since abandoned a commitment to intellectual freedom and the unhindered pursuit of truth. Schools and museums swapped the passing on of knowledge for moralising more than a generation ago. Theatres and art galleries were converted to identity-driven goals long before Gen Zers (those born between 1997 and 2012) were even born. Youngsters with Twitter accounts did not invent cancel culture, and its roots extend far beyond the invention of the smartphone.

As JK Rowling acknowledges, cancel culture makes intellectual freedom the preserve of those with independent means, tolerant sponsors or the guts to go it alone. That is, people like her. Although the cases discussed here are those that have attracted the most headlines, people without a public profile are just as likely to find themselves out of work for expressing the wrong views. In September 2020, train conductor Jeremy Sleath was dismissed after 17 years of loyal service with West Midlands Trains. His crime? He had celebrated the end of lockdown by posting on his personal Facebook account: 'Thank f*** our pubs open up today. We cannot let our way of life become like some sort of Muslim alcohol-free caliphate just to beat Covid-19.'[29] One anonymous colleague complained and Sleath was summarily dismissed. He later won a case for unfair dismissal, but the process of being dismissed and having to appeal his case still sent a message to others to keep controversial opinions to themselves.[30]

In June 2020, Nick Buckley was sacked from the Manchester-based charity he founded after he wrote a blog post criticising Black Lives Matter. Buckley was dismissed within days of an online petition gathering momentum.[31] After a backlash, Buckley was reinstated and the trustees involved stepped down.[32] In 2019, supermarket greeter Brian Leach was fired by an Asda in Yorkshire after he shared an 'anti-religion' sketch by Billy Connolly on his Facebook page. A colleague at the store where Leach had worked for five years complained that the sketch was anti-Islamic. Leach deleted the post and wrote an apology to his bosses and colleagues, but was still fired for breaching the company's social-media policy.[33] He was reinstated after outrage over the case.[34]

Despite all the examples detailed above, those championing cancellation often deny that cancel culture even exists. It is, they argue, a figment of the right-wing imagination, the death cry of those aggrieved that they have had to make way for those from historically less privileged backgrounds. The cancellers are not easily offended 'snowflakes', they insist. Rather, it is those shouting 'cancel culture' who melt when challenged about their own bigotry. And in any case, the cancel-culture deniers contend, those who claim to have been cancelled often go on to gain sympathy, publicity and money by writing all about their experiences in the pages of national newspapers.

This is dishonest. Denying the existence of cancel culture, or saying it doesn't really matter much anyway, is just a means for the new woke elites to deny the power they possess, even as they are in the process of wielding it. It is only possible for them to deny the existence of cancel culture because it is rarely a coordinated process. Rather, it is something that occurs spontaneously, in a society where emotional safety and not giving offence have become highly prized. The petty authoritarianism of cancel culture speaks to the intellectual fragility of woke values, and the fact that they are not grounded in popular support.

The battle for the past

A key component of the culture wars is the battle for the past. We see this being played out in disputes over statues, the names of schools, streets and public buildings, as well as in museums. There are demands for anything with the merest whiff of a connection to past social injustices – with the slave trade and colonialism to the fore – to be erased from public life and replaced with something more politically acceptable, or placed 'in context' with explanatory texts flagging up exactly what is 'problematic'.

Following the murder of George Floyd at the hands of police officer Derek Chauvin in Minneapolis on 25 May 2020, Black Lives Matter protests took place in towns and cities around the world. In Bristol in the UK, a demonstration on 7 June ended with the toppling of a statue of Edward Colston. Colston (1636-1721) was a merchant and slave trader. He was born in Bristol and served as the city's MP for a short time. He also donated some of his considerable wealth to the building of churches and hospitals and founded two almshouses and a school in the city. His legacy was enshrined in the names of streets and buildings, as well as a large bronze statue. In more recent years, campaigners began to question whether such memorials were appropriate, given that the source of much of Colston's wealth was slavery. They petitioned for buildings to be renamed and for Colston's statue to be removed.

The crowds that gathered in Bristol on 7 June quickly directed their anger at Colston's statue. The monument had been covered up ahead of the protest, but protesters still pelted it with eggs. The covering was then torn off as, according to the BBC, some protesters said 'they wanted to look the man in the eyes'. Protesters climbed on to the statue and fastened ropes around its head. Just 30 seconds later the statue toppled to the ground. Some people jumped on the statue, while others, including Jen Reid, whose image would soon be beamed around the world, climbed on to the now empty plinth, fists raised. The statue of Colston was dragged to Bristol Harbour and pushed into the water.[35]

In January 2022, a small group of the protesters stood trial and were found not guilty of criminal damage by a jury, despite admitting to their role in toppling the statue.

There is something medieval about attacking an inanimate object in this way. In the minds of these protesters, the line between the bronze representation of Colston and the man himself was sketchy. Looking him 'in the eyes', stomping on him and dumping him in the water seemed like ritualistic acts of retribution, designed to be enacted on a real live person rather than a lump of metal. Reid, who stood on the empty plinth, later explained what it all felt like. 'It just felt like I was cleansing it', she said. 'I had a surge of power.' It's easy to forget that people walked past that statue for over a century, most without batting an eyelid.

In Bristol, the empty plinth soon became home to a new statue: a model of Jen Reid, complete with raised fist, created by sculptor Marc Quinn. It made for a striking and beautiful image. But it is interesting that a protest movement that purported to care about social change so quickly morphed into a celebration of the protesters themselves. It is difficult to understand how people who live in parts of Bristol that suffer severe economic deprivation benefit from such displays of performativity. Quinn's statue of Reid lasted only a day on the plinth before it was taken down by the city council.[36] Colston's statue, meanwhile, was retrieved from the harbour and placed in a new exhibition in the city's museum, where it is displayed horizontally with Colston's face still daubed with red paint.[37] It effectively serves as a monument to the June 2020 protesters.

Clearly, people have a right to demand change in their towns and cities. Just because a statue has stood for a hundred years does not automatically mean it should remain in place for the next century. But it is worth asking why statues have become such a focus of attention, especially as racism has become less of a force in public life. The woke war on statues seems to be only in part a struggle over lumps of bronze or stone; it is primarily a fight over history. Demanding the removal of statues serves to remind the public of a minority group's historical experience of suffering and oppression, and draws a direct line between past discrimination and injustices today.

As Christopher Lasch wrote in *The Revolt of the Elites and the Betrayal of Democracy*: 'For many people the very term "Western civilisation" now calls to mind an organised system of domination designed to enforce conformity to bourgeois values and to keep the victims of patriarchal oppression – women, children, homosexuals, people of colour – in a permanent state of subjection.'[38] Attacks on statues today demonstrate a disconnect from, and a visceral loathing of, Western civilisation in general, and national history and identity in particular.

Cleansing the public sphere of statues is a practical means of erasing not just the historical figures represented, but also the fact that previous generations of citizens thought these figures were worthy of commemoration. It allows for history to be rewritten without public debate. What's more, when such debate does occur, it tends to centre on a simplistic and one-sided view of history. Just as in the discussion of literature, historical figures are also, in general, morally complex beings and products of the times in which they lived. Few humans are objectively and entirely good or bad in ways that transcend the social and cultural norms of their era. Colston made money in ways that are today considered morally reprehensible and criminal, yet he also spent his money in ways that benefitted the people of Bristol. Tearing down statues does not acknowledge this nuance.

One consequence of the war on the past is that people can no longer look to history for heroes or figures whose legacy can unite the nation. Plymouth is home to a statue of Sir Francis Drake, the English sea captain best known for his circumnavigation of the world and for serving as second-in-command of the English fleet when it defeated the Spanish Armada. Feted in his lifetime, Drake was central to patriotic stories of English heroism for over four centuries. Critics have rightly argued that such accounts too often ignored the crucial role Drake's exploits played in establishing the transatlantic slave trade. But the rush to condemn and erase overlooks the potentially more positive role that Drake played in cohering a sense of national identity – one that could transcend divisions of race, gender and sexuality. The myth of Drake instilled national pride and also promoted values of heroism, bravery, valour and determination. But now his status in English culture has been called into question.

In June 2020, Drake's statue in Plymouth was placed in shackles and had a poster bearing the legend 'decolonise history' attached to it. Campaigners wanted the statue removed entirely, but council officials pledged to keep it in place and to install a plaque alongside it, providing historical context. This fits with the UK government's 'retain and explain' policy for historical monuments. But focusing intently on the sins of former national heroes – and only rarely acknowledging their achievements – robs them of their capacity to provide a shared historical and cultural reference point. We learn to view the past only with shame and disgust.

Sir Winston Churchill is another national hero whose legacy has been challenged. Churchill's critics are not concerned with bringing us to a better, more nuanced understanding of either his character or his role in the Second World War. They just want to paint him as an irredeemable racist, pushing a view of the past as tainted and immoral. Once, Churchill's legacy served a useful purpose for Britain's cultural elite in rallying national pride. Nowadays, when Black Lives Matter protesters daub his statue with the word 'racist', we see that Churchill serves a purpose for a new cultural elite. He is used to alienate children from the recent history of their society, and from the values of their parents and grandparents.

Those exploiting the past in order to fight a culture war in the present refuse to allow us to reach our own conclusions, or to consider historical figures in the round. We are not permitted to see people as products of their time and circumstances. All must be judged by the standards of the present, and all, inevitably, fall short. Pride and patriotism are replaced with shame and guilt. In the process, our links to the past, connections that bind us into society along with our fellow citizens, disappear. We exist in an atomised and alienated ever-present.

The culture war is about projecting woke values, through a particular interpretation of history and culture, on to society at large. This cultural shift becomes a 'war' because it is imposed, top down, by a new elite on the majority of citizens. The elite imposition of woke values is interpreted by many as an attack on national identity, patriotism and tradition. But they find themselves dismissed whenever they raise their concerns.

The BBC frequently acts in such a way that reflects the views and interests of a woke elite, rather than the bulk of the population. The singing of 'Rule Britannia' at the Last Night of the Proms, for example, is not something that particularly concerns most people. However, it clearly troubled BBC producers who appeared to be embarrassed about overt displays of nationalism in the wake of Brexit. In 2020, without consulting the public, BBC higher-ups briefly considered dropping 'Rule Britannia'.[39] Yet, when there was a backlash, it was the people who protested who were accused of waging a culture war.[40]

The same is true for statues. Although woke campaigners launch crusades against statues and demand their removal, it is the British public who are accused of having a strange obsession with inanimate objects. *Guardian* journalist Gary Younge argues: 'In Britain, we seem to have a peculiar fixation with statues, as we seek to petrify historical discourse, lather it in cement, hoist it high and insist on it as a permanent statement of fact, culture, truth and tradition that can never be questioned, touched, removed or recast.' Presumably, on his side of the fence sit good people who have a far more critical and questioning view of history – people who are not remotely obsessed with statues. But this view is belied by Younge himself, who concludes that all statues of historical figures are 'lazy and ugly' and should be taken down.[41]

This game of 'you started it!' is unedifying, but it hints at the shift that is taking place between an old elite, with a traditional set of values, and a new cultural elite seeking to impose woke values on society. This battle between an old, establishment elite and a new, woke elite can be seen in institutions like the National Trust. The National Trust was, until very recently, the epitome of conservative respectability. With the help of volunteers and donations it safeguarded historic properties on behalf of the nation. But things have changed. In 2021, the National Trust even asked its army of largely elderly volunteers to don rainbow clothing and glitter in honour of Pride month.[42] Unsurprisingly, there were objections. Perhaps some volunteers have Christian beliefs about marriage. Perhaps some just don't fancy getting glitter in their hair. But for the National Trust's newly woke leaders, simply conserving the past is not enough. They need a new moral purpose, and they have apparently found one.

Woke thinking makes culture a minefield. It replaces beauty with political hectoring and shades-of-grey complexity with black-and-white worthiness. Creativity and experimentation are killed off with instructions to stay in your lane. All art becomes subjugated to a political purpose. The result is nihilism and conformity, where no one dares step out of line, and little in the human potential can be celebrated. Art now expresses contempt for the past and for humanity in the present. This is perhaps best typified by the debates that surround London's empty fourth plinth in Trafalgar Square. On 30 July 2020, a new sculpture was unveiled. Entitled *The End*, it depicts a giant swirl of whipped cream, with a cherry on top and a fly stuck to the side.[43] Observers are seemingly meant to feel an overriding sensation of disgust.

Whether culture is funded by the state or private finance makes little difference. As Christopher Lasch once noted, 'the market's effect on the cultural infrastructure is just as corrosive as that of the state'.[44] The same cultural elite, sharing and enforcing the same woke political outlook, is in charge in both instances today. That cultural elite is the focus of the next chapter.

Endnotes

[1] Cultural Conflict in America, James Davison Hunter, republished in *Culture and Politics: A Reader*, Lane Crothers and Charles Lockhart (eds), Palgrave Macmillan (2002)

[2] Cited in: Culture wars uncovered: most of UK public don't know if 'woke' is a compliment or an insult, Bobby Duffy and Ben Page, *Conversation*, 26 May 2021

[3] *Keywords: A Vocabulary of Culture and Society*, Raymond Williams, Fourth Estate Ltd (2nd edition, 1988)

[4] *Keywords: A Vocabulary of Culture and Society*, Raymond Williams, Fourth Estate Ltd (2nd edition, 1988)

[5] 'It's dangerous not to see race': is colour-blind casting all it's cracked up to be?, Micha Frazer-Carroll, *Guardian*, 11 August 2020

[6] Ghost in the Shell's whitewashing: does Hollywood have an Asian problem?, Steve Rose, *Guardian*, 31 March 2017

[7] The Battle of 'Miss Saigon': yellowface, art and opportunity, *New York Times*, 17 March 2017

[8] 'It's dangerous not to see race': is colour-blind casting all it's cracked up to be?, Micha Frazer-Carroll, *Guardian*, 11 August 2020

[9] The backlash against In the Heights, explained, Aja Romano, *Vox*, 15 June 2021

[10] Two years after Scarlett Johansson controversy, Rub & Tug gets reimagined for TV, *Vanity Fair*, 21 July 2020

[11] American Dirt: why critics are calling Oprah's book club pick exploitative and divisive, *Guardian*, 22 January 2020

[12] Lionel Shriver's full speech: 'I hope the concept of cultural appropriation is a passing fad', *Guardian*, 13 September 2016

[13] As Lionel Shriver made light of identity, I had no choice but to walk out on her, Yassmin Abdel-Magied, *Guardian*, 10 September 2016

[14] Edinburgh school cancels To Kill a Mockingbird as book 'promotes white saviour narrative', *Independent*, 6 July 2021

[15] *100 Years of Identity Crisis: Culture War Over Socialisation*, Frank Furedi, De Gruyter (2021)

[16] Hoop earrings are my culture, not your trend, Ruby Pivet, *Vice*, 10 October 2017

[17] *Who Owns Culture?: Appropriation and Authenticity in American Law*, Susan Scafidi, Rutgers University Press (2005)

[18] Classical Music's Suicide Pact (Part 1), Heather Mac Donald, *City Journal*, 1 August 2021

[19] Classical Music's Suicide Pact (Part 2), Heather Mac Donald, *City Journal*, 8 August 2021

[20] Planet of Cops, Freddie deBoer, Substack (originally published on Medium, May

2017)

[21] England's Ollie Robinson apologises after racist and sexist tweets emerge, *Guardian*, 2 June 2021

[22] Green Party pull candidate from crucial Batley and Spen by-election over 'highly offensive' homophobic tweets, *Pink News*, 7 June 2021

[23] Marc Bola charged with 'aggravated' misconduct for historical social media post, *Independent*, 3 September 2021

[24] Royal Academy pulls artist's work from gift shop over 'transphobic' views, *Telegraph*, 17 June 2021

[25] Royal Academy of Arts apologises to Jess de Wahls in transphobia row, *Guardian*, 23 June 2021

[26] Bari Weiss's New York Times resignation letter in full, *The Times* (London), 14 July 2020

[27] BBC journalists addicted to 'toxic' Twitter, says boss, *The Times* (London), 15 July 2020

[28] Backlash as BBC podcast asks 'How can white women not be Karens?', *Evening Standard*, 6 July 2020

[29] Jeremy Sleath – dismissed by his employer for celebrating the end of lockdown, Free Speech Union, 2021

[30] 'Secular atheist' train conductor who celebrated pubs reopening by declaring he didn't want to live in an 'alcohol-free caliphate' wins unfair dismissal claim, *Daily Mail*, 26 November 2021

[31] Award-winning charity boss who helped thousands of disadvantaged children is SACKED for criticising Black Lives Matter's 'neo-Marxist' agenda, *Daily Mail*, 27 June 2020

[32] 'Cancellers are cowards – their beliefs are built on sand', *spiked*, 25 September 2020

[33] Disabled granddad sacked from Asda for sharing Billy Connolly sketch on Facebook, *Metro*, 24 June 2019

[34] Sacked Brian gets his job back in Asda u-turn, *Press*, 26 July 2019

[35] Bristol George Floyd protest: Colston statue toppled, BBC News, 7 June 2020

[36] 'I had a surge of power': the Bristol woman whose statue replaced Edward Colston's, *Guardian*, 18 December 2020

[37] Edward Colston statue on display in Bristol exhibition, BBC News, 4 June 2021

[38] *The Revolt of the Elites and the Betrayal of Democracy*, Christopher Lasch, WW Norton & Company (1996)

[39] BBC considers dropping Rule Britannia from Last Night of the Proms, *Guardian*, 23 August 2020

[40] The Rule, Britannia! row is too important for anti-racists to ignore, Joseph Harker,

Guardian, 2 September 2020

[41] Why every single statue should come down, Gary Younge, *Guardian*, 1 June 2021

[42] National Trust is criticised after asking volunteers to wear rainbow colours for Pride month amid growing backlash over its 'woke' policies, *Daily Mail*, 15 June 2021

[43] Unveiling the Fourth Plinth – THE END, Mayor's Office London, YouTube, 30 July 2020

[44] *The Revolt of the Elites and the Betrayal of Democracy*, Christopher Lasch, WW Norton & Company (1996)

3 A New Cultural Elite

They move between state, private and voluntary sectors of the economy. They move between politics, government, the arts world and the media. They move from business trips to climate summits to forums on tackling obesity.

This chapter explores where today's cultural elite emerged from, who its members are, what qualifies someone for membership, and how these members operate and sustain their position. Of course, there are no entrance tests, secret handshakes or badges to show who is in the cultural elite. But demonstrating woke opinions allows its members to differentiate themselves from the masses. Expressing such views is how a would-be member advances. Most importantly of all, such views also provide morally vacuous leaders with a sense of purpose.

Who is the new cultural elite?

The word 'elite' has long been used by political theorists to denote a small section of society that holds a disproportionate amount of wealth, privilege or political power over everyone else. This group may include Plato's philosopher kings, Marx's bourgeoisie or C Wright Mills' 'power elite'. In every society, the size and composition of the elite, the source of its power and the extent of its influence change over time. Whereas Marx emphasised the role of economic capital (ownership of the means of production or a need to sell labour) in distinguishing the elite from the masses, French sociologist Pierre Bourdieu argued that cultural capital is also important. Writing in *Distinction*, he defined cultural capital as familiarity with the legitimate culture within a society, explaining that legitimacy is a fundamentally arbitrary product of elite taste. At the time Bourdieu was writing, in the late 1970s, high culture was legitimised by the elite. Familiarity with it was reproduced through family and social networks and credentialised through the education system. Crucially, Bourdieu noted that possessing cultural capital paves the way for meeting others who share similar knowledge, experiences and tastes, and those who control access to high-paying professions and prestigious leadership roles.[1] He considered economic, cultural and social capital to be convertible and exchangeable.

As such, it makes more sense to talk of multiple, overlapping elites, rather than a singular elite. Writing in 1916, Italian economist and political theorist Vilfredo Pareto divided the elite into two classes: 'a governing elite, comprising individuals who directly or indirectly play some considerable part in the government, and a non-governing elite, comprising the rest'. He further divided the 'governing elite', or the 'political class', into military, religious and commercial interests.[2] In his 1956 book, *The Power Elite*, C Wright Mills similarly described a triumvirate of power groups – political, economic and military. Each had 'a noticeable degree of autonomy', he argued, but all were drawn from a socially recognised and highly interconnected upper class.[3] Today we might similarly subdivide the non-governing elite and consider the media, academia or the arts as wielding different forms of power.

Together, the different sectors that comprise the governing and non-governing elite constitute a large group of interconnected people. Only a tiny proportion of this much bigger group rules directly, while the majority provide intellectual or moral expertise to support the ruling class. This brings us to Gaetano Mosca's view, which is summarised by TB Bottomore in his 1964 book, *Elites and Society*:

> *In modern times, the elite is not simply raised high above the rest of society; it is intimately connected with society through a sub-elite, a much larger group which comprises, to all intents and purposes, the whole 'new middle class' of civil servants, managers and white-collar workers, scientists and engineers, scholars and intellectuals. This group does not only supply recruits to the elite (the ruling class in the narrow sense); it is itself a vital element in the government of society.*[4]

It is this very broad-based group of the elite and the sub-elite that I define as the cultural elite. I am using culture in the broad sense outlined by Raymond Williams, as noted in the previous chapter, and I am using the word 'elite' rather than 'class' to suggest that this large group often has little sense of its own identity or a coherent sense of purpose. However, as we will discuss below, this lack of a coherent sense of purpose began to change with the 2016 votes for Brexit in the UK and Trump in the US.

Changes in the composition of the cultural elite and the ideas that motivate its members occur over time and are often reflective of broader social, political or economic shifts. Today's elite is a product of political trends that have been gathering pace since at least the mid-1970s. In the decades after the end of the Second World War, the governing class of many Western nations was pushed into a compromise with the working class. In the UK, this led to the development of the welfare state and the National Health Service. Members of the traditional ruling class found they had to accommodate the demands of a powerful trade-union movement, which led to a boom in workers' rights and higher wages.

This was not to last. As Michael Lind, writing in *The New Class War*, explains: 'For many members of the managerial overclass, the need to share power, wealth and cultural authority with petty tribunes of the working class, like trade-union officials and small-town politicians and religious leaders, was an indignity to be endured only under duress, until they could liberate themselves from constraint.'[5] The break came with what Lind describes as 'technocratic neoliberalism': a new 'orthodoxy of the credentialed managerial overclass'.[6]

Barbara and John Ehrenreich – writing in the mid-1970s, just as technocratic neoliberalism was beginning to replace the postwar compromise – pointed to the emergence of a more politically radical professional-managerial class (PMC), which they argued was 'not found in earlier stages of capitalist development'. Its primary function, they argued, was the direct or indirect management of working-class life, but the PMC also mixed 'hostility toward the capitalist class with elitism toward the working class'.[7] The Ehrenreichs estimated the PMC to be around 25 per cent of the US population.

Technocratic neoliberalism took whole areas of political decision-making out of the hands of elected representatives and gave them over to experts, such as judges or newly formed quangos. Meanwhile, previously state-owned industries were privatised. This created lucrative employment for a new managerial class who no longer simply supplied intellectual support to the governing elite, but also wielded power directly as managers of industry and workers. At the same time, technocratic neoliberalism degraded the votes of millions of ordinary citizens by placing political decision-making beyond the realm of elected representatives. As Christopher Lasch noted, 'the reign of specialised expertise… is the antithesis of democracy'.[8]

Three things have changed since then. First, the professional-managerial class has expanded beyond the Ehrenreichs' estimate. One way to consider its size is in relation to the number of university graduates. In the UK in 1980, only around 15 per cent of young adults stayed in any kind of full-time education or training after the age of 18; in the past decade, close to 50 per cent of those aged under 30 have gone on to university.[9] In the US, around 10 per cent of the total population aged 25 or more had graduated from college in 1970; this rose to around 37.5 per cent by 2020.[10] If graduates are less likely than the general population to be employed in manual work or unskilled labour, then this would suggest growth in the numbers working in professional, managerial or senior administrative roles. Second, technocratic neoliberalism had no moral or political mission distinct from its emphasis on science and expertise. By contrast, woke thinking provides a set of values that today's cultural elite can cohere around. Third, while the professional-managerial class in previous decades had its own interests, distinct from both the working class and the capitalist class, today's woke values are often shared by the capitalist class – something we will explore more fully in Chapter Seven.

Lind describes a 'revolution from above' that, he argues, 'promoted the material interests and intangible values of the college-educated minority of managers and professionals, who have succeeded old-fashioned bourgeois capitalists as the dominant elite'. We might argue that there has been less a process of succession from capitalists to professionals and more a process of blurring boundaries between the two groups. Lind defines a 'college-educated managerial class' as comprising roughly 10 to 15 per cent of the population, but owning 'roughly half the wealth in the United States'. In common with Bourdieu's notion of reproduction, Lind notes, 'overclass families will do anything they can to make sure that their offspring remain in the university-credentialed elite into which they were born'.[11]

Unlike the Ehrenreichs, many on the left had little problem with the emerging professional-managerial class. Indeed, they could find a useful role for themselves within its ranks. The blows dealt to the working class throughout the 1970s and 1980s pushed activists to seek power not in mass movements, but through instigating change from within state institutions, workplaces and supranational organisations.

Forget standing on picket lines, there are human-resources policies to be written. Forget winning the backing of unemployed coal miners, there are European Union bureaucrats to persuade. This move into HR departments, schools, the cultural industry and universities allowed left-wing activists to discover a new sense of purpose. In turn, they found that many of these institutions had lost their sense of moral and intellectual mission. The path was cleared for them to sell their newfound expertise and import their values.

Eventually, UK voters got to have their say on the most clear and tangible form of technocratic neoliberalism: the EU. And, as we all know, to the dismay of most on the political left, they rejected this supranational institution in favour of national sovereignty and the power to hold their own governing elite to account. But the enduring legacy of technocratic neoliberalism is that we still have an overly large cultural elite that comprises numerous smaller, often overlapping, groups. There is a governing elite made up of a tiny number of elected representatives and a larger cohort of political journalists, think tankers and lobbyists, civil servants and special advisers. Alongside this, there is a non-governing elite that runs business, academia, the arts world, leading charities and campaigning organisations, the church, the education system and mainstream as well as social media. Then there are junior members of the professional-managerial class who are employed in human-resource departments and local government, and as doctors, teachers, lecturers and social workers. The boundaries between all these groups are increasingly fluid. Individuals within the elite either wield political power or influence or they work closely alongside those who do.

At its broadest, this loose assortment of people aligns with David Goodhart's description of 'Anywheres', which he defines in opposition to a numerically larger but less powerful group of 'Somewheres'. 'The most typical Anywhere is a liberally-inclined graduate', Goodhart writes. He notes:

They generally belong to the mobile minority who went to a residential university and then into a professional job, usually without returning to the place they were brought up. They are mainly in the upper quartile of the income and social-class spectrum and include a disproportionate number of people who feel a special responsibility for society as a whole. They predominate among decision makers and opinion formers.[12]

Goodhart argues that 'Anywheres are highly concentrated in London and the other main metropolitan centres, as well as university towns'. There is a growing sense that the cultural elite is not just geographically remote, but also politically distant from the masses. Peter Oborne describes the elite as perceiving life only 'through the eyes of an affluent member of London's middle and upper-middle classes'. He explains: 'This very restricted perspective on life is made very much worse by the tendency of members of the Political Class to marry or form partnerships with each other.'[13] Lasch described the new elites as living 'in a little world of their own, far removed from the everyday concerns of ordinary men and women'.[14]

Perhaps the most important role of today's cultural elite is the management of the masses through health, education and social care systems, but also through employment. A whole cadre serves as managers or high-level administrators, and notions like diversity provide the moral justification for this management. Ben Cobley, in his book *The Tribe*, notes the apparent contradiction of having a system that emphasises diversity at every turn and yet is largely run by 'people who appear as unfavoured group members, notably many white-skinned men'. He notes that 'these overseers, or "administrators", of diversity, take on a role distributing power to the favoured groups via prominent members of those groups'.[15]

Institutions now spend vast sums of money on activities that have nothing to do with the services they provide. To take one example, Camden Council in London was reported to have spent £93,000 on an anti-racism training contract, despite cutting £230,000 worth of frontline jobs, including librarians.[16] The NHS and the BBC likewise spend vast sums on diversity and inclusion training programmes, publicity materials and resources. This is public money, commandeered by the cultural elite, that is not being used to cut hospital waiting lists or produce high-quality television programmes, but to inculcate woke values in employees and then, through the services provided, in the general public.

Today's cultural elite has moved away from the idea of public service that characterised the governing class of the Victorian era. In contrast, as Peter Oborne notes, today's elite is comfortable pursuing 'its own sectional interest oblivious to the public good'. Oborne points to the breakdown of 'the old barriers against factionalism, patronage and corruption' as one explanation for this turn to expediency.

Nowadays, the barriers between private and public interest, and between the domains of the state, business, politics, academia and charities, are highly permeable. All are interconnected and interdependent. The cultural elite in all its many forms becomes, to a considerable extent, a manifestation of the state. Both businesses and charities dedicate time and money to cultivating relationships with politicians. Where the state stops and commercial enterprises begin is no longer entirely clear. This was revealed starkly in the midst of the Covid-19 crisis, when government money was used to fund businesses supplying equipment and services, all with little apparent scrutiny. Members of the cultural elite are often paid directly or indirectly from state revenue, whether through salaries, government grants, contracts or public / private finance initiatives.

Irrespective of which sector they are employed in, members of today's cultural elite have much in common. In the arts world, they are only rarely creatives or producers themselves and are more likely to work as curators or in managerial or senior administrative roles. They are almost universally graduates of high-ranking universities, and are more likely to have studied arts or social-science subjects than technical or vocational courses. They share similar tastes in fashion, music, food and holiday destinations. They speak in a vocabulary that is immediately recognisable to fellow members of the cultural elite. They know instinctively that saying 'coloured people' is taboo, but saying 'people of colour' is correct. They know that the acronym 'BAME' might have been acceptable two years ago, but is now frowned upon. They know all the letters that are now supposed to come after LGBT.

When Bourdieu wrote about the inheritance and reproduction of capital, he was referring not just to financial assets but also to cultural capital. Tastes in food, drink, music and art are often handed down from family members. In the same way, some of today's left-wing progressives have inherited their political views, as Owen Jones makes clear when describing his own upbringing:

> My parents met while canvassing for the Labour Party in a snow-storm outside Tooting Bec station in 1969. I was babysat by striking miners in South Yorkshire and strapped to my dad's chest at rallies in which the voice of miners' leader Arthur Scargill would boom defiantly; as a five-year-old I marched with my family against Thatcher's hated poll tax.

Other members of today's woke elite tell a similar story. This sort of upbringing creates distance between members of the cultural elite and ordinary people. As David Swift puts it in *A Left for Itself*: 'If, instead of hearing complaints about immigrants from your older relatives every Christmas, as is the experience of millions of Britons, you instead heard tales about marches and demonstrations, this gives you a distorted view of reality. Indeed, I believe that hailing from a family of devoted leftists can be just as insulating from the realities of the world as growing up surrounded by wealth and privilege and attending top public schools.'[17]

At its smallest, the political class can be especially inward-looking. Members live in city centres away from the places they grew up. They marry fellow members of the cultural elite and send their children to the same schools. Just as with an older establishment, many members of today's cultural elite also find they can fall back on inherited wealth. But all of them enjoy extensive connections and cultural capital.

After leaving university, Owen Jones worked for the Corbynite Labour MP and future shadow chancellor of the exchequer, John McDonnell. This aligns Jones far more with the Westminster bubble than with the working-class miners his family used to rub shoulders with. In the past, being radically left-wing put you on the fringes of society. Today, it is where cultural power lies.

Where did the new cultural elite come from?

Culture has always been shaped by an elite with its own specific tastes and values. Go back more than a century and this elite was predominantly composed of upper-class, public-school-educated white men. They relied upon their apparently superior tastes to distinguish themselves from the masses, including a vocabulary superbly identified by Nancy Mitford in her list of 'U' and 'Non-U' words.[18] Just like today's cultural elite, members of this upper-class group shared a worldview, shared tastes in art and culture, and moved in the same social circles.

The woke domination of culture today hints at a straightforward transition from one elite to another. Old, white, upper-class men, who preferred high art, opera and classical music, have been ousted by a younger cohort who are more sexually, ethnically and gender diverse, and who champion pop music and pop art. But this portrayal of cultural upstarts toppling a stuffy and staid establishment rewrites history to flatter the young. This transition from one cultural elite to another has taken place slowly, within the elite itself, over the course of a century. It can be spotted in modern art movements, the modernist novels of Virginia Woolf and DH Lawrence, New Wave cinema, theatre's Angry Young Men and, of course, pop music. Yesteryear's rebels became the establishment figures, and then held the door open for today's cultural elite.

But even this historical account smooths over important distinctions. The movements that began pushing back against an older elite may have been predominantly made up of white heterosexual males, in contrast to today's far more diverse array of artists and musicians, but at least a few were from working-class backgrounds. There was until recently some scope for talented working-class youngsters, from Alan Sillitoe to Oasis, to battle their way into public prominence. Once there, they found an elite that had lost confidence in its former pursuits and beliefs. They found an elite that no longer possessed the moral authority to defend its own tastes or position. They found, in short, an open door.

In other ways, we have come full circle. The shift from white men in suits to trendy, young, transgender, bisexual people of colour has been rather superficial. Today's woke cultural elite has more in common with the century-old establishment the Angry Young Men pushed back against in the 1950s than with the Angry Young Men themselves. Today, just as it was a century ago, the privately educated are overrepresented in the media, music and arts worlds.[19] Just like a century ago, today's elite shares a political outlook and is hostile to those with different views. And, just as it was a century ago, shared tastes and language allow members of the cultural elite to distinguish themselves from everyone else.

One important difference between today's elite and an older establishment is the readiness of today's cultural gatekeepers to deny their status. Many figureheads of the new woke elite – prominent journalists like Afua Hirsch, Shon Faye and Laurie Penny – enjoyed middle-class, privately educated upbringings, yet they use their identities to distract from their social-class privileges and claim victimhood. Denying their privilege enhances their status within the cultural elite.

What does the new cultural elite believe in?

It is possible to identify a set of woke values that many within the cultural elite espouse. This might include the belief that racism, sexism, homophobia and transphobia are structurally endemic; that white people are inherently privileged and are racist if they deny this; that gender identity is more important to a person's sense of themselves than their sex; that Britain's past is a source of shame; that national borders are an oppressive construct; that community and tradition are regressive fictions; that masculinity is toxic; and that most people are mentally vulnerable. Most fundamentally, the cultural elite shares an assumption that we all have identity-based, historically accumulated privileges and disadvantages. We must all learn where to position ourselves and others within an intersectional hierarchy of privilege and oppression, and performatively support those less privileged than ourselves. The new elite's authority comes from acting on behalf of the oppressed.

Of course, not every member of the cultural elite is on board with all these beliefs, and many of these beliefs are held by people who can in no way be described as elite. Woke does not constitute a coherent ideology – at least not yet. As Frank Furedi argues in *100 Years of Identity Crisis*: 'Unlike the well-known ideologies, the different strands of countercultural forces did not and still do not have a recognisable name.'[20] The woke outlook comprises a set of fluid and evolving positions that are often presented as value-neutral statements of fact, or as opinions any right-thinking person would accept. Woke is not a fully worked-out political agenda, but something far more nebulous: it is a set of values and a way of thinking that has emerged over several decades, and that many cohorts of university graduates have been socialised into accepting as morally correct.

Woke values are not solely associated with one political party. They often transcend old divisions of left and right. Both the prime minister of the UK, Boris Johnson, and the leader of the Labour Party, Sir Keir Starmer, show deference to woke values to a degree. For instance, in the 2021 party conference season, the question as to whether only women have a cervix became a hot-button issue. Yet neither Johnson nor Starmer was able to provide a convincing answer. The best Johnson could muster was: 'Biology is very important, but…'[21] Starmer was more emphatic: 'It is something that shouldn't be said. It is not right.'[22] During the Conservative Party conference, Carrie Johnson, the prime minister's wife, declared herself to be an 'ally' to 'LGBT+ people' and suggested the government was committed to extending trans rights.[23]

As David Goodhart says of 'Anywheres': 'There is a left-of-centre wing – in caring professions like health and education, and the media and creative industries – and a right-of-centre wing in finance, business and traditional professions like law and accountancy.'[24] Woke's establishment within the cultural elite – and, therefore, the state infrastructure more broadly – means it has the power to transcend the wishes of the tiny number of elected politicians. The Conservative Party under Boris Johnson may, on occasion, try to push back against the institutional excesses of woke, but such attempts often fall flat because the state is run not by government ministers, but by a technocratic civil service in conjunction with a managerial class, drawn exclusively from within the cultural elite.

Woke may not have explicit party affiliations, but woke views are nonetheless more prevalent among left-wing progressives. This holds true even when embracing woke means overturning traditionally left-wing positions. For example, it was once the left that supported extending gay rights and the right that supported laws such as the infamous

Clause 28, which prevented the promotion (often interpreted as mere discussion) of homosexuality by local authorities. Today, in stark contrast, it is the left that has problematised same-sex relationships, due to its wholehearted embrace of gender ideology and rejection of the importance of biological sex. Some even argue it is 'transphobic' if a lesbian doesn't want to have sex with a transwoman. Similarly, the more the left aligns with woke values, the more it finds itself at odds with its traditional constituency – the working class.

Woke values have not appeared out of thin air. As we explore in this book, woke thinking about race, gender and identity has developed over a very long period of time. As we noted in Chapter One, the word woke itself has a lengthy history. However, it is only really in the past five years that both the word woke and efforts to promote woke values have burst into public consciousness. This coincides with the period since Britain voted to leave the EU and overlaps with Donald Trump's time as president of the United States. In 2016, voters in both nations took to the ballot box to signal their rejection of a jaded technocratic neoliberalism. Voters wanted change and they wanted their voices to be heard. The political elites in both nations recognised that this nascent populism threatened their material interests. What's more, it challenged the very foundations of the system they had put in place to keep politics away from ordinary people and in the hands of experts. Populism posed an existential threat to an elite that had long held the power to load the dice in its favour.

Since 2016, sections of the cultural elite have felt more able to express a long-held but once carefully couched contempt for the masses. The rise of populism lent them a renewed sense of purpose. Having something to fight against – be it Trump or Brexit – gave them a certain zeal. So if Brexit and Trump represented a populist, democratic uprising against technocratic government and neoliberal economic policies, then woke can perhaps be understood as a counter-revolution.

It is the means by which the cultural elite can discipline the unruly populace and retain its own managerial position. The rise of elite woke politics reminds citizens that, whoever they vote for, their views will not triumph without a fight.

Adopting woke values has become a pragmatic means for sections of the cultural elite to maintain their position. The tiny proportion of transgender people, for example, is not sufficient to explain the widespread reshaping of social institutions and cultural conventions that is being done in their name. Academics and medical practitioners have helped frame arguments around gender in order to lend intellectual and moral support to activists and put pressure on policymakers. At the same time, many in positions of power have been all too keen to embrace gender ideology.

People in key positions either believe the claims of the transgender activists – for instance, that 'woman' is simply an identity and that single-sex spaces are transphobic – or they are too cowardly to mount a challenge. Getting on board with woke can secure social-media affirmation and workplace promotions, whereas rejecting woke can lead to people being cast out of the cultural elite. And so the cultural elite comes to be comprised of people who go along with woke values without thinking too deeply about them, alongside militant enforcers who have a vested interest in the diversity industry and are often employed, in one way or another, out of the public purse.

Woke allows members of the cultural elite to carve out a role for themselves in managing the alleged division between oppressors and oppressed. As we will discuss more fully in later chapters, woke ideas and identity politics justify a system of mass bureaucracy. Left-wing activists who find they are unpopular on the doorstep can console themselves in their roles as managers and experts, bringing their expertise to bear on society safely removed from democratic accountability. Thomas Frank argues that the new elite breathes new life back into an old idea

– namely, that 'the ruling class ruled because it deserved to rule'.[25] Only now, as Frank puts it, 'the successful [are] not only more capable than those who toil; they [are] morally superior as well'. Significantly, woke not only gives members of the cultural elite a new role to play – it also provides them with a moral justification for their actions.

Class war

One lesson of the past five or six years is that, while citizens are free to reject political regimes that do not represent their interests, there are hefty consequences when they do so. We saw this in the elite hysteria that followed the votes for Brexit and Trump, which has continued to rage in one form or another ever since. The cultural elite will use all the instruments at its disposal – including workplace HR departments, the media, charities, universities, schools, businesses, health services, museums and art galleries – to remind the population where power truly lies. As Michael Lind puts it: 'There is no place in the public, private or nonprofit sectors where those who run afoul of the managerial oligarchy can hide from punishment.'[26] We are being told to shut up and acquiesce to those who claim they are morally superior.

The woke cultural elite is contemptuous of the masses for their alleged ignorance and incorrect beliefs. We saw this most starkly in the commentators who decried Brexit voters for being 'lizard brained', and fell over themselves to demonstrate a link between high levels of educational attainment and voting to remain in the EU. In newspaper op-eds and late-night BBC discussion programmes, Brexit voters were ridiculed for being nostalgic for an age of Empire, despite a lack of evidence to suggest such a sentiment existed. In the imagination of the cultural elite, backward-looking Leavers were contrasted with intellectually superior Remainers who know that Britain's past is only ever a source of shame.

The cultural elite wants to save us from ourselves. We are deemed to be in need of elite instruction to prevent us from becoming obese, alcoholic, gambling addicts and bad parents – as well as racist, sexist and transphobic to boot. This project of moral re-education turns older progressive values on their head. Rather than freedom, people are offered dependency. Rather than gaining solidarity, we are made more suspicious of each other. Rather than equality, we have special treatment for some and punishments for others. Meanwhile, the public – as taxpayers – are expected to foot the bill for their state-backed woke overlords.

The following chapters explain where members of the cultural elite get their ideas from, why woke values have gained so much traction, and how they can be challenged.

Endnotes

[1] *Distinction: A Social Critique of the Judgement of Taste*, Pierre Bourdieu, Routledge Classics (2010)

[2] Cited in: *Elites and Society*, TB Bottomore, Penguin Books (1964)

[3] *The Power Elite*, C Wright Mills, Oxford University Press (2000)

[4] Cited in: *Elites and Society*, TB Bottomore, Penguin Books (1964)

[5] *The New Class War: Saving Democracy from the Metropolitan Elite*, Michael Lind, Atlantic Books (2020)

[6] *The New Class War: Saving Democracy from the Metropolitan Elite*, Michael Lind, Atlantic Books (2020)

[7] The New Left: A Case Study in Professional-Managerial Class Radicalism, Barbara and John Ehrenreich, *Radical America*, Volume 11, Number 3 (1977)

[8] *The Revolt of the Elites and the Betrayal of Democracy*, Christopher Lasch, WW Norton & Company (1996)

[9] The symbolic target of 50% at university reached, BBC News, 26 September 2019

[10] Educational attainment distribution in the United States from 1960 to 2020, Statista, 29 July 2021

[11] *The New Class War: Saving Democracy from the Metropolitan Elite*, Michael Lind, Atlantic Books (2020)

[12] *The Road to Somewhere: The Populist Revolt and the Future of Politics*, David Goodhart, Penguin Books (2017)

[13] *The Triumph of the Political Class*, Peter Oborne, Simon & Schuster (2007)

[14] *The Revolt of the Elites and the Betrayal of Democracy*, Christopher Lasch, WW Norton & Company (1996)

[15] *The Tribe: The Liberal-Left and the System of Diversity*, Ben Cobley, Societas (2018)

[16] Camden Council spends £93,000 on 'woke' training whilst cutting library staff, Guido Fawkes, 21 June 2021

[17] *A Left for Itself: Left-wing Hobbyists and Performative Radicalism*, David Swift, John Hunt Publishing (2019)

[18] The English Aristocracy, Nancy Mitford, *Encounter*, September 1955

[19] Former private school pupils 'dominate Britain's top jobs', ITV News, 25 June 2019

[20] *100 Years of Identity Crisis: Culture War Over Socialisation*, Frank Furedi, De Gruyter (2021)

[21] Help! I don't know what a cervix is, Cosmo Landesman, *Spectator*, 6 October 2021

[22] Labour conference: Wrong to say that only women have a cervix, says Keir Starmer, *Independent*, 26 September 2021

[23] Carrie Johnson says Boris is looking at 'extending' gay rights, *Telegraph*, 5 October 2021

[24] *The Road to Somewhere: The Populist Revolt and the Future of Politics*, David Goodhart, Penguin Books (2017)

[25] *The People, No: A Brief History of Anti-Populism*, Thomas Frank, Metropolitan (2020)

[26] *The New Class War: Saving Democracy from the Metropolitan Elite*, Michael Lind, Atlantic Books (2020)

4 Politicising Children

For many years now, 'school' has been the answer to every conceivable social problem – from climate change to childhood obesity, from teenage pregnancy to knife crime, 'put it on the curriculum' has been the stock response of politicians and campaigners. As a result, the remit of schools stretches wider than ever before. Children are taught about gender identity, sex and relationships, drugs and substance abuse, recycling and sustainability, how to open a bank account and manage personal finances, healthy eating and how to apply for a job. The list goes on and on, crowding out academic subjects. Some of these are, arguably, useful skills – albeit the kind of things most of us pick up as we go through life. But others are far more contested. Not everyone agrees that gender is on a spectrum and not all happy relationships follow the same instruction manual. The boundaries between school and home, between the responsibilities of teachers and parents, have been blurred. In the process, schools have become politicised. This chapter explores how this happened, and why it is to the detriment of children, families and education.

Individual teachers might not see themselves as political; they may reject the notion that schools adopt particular positions on a range of social issues. Some argue that teaching about diet, environmentalism and anti-racism is simply part and parcel of a well-balanced education and essential to socialising children into responsible citizenship. But not all parents agree. This disagreement between parents and teachers shows that when schools take on the role of imparting values, they move beyond promoting socially accepted codes of behaviour and into the realm of social engineering – that is, attempting to change society by moralising children into new values. These values might be taken for granted by the cultural elite, but they are not generally accepted by the bulk of the population.

When schools go down this route, the path is cleared for activist teachers with a missionary zeal in relation to their young charges to pursue their own agenda. Educational goals have become blurred with political aims to such an extent that the need to challenge racism, sexism and homophobia is not seen as an additional responsibility for already stretched teachers, but as fundamental to education itself. Clearly, teachers have a duty to protect children in their care and ensure a safe learning environment for all. Individual acts of bullying or discrimination should be dealt with immediately. Politicisation occurs when teachers come to see tackling broader social problems, as defined by them, as integral to their mission. This moves schools away from educational concerns and into political pursuits. It also sets school in opposition to home. Parents who object to their children being taught about concepts such as 'white privilege' or 'genderfluidity' not unreasonably come to see schools as a site for protest. Schools find themselves on the frontline of the culture war as well as the front pages of newspapers.

Schools are not embroiled in a culture war against their will (although that may well be the case for individual teachers). Just as campaigners have pushed to have their pet issues covered on the curriculum, so too have activist teachers, headteachers and union leaders embraced the opportunity to use the classroom to promote their favoured causes. The UK's biggest teaching union, the National Education Union (NEU), has published an anti-racism charter in which it claims that racism 'affects every single student' and that 'ideas about white superiority are still deeply influential and prevalent'.[1]

In the US, critical race theory underpins teacher-training workshops and classroom practice. Critical race theory is premised on the belief that racism is completely interwoven within society and culture, giving white people inherent privileges and leaving black people permanently disadvantaged. To challenge racism, according to this perspective, race must be made visible. In place of a colour-blind approach to teaching, children must be taught to see themselves as black or white, oppressed or privileged. Parents are understandably uncomfortable when their children are taught to see themselves in this way. In the US, angry parents, organised through Facebook groups, have taken to protesting at school-board meetings.[2]

In response, teachers appear shocked and angry that their domain should be tainted by angry demonstrations and their professional authority called into question. But schools did not become political only at the point at which parents became aware of what was happening in classrooms. In many academic subjects, such as history and English literature, knowledge has given way to the promotion of woke values.

Welcome to the woke school!

Moral engineering now begins in the nursery, with books that convey acceptable messages about the importance of gender equality, antiracism and same-sex relationships. Almost all of them have been published in the past five years. There's Ibram X Kendi's *Antiracist Baby* and Steve Herman's *Teach Your Dragon About Diversity*. Sophie Beer's *Change Starts with Us* teaches children to protect the environment, while Jo Hirst's *A House for Everyone* teaches children about gender identity. Such books may be good at promoting a particular viewpoint to children too young to raise questions, but they are unlikely to inspire a lifelong love of reading. Nor do they forge the intergenerational bonds that give family members shared points of reference. Of course, good teachers regularly update classroom reading material. But in the absence of selection criteria based on literary merit, individual teachers make personal choices grounded in their own priorities.

It's not just books. Nursery teachers are advised to use gender-neutral vocabulary and avoid the use of words and phrases such as 'boys and girls' or 'let's go, guys', which are deemed dangerously 'cisnormative' and sexist. At one primary school in Birmingham in the UK, children are co-opted into policing their classrooms and playgrounds. If a teacher misspeaks, pupils hold up brightly coloured posters highlighting the particular speechcrime that has been committed. They are praised for shaming the teacher, compelling an apology and alerting fellow pupils to the incident. Each week, the two children who pursue this task most enthusiastically are rewarded with a certificate.[3] Children are being trained to accept new values and, in turn, to carry these new values back into the home environment.

Nowadays, gender equality is largely accepted and parents tend to have similar ambitions for both their sons and their daughters. Yet parent protests suggest not all are on board with schools problematising the everyday language and practices of the home and wider society. Whether activist teachers like it or not, 'boys' and 'girls' remains the primary way adults and children categorise each other. Likewise, some parents are concerned that schools demonise boys and traditionally masculine character traits. The phrase 'boys don't cry' might seem old-fashioned nowadays, but it signifies the importance of being stoical and in control of your emotions. Some parents still consider this an important character trait.

What's your gender?

The problematising of 'boys' and 'girls' and the use of gender-neutral language suggest schools are moving from promoting gender equality towards a focus on gender identity. In Brighton in the UK, parents applying for a school place are encouraged to discuss their child's gender identity with them. The form they need to fill in states:

> We recognise that not all children and young people identify with the gender they were assigned at birth or may identify as a gender other than male or female, however the current systems (set nationally) only record gender as male or female. Please support your child to choose the gender they most identify with or if they have another gender identity please leave this blank and discuss this with your child's school.[4]

This sends a message to the very youngest children and their parents that starting school is the point at which all certainties are to be left behind and replaced by the word of the teacher.

Stonewall, the UK's leading LGBT charity, advises schools to replace 'boys and girls' with 'learners' and to hold mixed-sex PE classes. It recommends that transgender pupils should use toilets and changing rooms that match their gender identity rather than their sex. Hundreds of primary and secondary schools have paid to sign up to be Stonewall School and College Champions. According to the *Telegraph*, St Paul's Girls' School in London is reported to be one of them.[5] This elite school no longer has a 'head girl'. This honorific has been replaced by a more gender-neutral title, 'head of school', sending a message that the word 'girl' is outdated and offensive. At a recent training session, staff were taught that there are at least '150 gender identities'.[6] In many schools, personal, social and health education (PSHE) lessons and assemblies send children the message that a person's body does not provide any indication as to whether they are male or female, and that their gender identity is a matter of how they feel.

Changing the way teachers address children, altering school buildings to incorporate changes to the toilets and changing rooms, rewriting uniform requirements – all of this is expensive and time-consuming. Such is the level of commitment among schools today to gender ideology. Children are taught that gender is a matter of identity and must never be assumed. At present, only very small numbers of children claim to be transgender, but this cohort is growing rapidly. In the most recent year for which figures are available, the number of 13-year-olds referred to the UK's primary NHS gender clinic, the Tavistock, rose by 30 per cent on the previous 12 months, to 331. The number of 11-year-olds was up by 28 per cent. The youngest patients were just three years old.[7] Three quarters of children who wanted help to change their gender were girls – the highest proportion ever recorded. Children are being taught that gender ideology is a fact rather than a contested theory, so it should not surprise us when they apply such ideas to their own sense of identity.

Stephanie Davies-Arai, the founder of Transgender Trend, points to the particular risk posed to girls by the current approach to gender:

Children are being confused about biological sex, we are leaving them with no grasp of what is real and what is just a feeling. This mainly affects girls, who are no longer taught how to understand their own bodies. The female sex is being erased, we become reduced to 'menstruators' or 'uterus-havers'... When we define 'boy' and 'girl' as just subjective feelings we take away all boundaries between the sexes. No boundaries are possible, everything is mixed-sex: toilets, changing rooms, overnight accommodation. This is a red flag! It's taking away girls' rights to establish boundaries with the opposite sex, their right to say 'no'.[8]

In the woke school, girls learn that their need for privacy comes second to the rights of boys who identify as girls.

In Loudoun County, just outside of Washington, DC, a teenage girl was raped in the girls' toilets of her school by a boy allegedly wearing a skirt. He was assigned to another school where he sexually assaulted another girl. (He has since been convicted for the assaults and sentenced to supervised probation in a residential-treatment facility, where he will remain until he turns 18.)[9] At a subsequent school-board meeting with parents to discuss a new transgender bathroom policy, Loudoun County school superintendent Scott Ziegler said there was no record of sexual assaults having taken place in school toilets. Local reporting later revealed he had been fully aware of the rape when he said this. Ziegler says he misinterpreted the question he was answering. But parents have accused him of omitting the assault so as to push the policy through, putting gender ideology ahead of their children's safety – a charge the school board strongly denies.[10] The father of the girl who had been raped attended the meeting and got into a heated exchange. Police were called and he was dragged out and arrested. The National School Boards Association later likened him to a 'domestic terrorist'.[11]

Such institutionalised distrust of parents is just as apparent in the UK as it is in the US. Some teachers focus more on childrearing than imparting subject knowledge. Many primary-school teachers, for example, routinely check the contents of children's lunchboxes to make sure they meet standards set down by the school. But not even the very best, most caring or knowledgeable teachers have the same relationship with a child as his or her parents do. The intimate relationship of the home, characterised by family bonds and love, cannot be replicated in the sterile environment of the classroom.

Putting every social problem on the curriculum allows activists to bypass difficult arguments with adults and go straight to the easier task of convincing children. This is social engineering, not socialisation.

Parents are right to be angry when the state, via schools and teachers, tries to dictate how people should behave in the most intimate sphere of their lives. Demonstrating outside schools is ugly and shows children the divisions between the adults in their lives. But it is schools – not parents – that began the process of politicising education. This is not to place the blame at the feet of teachers, though. They are the product of a process that has been playing out for generations.

Teaching race

Identity concerns enter schools through teaching about race. We have already noted the growing influence of critical race theory in schools. This extends into the curriculum, with many schools engaging in projects to decolonise teaching resources and create lessons that 'reflect the achievements of black and minority-ethnic people and address the harmful legacy of colonialism'. The *Guardian* reports that more than 660 schools in England have signed up to an anti-racist curriculum programme developed by teachers and council staff in the London borough of Hackney. Entitled 'Diverse Curriculum – the Black Contribution', it provides pupils with nine weeks of lessons on subjects including the Windrush generation, activism, British identity, and diversity in the arts and sciences.[12] Brighton's schools have signed up to the city council's 'Anti-Racist Schools Strategy', which requires the teaching of 'key aspects of racial literacy', including an 'historical understanding of the construction of "race", an understanding of structural / systemic racism and an understanding of contemporary manifestations and reproductions of "race" both in and out of schools'. The scheme's authors are critical of 'colour blind' approaches to racial equality.[13]

In the UK, guidance produced by a coalition of teaching unions and charities, entitled 'Birth to 5 Matters', recommends that nursery staff should receive training in 'white privilege, systemic racism, and how racism affects children and families in early years settings'.[14] The key message is that under no circumstances must nursery teachers ignore differences in skin colour and treat all those in their care the same way. Doing this, the guidance warns, 'simply allows the continuation of bias in society which disadvantages people from black and minoritised groups. Instead of a colour-blind approach to race, more proactive anti-racism is needed.' This involves 'encouraging dialogue and conversation about difference' in order to 'evoke children's strong sense of fairness' through getting them to 'recognise racist behaviours and develop anti-racist views'. It also requires staff to 'break down false assumptions about everyone being able to succeed on their merits'.

Graduating from nursery does not mark the end of lessons in racial thinking for today's youngsters. For decades, schools have challenged racism and promoted multiculturalism. Following 2020's historic Black Lives Matter protests, this has been ratcheted up via staff training, curriculum reviews, revamped reading lists, special assemblies, workshops and guest speakers. Yet still the teaching unions argue that black history must be 'taught across all subjects including maths, geography, food technology, science and music'.[15]

In June 2020, UK TV station Channel 4 broadcast *The School That Tried to End Racism*, a documentary series that followed the progress of children made to undergo anti-racist training based upon the principles of critical race theory, a UK trial of a US programme.[16] It took place at a state secondary school in London with a diverse pupil intake. The children were filmed completing various tasks to explore racial identity. They had to attach certain negative and positive words to certain ethnic groups. Another task involved them taking up starting positions in a race according to their answers to certain questions. They were told, for example, to 'take a step forward if you've never been asked where you come from', 'step back if you have ever worried about stop and search' and 'step forward if you've never been the only person of your colour in a room'. This exercise was intended to introduce children to the concept of white privilege.

Such lessons teach children to see themselves and others as members of racial groups. For quite a few of the children, this is no easy matter – not least because those of mixed heritage are uncertain which group they are expected to join. Still, all are expected to put themselves in a group and find a label. The intended lesson here is that black and brown people are inherently disadvantaged and white people are inherently privileged. Children are taught to see themselves and their futures as entirely determined by social structures outside of their control.

This is racialising children. Such school programmes force young people to recite stereotypes, inculcating them in notions of victimhood and guilt, based on characteristics they have no control over. As the UK equalities minister, Kemi Badenoch, has argued: 'The repetition of the victimhood narrative is really poisonous for young people because they hear it and believe it.'[17] For black children, being told that they are at a disadvantage, and that a racist 'system' is stacked against them, may mean they are less inclined to make an effort to begin with.

Bari Weiss has written about 'woke weaning', the practice of 'grooming' children in woke thought, particularly around race. Disillusioned parents are getting together to work out how best to deal with schools that implement heavy-handed diversity programmes. One parent told Weiss: 'They are making my son feel like a racist because of the pigmentation of his skin.'[18] Clearly, no school should be supporting or condoning racism. But teaching based on critical race theory is less about challenging specific incidents of racism and more about promoting a particular ideological outlook – one that pushes children to see themselves as representatives of a racial identity.

Campaigners' relentless focus on children makes clear that they see systemic racism as a deeply ingrained part of a person's psychological make-up, which can only be overcome at a young age with input from professionals. Using schools and nurseries to promote critical race theory is bad for education and bad for children. The push to promote ideas around white privilege ignores class-based links to educational underachievement. Teaching black children that they cannot achieve on merit and effort alone sets them up to fail. And when children are taught to see and judge their classmates according to skin colour, racial thinking is rehabilitated among those least likely to care about race.

Schools have changed

For the most part, schools still teach children how to read, write and add up. But too often, woke values creep in – not at the hands of subject specialists or even zealous educationalists, but at the behest of bureaucrats who see the primary purpose of schooling as being to socialise children into state-approved values.

In taking children out of the home environment and placing them in formal institutions, schools have always played a role in socialising children, alongside imparting knowledge. If we look back over more than a century, we see that schools have, at different times, sought to instil in children obedience to authority, religious piety, national pride, respect for multiculturalism and gender equality, as well as teach them the skills needed by employers. In the past, these values were not written down in mission statements and only rarely attracted the ire of parents. They were values that most adults in society collectively shared. In this way, schools reflected the broader culture – they were not attempting to change it.

In the past, schools inculcated particular values, but not through timetabled classes taught by a particular teacher, or even in a weekly talk given in assembly. Instead, values were reflected in every aspect of school life. Pupils were not given formal lessons on the need to respect adults as figures of authority. Instead, they were taught to stand when a teacher entered the classroom, to use 'sir' or 'miss' rather than first names, and to be quiet when teachers were talking. Children were not taught theory around the benefits of competition – they had sports days, star charts, awards ceremonies and house rivalries. One value in particular drove much of what happened in schools: respect for knowledge. Children were expected to leave school knowing more than they did when they arrived. Discipline had a purpose: it was to mould character and encourage application and shape thought. For this reason, discipline in education refers to subjects as well as behaviour.

Just as there was general agreement in the past about the correct values to instil in children, there was also a general consensus about what schools should teach. Beyond the 'three Rs' – reading, writing and arithmetic – there was the literary canon, key periods in national history, scientific principles and geographical features to be mastered. Preserving and passing on canonical knowledge made schools inherently conservative institutions. Rather than seeking to change society in their own image, teachers looked to the past to determine what would be of value for the future. The ethos of many schools, represented in rules, uniforms and rituals, was rooted in tradition. The conservative nature of schooling does not automatically imply links to the ideology of the Conservative Party. Nonetheless, back in the 1970s, a majority of teachers in the UK did claim to be Conservative voters.[19]

Over several decades, traditional values have been questioned, rejected and replaced. Most fundamentally of all, the authority of the past has been called into question. When educationalists come to understand the role of schools not as conserving or transmitting the knowledge of the past, but as preparing children both intellectually and morally for life in a rapidly changing world, then there is no longer collective agreement about what children need to know. Indeed, when knowledge is contested and facts are easily 'Google-able', it becomes difficult to make the case for teaching anything in particular. Getting children to pass exams, rather than deepening their knowledge and understanding, has become the primary purpose of teaching. Curriculum planners seek to second guess the next generation of workplace skills and, because this is impossible, they get children to 'learn how to learn'. Teachers are no longer presented as a source of knowledge but as learners themselves, just like their pupils. And if teachers have no special knowledge to impart, they have little basis to command respect.

Unlike passing on knowledge, learning to learn is morally and intellectually vacuous. This vacuum has been filled by woke. Given woke is the dominant outlook of teachers today, it is what they automatically reach for. This is not to say that teachers are so in thrall to identity politics that they no longer see subject knowledge as important. Rather, it is because cultivating subject knowledge is no longer seen as an end in itself that woke values are invited in to lend a sense of purpose to education.

Woke schools focus on inculcating particular attributes and values into their young charges. This is done explicitly through assemblies and discreet lessons such as personal, social and health education (PSHE) and topics such as relationships and sex education (RSE). Schools promote a general ethos through the overall environment: the wall displays, book choices, rules around behaviour and uniform, and teachers' language use.

What's lost from this is any meaningful sense of education in relation to knowledge, attainment or standards. In California, campaigners have recently argued for changes to the teaching of maths. In a document on 'dismantling racism in mathematics instruction', they argued against 'upholding the idea that there are always right and wrong answers'.[20] Their demands were rejected, but a review of the California curriculum still called for an end to streaming maths classes by ability or achievement and the scrapping of 'gifted and talented' programmes because they are 'inequitable'.[21] The assumption that black children are disadvantaged by merit and marking demonstrates a bigotry of low expectations. This patronising approach has been around for some time now. As Christopher Lasch noted in the 1990s:

> *Today it is widely believed, at least by members of the caring class, that standards are inherently oppressive, that far from being impersonal they discriminate against women, blacks and minorities in general. Standards, we are told, reflect the cultural hegemony of dead white European males. Compassion compels us to recognise the injustice of imposing them on everybody else.*[22]

Today's teachers are themselves the product of a culture that sees no authority in the past and little value in knowledge. For this reason, standards appear arbitrary. Teachers trained in the ways of 'child-centred' rather than 'subject-centred' schooling see their role in the classroom as either technocratic instruction or shaping the values of the next generation. Subject knowledge is edged out. The losers are children and education.

Today's schools are the product of a long-running crisis in education. They also play a role in preparing children for a woke future. Mao saw in children and young people a zealous ideological purity and a desire to please that could be exploited for his own ruthless ends. For this reason, he gave students a central role in his Cultural Revolution. Now it seems that some educators in Western countries are also keen to manipulate children in the pursuit of their own political goals. Those using schools to promote woke ideas do so because appealing directly to children gives them a captive audience, one that is too young, powerless, inexperienced and lacking in knowledge to be able to challenge what they hear.

The result of all this is that children are taught to treat parents *and* teachers with suspicion – to see adults in general not as a source of wisdom, but as a source of outdated and problematic views. At the same time, adults learn to be suspicious of children who have been taught to play the role of informer. The headteacher at the Birmingham primary school mentioned earlier in this chapter recounted to *The*

Times with delight the day that the 'children ran into my office one playtime and said, "Miss, Miss, something terrible has happened… one of the supervisors has just taken a skipping rope off a boy and said boys don't skip". They were rightly absolutely horrified. It was brilliant that they ran in to tell me.'[23] The playground supervisor had to attend a professional-conduct meeting and now no longer works at the school. What's more, one of the American parents interviewed by Weiss noted that this culture of calling out ideological transgressions also means that 'kids are scared of other kids'.[24]

The demand for conformity to a particular viewpoint is, increasingly, a major focus of schooling. Sadly, when children become adults, leave school and arrive at university, they find that all of this is ramped up further, as we will discover in the next chapter.

Endnotes

[1] Anti-Racism Charter, National Education Union

[2] Inside the American schools being torn apart by controversial race teaching, *Sunday Telegraph*, 4 July 2021

[3] We're girls, not guys: pupils urged to protest against 'sexist' language, *The Sunday Times*, 25 April 2021

[4] Brighton pupils 'able to choose own gender', BBC News, 20 April 2016

[5] Stop using terms 'boy' and 'girl', Stonewall tells teachers, *Telegraph*, 18 June 2021

[6] St Paul's Girls' School ditches 'binary' head girl, *The Times* (London), 19 June 2021

[7] Tavistock clinic reveals surge in girls switching gender, *The Times* (London), 30 June 2019

[8] Interview with author, recorded in *The Corrosive Impact of Transgender Ideology*, Joanna Williams, Civitas (2020)

[9] Family of schoolgirl raped in girls' bathroom asked judge to SPARE Loudoun County 'boy in a skirt', 15, from jail to 'give him a fighting chance at becoming a better person': Judge grants probation despite blasting his 'scary' psych report, *Mail Online*, 12 January 2022

[10] Loudoun County parents demand superintendent and school board members resign over 'cover-up' of sexual assault in order to 'push school's pro-transgender policies', *Mail Online*, 27 October 2021

[11] Loudoun County assault victim's dad wants apology for being called 'domestic terrorist', ABC 7 News, 26 October 2021

[12] Hundreds of schools in England sign up for anti-racist curriculum, *Guardian*, 26 March 2021

[13] Brighton's battle over critical race theory, Adrian Hart, *spiked*, 26 July 2021

[14] *Birth to Five Matters: Non-statutory guidance for the Early Years Foundation Stage*, Early Years Coalition, 2021

[15] Black history 'should be taught across all subjects in UK schools', *Guardian*, 5 April 2021

[16] *The School That Tried to End Racism*, Channel 4 (2020)

[17] Kemi Badenoch: The problem with critical race theory, *Spectator*, 24 October 2020

[18] The miseducation of America's elites, Bari Weiss, *City Journal*, 9 March 2021

[19] *The Changing Urban School*, Robert Thornbury, Routledge (2012)

[20] *A Pathway to Equitable Math Instruction: Dismantling Racism in Mathematics Instruction*, May 2021

[21] 'Racist' California maths review is axed, *The Times* (London), 26 May 2021

[22] *The Revolt of the Elites and the Betrayal of Democracy*, Christopher Lasch, WW Norton & Company (1996)

[23] We're girls, not guys: pupils urged to protest against 'sexist' language, *The Times* (London), 25 April 2021

[24] The miseducation of America's elites, Bari Weiss, *City Journal*, 9 March 2021

5 Training the Elite

Higher education is structurally, systemically and irredeemably racist. Academics and students alike are sexist, homophobic, transphobic and ableist. All indicators show that this is clearly not the case. And yet we are told that a whole apparatus of diversity and inclusion is needed to make university a hospitable place for minorities. In the fevered imagination of university administrators, prejudice, discrimination and abuse would be inevitable were it not for an endless cycle of workshops, awareness-raising campaigns, anonymous reporting systems and institutional policies setting out exactly how staff and students should relate to each other – right down to which words they should use.

On campus, both staff and students receive formal instruction in how to think about race, gender identity and sexuality through policies, student workshops and staff-training programmes. This instruction combines with an atmosphere that is hostile to allowing opposing views to be raised. Censorship can be explicit: speakers viewed as controversial may be subject to petitions and protests – fronted by students, but often supported by academics – calling for their invitations to be withdrawn. The blurring of the line between education and political activism means new recruits quickly become aware of which views are socially acceptable and which are considered beyond the pale. More harmful than No Platforming campaigns is a culture of self-censorship and political conformity. The upshot is that universities, as institutions, become less concerned with the pursuit of truth, or knowledge, and more concerned with the inculcation of woke values. They provide training in woke thinking for future members of the cultural elite. This will be the focus of this chapter.

Woke on campus

It is largely down to events that occurred in American colleges that woke ideas first began to enter public consciousness. In the two academic years either side of Donald Trump's presidential victory, student protests swept colleges across the US. Many of them were focused on what students claimed was systemic campus racism. A small number garnered global media coverage. Three, in particular, stood out.

In October 2015, as undergraduates at Yale began to pick out their Halloween costumes, campus administrators decided to offer them explicit guidance about which outfits would not be considered appropriate. Erika Christakis – a lecturer at the university whose husband, Nicholas, was then master of Yale's Silliman College – sent an email to students defending their right to choose their costumes without interference. In response, hundreds of Yale students joined protests calling for the Christakises to be fired for making them feel unsafe in their own home. Video footage showed students screaming and shouting abuse at the couple. They resigned from their posts the following year. [1]

Around the same time, the University of Missouri hit the headlines. Campus tensions over alleged incidents of racism had been simmering for several years and grew louder in the autumn of 2015. On 3 November, student Jonathan Butler began a hunger strike, claiming he would not eat until the university's president, Tim Wolfe, resigned. An anti-racist group, Concerned Student 1950, backed Butler's demands and other students joined in the protest. Encampments were set up.

Eventually, the students got their way and Wolfe resigned.[2] That day a reporter was forcibly stopped by faculty member Melissa Click from covering the demonstrations.

Then, in 2017, protests erupted at Evergreen State College, a small liberal-arts college in Olympia, Washington. Each year, Evergreen had marked a 'Day of Absence' when minority staff and students would stay away from campus in order to highlight the contribution they make to university life. In 2017, it was requested that white people leave the campus instead. Biology professor Bret Weinstein refused and described the event as 'an act of oppression'. He became the target of 'anti-racist' protesters who demanded he be fired. At one point, he was advised by police to stay away from campus for his own safety[3] as students, some reportedly wielding bats, ran riot.[4] Weinstein later sued Evergreen and resigned after receiving a settlement.[5]

These three incidents had a lasting impact on universities across America and the UK. Social media disseminated the viciousness of some of the protesters' tactics and their targeting of specific individuals. The world watched as university leaders seemingly acquiesced to the students' every demand. These campus protests also put woke ideas at the heart of broader political debate for the first time. One particular trend that emerged was the newfound privileging of emotional safety. A previous generation of student activists fought for the lifting of over-bearing restrictions on their political and social lives. Today's young people demand to be better protected. Where students once demanded freedom of speech, woke students want freedom *from* speech.

Teaching students what to think

At the University of Kent in the UK, all new students are expected to sit a four-hour mandatory online module called Expect Respect, which covers topics such as white privilege, microaggressions and pronouns.

Students are tested to check they understand that, for instance, being able to wear second-hand clothes without being held up as an example of 'the bad morals of my race' is an example of white privilege.[6] Meanwhile, at the University of St Andrews, students sitting a similar test are asked to agree with statements including: 'Acknowledging your personal guilt is a useful start point in overcoming unconscious bias.' Those who tick 'disagree' are marked as having answered incorrectly, and too many incorrect answers can mean having to retake the module.[7] Being asked to sit such tests prior to embarking upon any academic work sends a message to incoming students that there are correct views to be held on campus and that disagreement is an unacceptable moral failing.

Staff are also being told what to think. In the US, the University of Iowa's College of Law responded to the Black Lives Matter protests of 2020 by forming an Anti-Racism Action Committee. The committee recommended that the college's staff be asked in annual evaluation forms about their contribution to 'diversity, equity and inclusion'. Responses would impact on promotion and tenure consideration.[8]

Back in the UK, at the University of Manchester, staff have been advised not to use terms like 'mother' and 'father' and instead to use more inclusive and gender-neutral terms like 'parent' or 'guardian'. Likewise, 'men' and 'women' should be replaced with 'individuals', while 'manpower', 'mankind' and 'chairman' should be replaced with 'workforce', 'humankind' and 'chair'.[9] The University of Edinburgh provides a list of transphobic statements that academics and students are urged not to say. It includes 'all women hate their periods' and 'you're either a man or a woman'.[10] In the US, Northwestern University advises that rather than greeting friends with 'Hey, guys', people should say 'Hey, everyone'. It also issues guidance for 'socioeconomic language', recommending 'under-resourced' rather than 'inner-city' and 'working hard to make ends meet' rather than 'working poor'.[11]

These lists reveal what passes as offensive on today's campuses.

Universities are not simply outlawing racial epithets or gross insults. Staff and students are far too polite and well-intentioned to utter such phrases. Rather, universities are proscribing common words that are part of most people's everyday vocabulary. Campus bureaucrats dictate the limits of acceptability in line with their cultural-elite prejudices. Spontaneous interactions are replaced by a stilted deference to the rules. Personal behaviour, even unconscious actions, are labelled as 'microaggressions' and can get you into trouble. Cambridge University hit the headlines in 2021 after students were encouraged to report professors who raise an eyebrow, give backhanded compliments, or refer to women as girls. The university's Report and Support website permitted anonymity, meaning alleged offence-givers would have no idea who they upset.[12]

We might assume that when insults are so 'micro' as to be barely perceptible, students have little to worry about. Or we might think they should be encouraged to give the offender the benefit of the doubt, or even strike up a conversation and explain why they are upset. Instead, students are given training in the sin of unconscious bias and taught to see themselves as too vulnerable ever to risk an off-the-cuff conversation. Meanwhile, professors – particularly the older, pale and male variety – are made fearful of anonymous accusations because they suspect the university will not side with them, nor with the principles of academic freedom.

Cambridge's plans were met with a backlash. Following national publicity, professors launched a revolt over the snitching site. In an open letter, they accused the university of trampling on free speech, denouncing the reporting system for fostering a culture 'akin to that of a police state'. The university subsequently took its Report and Support system offline, saying that some material 'was included in error'. However, one in four of the UK's top universities reportedly allows for the anonymous recording of microaggressions. Durham University lists 'not giving someone eye contact' and 'constantly criticising and never praising' as examples of behaviour worthy of further investigation.[13] Schemes like Expect Respect and Report and Support call into question who runs universities and to what end. Administrators – often led by a new cohort of professionals offering instruction in teaching and managing the learning environment, and lent credibility by charities and sector-specific organisations such as Athena SWAN, Stonewall and Advance HE – wield huge influence. The practices they promote have become widely accepted.

Trigger warnings are a good example. Once considered outlandish, they are now routinely used. Trigger warnings are statements giving advance notice that a book, course or text might upset, offend or trigger panic attacks among those who have suffered trauma. They have been subject to much discussion, but they are perhaps best understood as a disciplinary mechanism. When academics issue trigger warnings, they demonstrate compliance with the regime imposed by administrators and managers.

Psychologists have questioned the efficacy of trigger warnings in helping victims of abuse.[14] But this misses the point: abuse and trauma are now defined so widely that actual victims of specific incidents are lost in the disarray. Instead, trigger warnings teach all students that they are psychologically vulnerable in the face of any discussion about race, sex or gender, no matter how historical the material or abstract the discussion. In turn, mandatory trigger warnings remind lecturers to view students as extremely sensitive and easily offended. One lesson higher education offers students today is that cries of psychological harm often lead to political wins, particularly when they are backed up by menace. We saw this with the case of Professor Kathleen Stock. Students accused her of transphobia and sought her removal from the University of Sussex. The harassment and abuse they meted out ultimately led to her resignation.

The assumption that students are so vulnerable as to find even mundane aspects of campus life psychologically harmful is matched by the belief that potential sources of trauma lurk everywhere – in course reading lists, the architecture of campus and myriad daily interactions. Such sensitivity is not challenged – it is cultivated. This drives demand for colouring books, cookies, petting zoos and meditation workshops at exam time – or, better still, the replacement of exams with less intensive forms of assessment. At Goldsmiths, University of London, black and ethnic-minority students are allowed to defer essay deadlines and exams if they suffer from 'racial trauma' during their time at university.[15] This assumption of racially traumatised staff and students underpins demands for statues, like those of Cecil Rhodes at Oxford, to be pulled down and for buildings to be renamed on supposedly anti-racist grounds.

In September 2020, the University of Edinburgh renamed its David Hume Tower '40 George Square' after the philosopher was accused of racism. The university said that Hume's comments on race, 'though not uncommon at the time, rightly cause distress today'.[16] Few saw a need to explain to students the significance of Hume's work. Instead, it was accepted that students were 'rightly' distressed, that distress was the 'correct' emotional response. This begs the question: are the many people who were not distressed by the existence of David Hume Tower racist? Emotions seem to be as important as words in the woke university.

Education or activism?

This deference to a minority of overly sensitive students and obedience to administrative edicts leaves universities open to activists with a political agenda. Surveys suggest that a growing proportion of academics back left-wing parties. A survey of university staff conducted immediately prior to the UK's 2019 General Election revealed that 54 per cent intended to vote for the Labour Party, 23 per cent for the Liberal

Democrats, eight per cent for the Conservative Party and five per cent for the Green Party. This was almost unchanged from a similar survey conducted prior to the 2017 General Election.[17]

Similar findings have emerged when polling academics in the US. A report from the National Association of Scholars in 2020 suggested that the ratio of college-professor donations to Democrats as opposed to Republicans was 95:1.[18] Such findings reveal a political bias that is profoundly at odds with the political landscape of the respective nations, and a growing homogeneity of views within academia that prompts concerns about groupthink or confirmation bias in research. All this makes it possible for views that are politically partisan to become accepted as common sense. The political views of individual academics would not be a concern if there was a culture of tolerance and a welcoming of debate and intellectual challenge on campus. Unfortunately, that is often far from the case.

Much like in schools, the politicisation of universities has less to do with the strength of arguments or cunning tactics deployed by activists than it does with the hollowing out of an older sense of purpose. This is well illustrated by the widespread campaign to 'decolonise' higher education. The decolonise movement has spread from the US to South Africa and the UK. It builds on ideas that emerge from critical race theory. A key demand is that universities acknowledge and take steps to rectify the legacy of colonialism which, campaigners argue, can be found in the structure of universities and how knowledge is taught and pursued. In practice, this often means arguing for the removal of statues and plaques from campus and the rewriting of reading lists and course content so as to 'de-centre' work that foregrounds 'white' knowledge. The content of the curriculum, campaigners argue, reflects and perpetuates a colonial legacy, through the presentation of a white, Western intellectual tradition as universal. The privileging of Kant, Shakespeare and Pythagoras, they suggest, normalises a Eurocentric and Enlightenment-focused view of the world.

Decolonisers ignore the fact that prominent black intellectuals, like WEB Du Bois and CLR James, revelled in access to canonical works. 'I denounce European colonialist scholarship', James told a conference in 1966, 'but I respect the learning and profound discoveries of Western civilisation'.[19] Even as James was making this statement, decades before today's woke young students were even born, academics themselves were at the forefront of disparaging the 'profound discoveries of Western civilisation'. For this reason, those now wanting to decolonise the curriculum find that university managers already endorse their cause. The days of expecting students to imbibe the great works of the Western canon are long gone.[20] Postmodernism dictates that works of literature and philosophy are simply 'texts' and neither intellectual content nor stylistic beauty particularly matter. In the woke university, both staff and students share the same intention: to disrupt the Western intellectual tradition in favour of teaching content that is superficially diverse but completely lacking in intellectual diversity.

Censoring wrongthink

There is nothing new about universities being hotbeds of political radicalism. The Sorbonne in Paris and the University of California at Berkeley became global cultural reference points following the student protest movements of the 1960s. But where those movements fought for free speech, just a decade later radical students had started to launch campaigns to curtail speech on campus. There has never been a golden age of unfettered free speech on campus. When the very first universities were established over 800 years ago, the all-powerful church dictated what could and could not be discussed. When the church stepped back, the state stepped in. In the UK, universities had *in loco parentis* responsibilities when the age of majority was still 21. When this was lowered to 18, students took over the policing of debate themselves, with the first 'No Platform' campaigns waged against far-right speakers in the 1970s. Since this time, campaigns to prevent the far right from speaking have extended to encompass anti-abortion groups, mainstream right-wing politicians and gender-critical feminists. In this way, activists within universities have mirrored the increasingly censorious turn within left-wing politics more broadly.

Despite a long history of student agitation and campus censorship, something has clearly changed in the past few years. Today, threats to academic freedom come from multiple directions. Students who campaign to have lecturers sacked and invited speakers No Platformed are backed up by diversity officers and administrators happy to maintain the campus as a 'safe space'.[21] Legal provisions, such as the Prevent duty, compel UK universities to monitor students deemed at risk of radicalisation and to vet external speakers.[22] Meanwhile, academics themselves sign petitions and share social-media posts calling for their colleagues to be fired or, at the very least, silenced.[23]

Institutional speech codes and language guides, as well as training in unconscious bias and microaggressions, all send the signal that words are powerful and can give offence – that they must be used carefully rather than thrown around spontaneously. Words do, of course, have immense power to provoke and persuade. But there must be room for people to speak freely, disagree, change their minds and test received wisdom, particularly in a university. Learning depends upon putting your own ideas into words, understanding how language conveys emotions, and honing arguments in response to ideas with which you disagree. The woke university chills speech and prevents students from learning these invaluable lessons.

On both sides of the Atlantic, there are numerous examples of speakers being disinvited from taking part in previously agreed events. Students at Elizabethtown College in Pennsylvania invited Joe Basrawi, a conservative political commentator, to speak at an event in September 2021. Basrawi's chosen topic was critical race theory. After his talk had been advertised, an administrator objected to the title of a flyer for the event ('Critical Hate Theory') and informed the organisers that the college needed to approve guest speakers. According to the Foundation for Individual Rights in Education (FIRE), once the students submitted the required information, 'administrators denied the request on the basis that Basrawi would promote a "negative" view of critical race theory and "cause division and disorder" on campus'.[24]

In 2021, Lisa Keogh, a law student at Abertay University in Scotland, faced formal disciplinary proceedings and possible expulsion from her course for stating, in the context of a seminar on gender, feminism and the law, that 'women have vaginas'. This may be a simple biological fact and something almost every person knows to be true. But according to lecturers in the grip of gender ideology, and institutions in thrall to LGBT campaign groups, sex is nothing more than a label arbitrarily assigned at birth and arguing otherwise is akin to heresy. Keogh told *The Times*: 'I didn't intend to be offensive, but I did take part in a debate and outlined my sincerely held views. I was abused and called names by the other students, who told me I was a "typical white, cis girl".[25]

Keogh was cleared of misconduct, but only after a formal investigation into the potentially 'offensive' and 'discriminatory' nature of her comments. This makes little educational sense. Her comments were scientifically correct and echoed the views of radical feminists. Was this entire strand of feminist thought outlawed from this module on feminism? The government has launched repeated inquiries into the law around gender recognition. If law students are prevented from discussing these questions then speech is apparently less free on university campuses than it is in the rest of society. Debate should be at the very heart of higher education. Keogh knows this better than her lecturers. 'You have got to be able to freely exchange differing opinions, otherwise it's not a debate', she told *The Times*. But in the woke university, dissent is forbidden.

We now have a campus culture where debate is discouraged and 'correct' speech – be it declaring pronouns or pledging allegiance to Black Lives Matter – is compelled. Academics and students alike quickly learn that when the costs of misspeaking are so high, it is better to say nothing.[26] Academic freedom is, at best, an empty slogan to be wheeled out only when politically expedient.[27] At worst, it is stigmatised as a right-wing trope.[27] At the Maryland Institute College of Art in 2020, faculty member Saul Myers was investigated for harassment, all because he argued in defence of academic freedom and dissent. The college did not uphold the harassment claim against Myers, but it did issue him with a written disciplinary warning based on the college's expectation of 'respectful interactions among members of its community'.[28]

It is easy to blame overly sensitive students for restricting free speech, but in the woke university many professors undermine academic freedom in practice and degrade it as a value. Too many lecturers either join in with or fail to speak out against attempts by students to target individual academics. The campaign against Eric Kaufmann, a professor of politics at Birkbeck, University of London, is a good example. In 2021, he was the subject of a letter, signed by both staff and students, calling for university management to 'investigate' his 'activities' and 'make public its findings'. It read:

> Birkbeck prides itself on its commitment to inclusion, diversity and critical scholarship. The university claims that the college community is 'safe, supportive and inclusive of all' and, furthermore, was 'committed to addressing racism and challenging injustice in all that we do, including our educational programmes'.

> Clearly, Kaufmann does not align with these core values.[29]

Here the signatories take for granted that a university should have values above and beyond the pursuit of knowledge. But this is a strange assumption. Who can lay claim to speak on behalf of a university? Who gets to decide what exactly are institutional values? What is clear is that holding opposing values is considered justifiable grounds for public denunciation. Heterodox views are not welcomed as a prompt for debate; they are publicly rejected in a display of moral outrage and political conformity.

Kaufmann's case came hot on the heels of Neil Thin's suspension from the University of Edinburgh, following complaints from students about his social-media posts.[30] Thin, a senior lecturer in social anthropology, stood accused of making racist and sexist comments and writing tweets 'variously described as "triggering", "offensive", "bigoted", "racist", "misogynistic" and "transphobic"'. The evidence against him amounted to a declaration that 'civilisation is for everyone', a defence of JK Rowling, and a joke questioning whether NASA will announce that the 'man in the moon' is 'actually non-binary'. Rather than defend a member of its academic staff against these ridiculous allegations, the university launched an investigation into Thin, before clearing him of any wrongdoing.

The group most often targeted for campus censorship in the UK today is gender-critical feminists. Back in 2019, Jo Phoenix, then professor of criminology at the Open University, was scheduled to speak at the University of Essex on the topic of trans rights in the criminal-justice system. Students duly protested. A leaflet headlined 'SHUT THE F*** UP TERF', alongside a picture of a gun, was circulated.[31] Another flyer read: 'Delegitimising trans people is part of a misogynistic, colonialist and violent ideology. She is covering up her bigotry in academic jargon and claiming to just "raise questions", but this is a typical disguise for prejudice.'[32] The university acquiesced and cancelled Phoenix's lecture.

A subsequent independent review of the cancellation led to a public apology from Essex University's vice-chancellor, and the wider revelation that staff and students at Essex felt 'constrained to self-censor their speech and activity because of concerns about how we manage the balance between freedom of speech and our commitment to diversity, equality and inclusion'.[33]

The findings of the review revealed the extent to which Essex University had been 'captured' by LGBT campaign group Stonewall. It pointed out that 'the university's equality, diversity and inclusion annual report for 2018-19 states that one of the university's equality objectives is to consistently be ranked in the Stonewall Top 100 employers list'. The review noted that the definition of harassment contained within the university's policy on supporting trans and non-binary staff 'states the law as Stonewall would prefer it to be, rather than the law as it is. To that extent the policy is misleading.' The relationship between Stonewall and the university appeared 'to have given university members the impression that gender-critical academics can legitimately be excluded from the institution'.[34] Perhaps inevitably, Essex faced a backlash for publishing such a critical review. The university's vice-chancellor, Professor Anthony Forster, later responded: 'I have been asked to provide a number of apologies, including: to anyone who felt excluded from or affected by the process of contributing to the review; for the manner in which the [report] was released, and in particular for the timing of the release.'[35]

The lecturers' union, the University and College Union (UCU), has also failed to protect members who have been targeted by woke mobs of academics and students. In the case of Kathleen Stock, her Sussex UCU branch issued a statement essentially defending the students who accused her of transphobia.[36] Likewise, in response to the government's proposed Higher Education (Freedom of Speech) Bill, UCU said: 'There are serious threats to freedom of speech and academic freedom from campus [sic], but they come from the government and university managers, not staff and students.'[37] It would undoubtedly be better not to have academic freedom policed and enforced by a government that shows scant regard for the importance of free speech – and, indeed, little understanding of what academic freedom actually entails. But many in our universities are denying there is even a problem. We cannot underestimate the scale of the cultural change that is needed to uphold academic freedom.

Changed goals

Academic freedom is not just a platitude. It is crucial to the unfettered pursuit of knowledge, to what should be the fundamental purpose of a university. Put simply, academics need to be able to ask questions that challenge the consensus in their disciplines, and in the public sphere beyond the university, without fear of disapprobation from their own institutions. Without such safeguards, academics are limited to researching and teaching only that which confirms received wisdom. The fact that this is so rarely raised as an issue suggests that many in universities no longer see the unfettered pursuit of knowledge, still less of truth, as their primary goal. This calls into question the nature of education and the capacity for universities to maintain standards.

Elite universities have traditionally been bastions of privilege, with a student body that was predominantly white, male and wealthy. Countless talented individuals were previously denied admission and, in turn, access to the well-paid professional roles that a degree from a top institution opens up. But attempts to compensate for disadvantage at a community level, often through lower entry requirements for individuals, are not without problems. Today's anti-racism campaigners argue that meritocracy is a disguise for white privilege and that black students should not be penalised for spelling or grammatical errors. This suggests they have little faith in the intellectual capacity of black students. If black students are receiving a lower standard of schooling, then it is that which must change; black students are ill-served by differential, low expectations.

Rather than looking to broaden the educational horizons of all students, universities run training sessions in 'concepts of white privilege, fragility and allyship, and intersectionality'.[38] Black students are taught to see themselves as victims of racism, while white students are cast in the role of oppressor and invited to undertake unconscious-bias training. Challenging racism on campus today seems to be less about serving the best interests of black staff and students and more about shoring up the moral authority of institutions that have lost sight of their real purpose.

Higher education has become a business like any other. Vice-chancellors do not like to think of themselves as mere purveyors of a commodity, yet they seem incapable of articulating the intellectual importance of universities. Unable to defend academic disciplines that stand accused of being 'Eurocentric' or elitist, university leaders now see shaping 'the minds and attitudes of the next generation' and 'driving cultural change' as their mission.[39] We need to ask whether racialising staff and students is a price worth paying for university leaders to feel good about themselves.

Such disregard for academic freedom shows the extent to which the purpose of higher education has changed. Rather than intellectual risk-taking, we have a culture of conformity. Rather than dissent, we have consensus. Rather than challenging the status quo, we have adherence to predetermined values – and so often nowadays, those values are woke.

Training a woke elite

Some argue that woke values took off in universities due to the dominance of critical theory and postmodernism. But this can make it seem as if these ideas won out because of their sheer intellectual strength, or because their adherents achieved success through a Gramsci-inspired 'long march through the institutions'. In reality, the ascendancy of woke has less to do with the intellectual authority of critical theorists and more to do with the abject failure of an intellectual elite to defend Enlightenment values such as rationality, reason, liberty, progress and tolerance. Even in the 1960s, radical young scholars often found themselves pushing at an open door. An older generation of professors no longer had the confidence to maintain traditional scholarly principles, which they saw as tainted following the experience of war in general and the Holocaust in particular.

Universities, unable to pursue knowledge and preserve culture as ends in themselves, sought out a new moral mission. In the years after the Second World War, it seemed clear that universities could, through championing science, contribute to both the public good and national prosperity. But by the 1990s, the public good was being defined along far more individualistic lines. Rather than national prosperity, the goal was for individuals to achieve social mobility. The job of the university was to take students from disadvantaged backgrounds and provide them with sufficient credentials to enable them to get a job with a fractionally higher salary than they would have got without higher education.

This mission was later sold to fee-paying students as a means of securing a return on their investment. Employability skills came with a side order of customer satisfaction. One thing students, already perceived as vulnerable, are assumed to desire today is safety. Across the higher-education sector, this has come to be understood as emotional safety. This means universities now swiftly acquiesce to demands premised upon claims of vulnerability. And so, by accident rather than by design, universities have found themselves with a new moral purpose: the pursuit of woke.

Universities should be places for the brightest students to learn from professors at the forefront of their discipline. However, if universities are not all that invested in the pursuit of knowledge, and are not especially keen on a commitment to truth, then academic attainment becomes less of a concern. If universities are more concerned with bringing about social justice, or the promotion of diversity and inclusion, then it matters less that students have the correct credentials and more that they contribute to the creation of a diverse student body.

The woke university has a superficially diverse but values-aligned student body, taught by politically homogeneous instructors. Induction and ongoing training sessions reinforce the importance of holding the correct views and using the correct terminology. Dissent is quashed, consensus insisted upon. The decolonised curriculum struggles with Newton, Darwin and Hume, but embraces unconscious-bias training and diversity workshops. Education can still be found, but both academics and students have to search long and hard for it. Nonetheless, grades keep rising and certificates keep on coming.

Universities' primary role in the 21st century is preparing young adults for the woke workplace. Students might leave university having read little, discussed less and unable to formulate a critical thought. They may have become illiberal, intolerant and ignorant. But they will be fluent in an ever-shifting woke vocabulary and know the phrases that mark out transgressors. A century ago, universities trained up young men to work in the colonies and 'civilise' the 'natives'. Today, universities play a similar role, only now the 'natives' are at home.

Endnotes

[1] The perils of writing a provocative email at Yale, Conor Friedersdorf, *Atlantic*, 26 May 2016

[2] Jonathan Butler: Meet the man whose hunger strike flipped the script at Mizzou, CNN, 10 November 2015

[3] Professor told he's not safe on campus after college protests at Evergreen State College, Eugene Volokh, *Washington Post*, 26 May 2017

[4] Evergreen State College resumes classes after students with 'sticks and baseball bats' caused $10,000 of property damage, *Insider*, 7 June 2017

[5] Evergreen professor at centre of protests resigns; college will pay $500,000, *Seattle Times*, 16 September 2017

[6] Wearing second-hand clothes 'an example of white privilege', students told, *Telegraph*, 27 September 2021

[7] St Andrews university sets bias test for entry, *The Times* (London), 1 October 2021

[8] Memo to the dean of the College of Law from Iowa Law Anti-Racism Action Committee, 21 August 2020

[9] Now Manchester University gives in to woke brigade as it advises lecturers to replace 'mother' and 'man' with terms like 'guardians' or 'individuals' in bid to be more inclusive, *Daily Mail*, 14 March 2021

[10] University of Edinburgh staff given banned list of transphobic microaggressions they can't say to students, *Pink News*, 3 May 2021

[11] Inclusive Language Guide, Family Institute, Northwestern University, 16 October 2019

[12] Cambridge accused of creating 'police state' where dons can be reported for raising an eyebrow, *Telegraph*, 20 May 2021

[13] Lecturers who avoid eye contact could be reported as 1 in 4 top universities monitor 'microaggressions', *Telegraph*, 29 May 2021

[14] Helping or Harming? The Effect of Trigger Warnings on Individuals With Trauma Histories, PJ Jones et al, *Clinical Psychological Science*, 1 June 2020

[15] Black and ethnic minority students can use 'racial trauma' to defer exams, *Telegraph*, 17 June 2021

[16] Edinburgh University renames David Hume Tower over 'racist' views, BBC News, 13 September 2020

[17] Labour vote set to hold up among HE staff, THE survey suggests, *Times Higher Education*, 4 December 2019

[18] *Partisan Registration and Contributions of Faculty in Flagship Colleges*, National Association of Scholars, 17 January 2020

[19] The Making of the Caribbean People, CLR James, lecture to the Second Montreal Conference on West Indian Affairs, 1966

[20] *Cynical Theories: How Activist Scholarship Made Everything About Race, Gender, and Identity – and Why This Harms Everybody*, Helen Pluckrose and James Lindsay, Swift Press (2020)

[21] University speakers with gender-critical views are most likely to be banned from addressing students, *Telegraph*, 20 February 2021

[22] Counter-terrorism – the Prevent duty, Office for Students

[23] Selina Todd and the rise of academic mobs, Joanna Williams, *spiked*, 11 February 2020

[24] Elizabethtown College: Conservative Student Group Denied Permission to Host Speaker Opposed to Critical Race Theory, Foundation for Individual Rights in Education (FIRE), 23 November 2021

[25] Student investigated for saying women must have vaginas, *The Times* (London), 15 May 2021

[26] 'Racist and sexist' Edinburgh lecturer removed from 'all academic matters', *Tab*, 26 April 2021

[27] The right-wing defence of 'academic freedom' masks a McCarthyite agenda, Jonathan Portes, *Guardian*, 4 August 2020

[28] Maryland Institute College of Art: faculty member disciplined for comments about free expression, Foundation for Individual Rights in Education (FIRE), 17 November 2021

[29] #HelloBBK, we need to talk about Eric, Birkbeck Students Anti-Racism Network

[30] Students accuse Edinburgh lecturer of spouting 'racist and sexist' comments, *Tab*, 9 April 2021

[31] A backlash against gender ideology is starting in universities, *The Economist*, 5 June 2021

[32] Quoted in: Stonewall and the silencing of feminist voices at universities, Julie Bindel, *Spectator*, 19 May 2021

[33] Review of the circumstances resulting in and arising from the cancellation of the Centre for Criminology seminar on Trans Rights, Imprisonment and the Criminal Justice System, scheduled to take place on 5 December 2019, and the arrangements for speaker invitations to the Holocaust Memorial Week event on the State of Antisemitism Today, scheduled for 30 January 2020, Akua Reindorf, 17 May 2021

[34] Essex apologises to academics disinvited over gender views, *Times Higher Education*, 18 May 2021

[35] Essex University makes further apology in trans rights row, *Guardian*, 4 July 2021

[36] Professor says career 'effectively ended' by union's transphobia claims, *Guardian*, 12 October 2021

[37] UCU response to Queen's Speech, University and College Union, 11 May 2021

[38] *Tackling racial harassment in higher education*, Universities UK, 15 October 2021

[39] *Tackling racial harassment in higher education*, Universities UK, 15 October 2021

6 Thought Crimes

Police officers have had a change of image. The British 'bobby on the beat' is now a rare sight; today's cops are as likely to spend their time sitting in front of a computer screen as walking the streets. Go back a couple of generations and 'hate crime' had yet to be invented. Now, equality, diversity and inclusion are key parts of formal police training. Meanwhile, the demand from every identity-based activist group is for more laws to better protect their particular interests. The very notion of policing has become politically contentious just as police officers are pushing – or have been pushed – into more explicitly political terrain. Officers in the UK now attend Pride marches, take the knee at Black Lives Matter protests, make social-media videos to mark International Pronouns Day, and patrol Twitter to root out hate speech. It is not that catching criminals is no longer a priority. It is that the justice system, shaped by woke values, is now a participant in the culture wars. This chapter explores how and why this has happened.[1]

Who should be in women's prisons?

Women prisoners, while undoubtedly criminals, are also vulnerable. The UK's Prison Reform Trust notes that women inmates have often been victims of crimes far more serious than those of which they have been convicted. It suggests that 57 per cent of women in prison report having been victims of domestic violence, while 53 per cent report having experienced emotional, physical or sexual abuse as a child, compared with 27 per cent of male prisoners.[2] Women prisoners are likely to have suffered abuse prior to having committed the acts for which they have been tried, found guilty and sentenced. This abuse will, more likely than not, have been perpetrated by men. Loss of liberty should not mean continued risk of abuse. Although convicts are incarcerated as a punishment, prison officers have a duty of care to protect them from assault.

A survey for the chief inspector of prisons in 2019 suggested that one in 50 prisoners in the UK – roughly 1,500 inmates – identifies as transgender.[3] No one knows for certain because some datasets record only gender identity and not sex. But if we assume the one-in-50 figure to be broadly correct, then there is a far higher proportion of transgender people in prison than there is in the general population. There are various explanations made for this. Some argue that a combination of prejudice and poverty makes survival for transgender people dependent upon criminal activity and that, at the same time, they are more likely to be criminalised and targeted by police officers. Others note that criminals may be incentivised to claim to be transgender in order to secure perks such as being able to shower alone or have their own cell, or to switch between male and female jails. Furthermore, taking on a new name and identity may permit personal histories to be rewritten, due to the growing taboo around 'deadnaming'.

Regardless of when or why a particular offender transitioned, there are clearly risks associated with incarcerating a male-bodied offender alongside female prisoners. Statistics show that transgender inmates comprise roughly one per cent of female prisoners in the UK, but they were responsible for 5.6 per cent of sexual assaults recorded in women's prisons between 2010 and 2018.[4] The stories behind the statistics are appalling. David Thompson, a convicted paedophile and rapist, was jailed for life in the early 2000s while on remand for grievous bodily harm, burglary, multiple rapes and other sexual offences against women. In 2017, Thompson, now identifying as a woman called Karen White, was moved to a women's prison.[5] Once there, he sexually assaulted two female inmates.

A female inmate, who alleges she was sexually assaulted by a transgender inmate, brought a legal action in 2021 against the government's policy of housing transwomen in female prisons. At the High Court, Lord Justice Holroyde acknowledged that 'the unconditional introduction of a transgender woman into the general population of a women's prison carries a statistically greater risk of sexual assault upon non-transgender prisoners than would be the case if a non-transgender woman were introduced'. He also accepted that:

> [S]ome, and perhaps many, women prisoners may suffer fear and acute anxiety if required to share prison accommodation and facilities with a transgender woman who has male genitalia, and that their fear and anxiety may be increased if that transgender woman has been convicted of sexual or violent offences against women.

Yet, despite these concessions, Lord Justice Holroyde concluded that the policy of incarcerating according to gender identity rather than sex should continue because he also 'had to take into account the rights of transgender women in the prison system'.[6] In other words, women inmates who may have good reason to fear men, and may be at greater risk when locked up alongside men, will still be incarcerated with men because a woman's right to physical safety is trumped by the rights of men who declare themselves to be women. Woke values replace basic common sense.

Allowing transgender inmates to choose between either male or female prisons is presented as a compassionate move that respects the identity and protects the safety of transgender prisoners. This view is driven by the mantra that 'transwomen are women' and a belief that people do not lie about their gender identity. Riding roughshod over the rights of women is considered a small price to pay for empathy towards an even more oppressed group. Lisa Nandy, a one-time Labour leadership contender, went so far as to argue that male child rapists, who subsequently identify as women, should be housed in a women's prison if this is their choice.[7]

In Scotland, gender ideology extends into all parts of the justice system. A freedom of information request sent by MurrayBlackburn-Mackenzie exposed Police Scotland's policy for dealing with rape suspects. If a rape or attempted rape has been perpetrated by a 'male who self-identifies as a woman... the male who self-identifies as a woman would be expected to be recorded as a female on relevant police systems'. This was backed by Humza Yousaf, then the Scottish justice secretary, who stated that Police Scotland should record a person's gender identity rather than their sex. Detective superintendent Fil Capaldi told *The Times* that: 'The sex / gender identification of individuals who come into contact with the police will be based on how they present or how they self-declare, which is consistent with the values of the organisation.'[8]

Describing a suspected male rapist as female fundamentally alters the nature of the crime committed. It makes an absurdity of the legal stipulation that only a man can commit rape.[9] And it trivialises and invalidates the experiences of the victim – the woman who has been violently penetrated by a penis. Now, if her rapist identifies as female, then she must accept that she was attacked by a woman. Allowing male rape suspects to declare that they are women also rewrites history and makes it more difficult for justice to be done. It is hard to track down a suspect when the police hunt is for a 'woman' – even if the description provided reads 'six-foot tall, beard'. And, if eventually tried and found guilty, these sex offenders may still get to serve their time in a women's prison.

Self-identification also distorts crime statistics. It makes it seem as if rape is a crime committed by men and women. This muddies our understanding of this particular offence and makes it more difficult to discuss why rape is carried out and what can be done to prevent it. Meanwhile, anyone who challenges this new orthodoxy increasingly runs the risk of being accused of transphobia.

Hate crime and hate incidents

In the UK, hate crime is defined as 'any criminal offence which is perceived, by the victim or any other person, to be motivated by hostility or prejudice towards someone based on a personal characteristic'. This definition was agreed in 2007 by the police, the Crown Prosecution Service (CPS), the Prison Service (now the National Offender Management Service) and other agencies that make up the criminal-justice system.[10] The element of subjectivity ('*perceived*... to be motivated') and the emphasis on the 'personal characteristics' of the victim, rather than the actions of the perpetrator, make hate crime different from other forms of crime. It is a vague and expansive category that is open to political exploitation. By focusing on the identity of the victim, rather than the offence committed, hate crime enshrines in law the idea that particular groups are deserving of differential legal protections. The law is no longer a neutral, objective arbiter of justice, but a politicised tool that intervenes according to interests and identities.

The UK government website urging people to report hate crime claims: 'Crimes committed against someone because of their disability, transgender identity, race, religion or belief, or sexual orientation are hate crimes and should be reported to the police.'[11] It specifies that hate must be directed at someone on account of their membership of these five particular groups, and not just at them as an individual. The Metropolitan Police specify that: 'With hate crime it is "who" the victim is, or "what" the victim appears to be, that motivates the offender to commit the crime.'[12] The elements of a person's identity that are singled out for protection under hate-crime legislation mirror some (but not all) of the 'protected characteristics' outlined in the Equality Act 2010.[13] However, there are continual calls to expand the definition of hate crime – for example, to encompass misogyny, too.

Hate crime can include verbal abuse, intimidation, threats, harassment, assault and bullying targeted at individuals or groups, as well as more general offences of 'stirring up' hatred. Speech is not just a component of hate crimes, but can also be a criminal offence in its own right. As the Law Commission notes: 'The term hate crime is sometimes also used to describe "hate speech" offences, such as offences of stirring up hatred under the Public Order Act 1986, and the offence of "indecent or racialist chanting" under the Football (Offences) Act 1991.' The UN defines hate speech as 'any kind of communication in speech, writing or behaviour, that attacks or uses pejorative or discriminatory language with reference to a person or a group based on who they are, in other words, based on their religion, ethnicity, nationality, race, colour, descent, gender or other identity factor.'[14]

In recent years, police officers in the UK have been investigating not just hate crimes and hate speech, but also 'non-crime hate incidents'. Non-crime hate incidents came to be defined as any speech or action that is perceived to be motivated by hostility or prejudice, either by the victim or anyone else, but which does not constitute a criminal offence. People have had non-crime hate incidents recorded against their names even when there was no actual evidence of prejudice. People have been visited by the police for saying something on social media that is completely legal to say. The practice was ruled unlawful at the UK's Court of Appeal in December 2021, but it may well live on in a modified, more discretionary form.[15]

Non-crime hate incidents reflect the rise of subjectivity in modern policing. Where hate incidents are concerned, it is not the perpetrator's speech or actions that matter. What matters is the perception of hate by the alleged victim or a more sensitive third party. As the Metropolitan Police spell out: 'Evidence of the hate element is not a requirement. You do not need to personally perceive the incident to be hate related. It would be enough if another person, a witness or even a police officer thought that the incident was hate related.'[16]

Non-crime hate incidents paved the way for people to report their political opponents to the authorities. In October 2016, a speech by the then home secretary, Amber Rudd, at the Conservative Party conference briefly became a police matter. Rudd said she wanted to ensure foreign workers 'were not taking jobs British workers could do'. She did not use racial slurs or name specific individuals. She expressed a legitimate political view that echoes similar remarks made by politicians from all parties. Joshua Silver, a British physics professor at Oxford University, was not present when Rudd made her speech. Indeed, he was not at the Conservative Party conference at all. Silver was, however, so alarmed by the media coverage of the speech that he contacted the police. 'I felt politicians have been using hate speech to turn Britons against foreigners, and I thought that is probably not lawful', he later told *The Times*. As patently ridiculous as the allegation was, the speech was still recorded as a hate incident.[17]

Rudd's case reveals the extent to which hate crime and hate incidents have become politicised. This understanding of hate crime as including the expression or representation of views we find objectionable seems to have entered the popular consciousness. In January 2022, four of the protesters responsible for toppling the statue of Edward Colston in Bristol (who we first met in Chapter Two) stood trial for criminal damage and were acquitted by a jury. They each admitted to their involvement but denied that their actions were criminal because, as they put it, the statue itself had been a hate crime against the people of Bristol.[18]

The successful Court of Appeal ruling against non-crime hate incidents was brought by Harry Miller. Miller, a former police officer from Humberside who now leads the campaign group Fair Cop, was investigated by the police in 2019. They had received a complaint about his tweets about transgenderism, including a poem he had retweeted. Another post, penned by Miller, read: 'I was assigned mammal at birth, but my orientation is fish. Don't mis-species me.' In response, a 'community cohesion officer' from Humberside Police telephoned Miller and told him that while his tweets had not broken any laws they had been recorded as a non-crime hate incident. The officer also gave him an impromptu lecture on transgenderism. 'I've been on a course and what you need to understand is that you can have a fetus with a female brain that grows male body parts and that's what a transgender person is', he reportedly told Miller.

Police also approached the directors of Miller's company. The complainant had managed to identify Miller's business and alleged his tweets made the workplace an 'unsafe environment' for trans people. 'My retweeting of a gender-critical verse had apparently so enraged someone from "down south" that they felt it their civil duty to act as Offended-in-Chief on behalf of my employees "up north"', Miller later said. 'Not that anyone from my firm of around 90 staff had complained, of course, but again… that's beside the point. A police constable rang my work, spoke to my managing director, and then spent 32 minutes lecturing me on hurt feelings and in-vitro body parts accidentally growing from a lady brain as I sat with my shopping at Tesco. Sarcasm, satire and talk of synthetic breasts was sufficient to prompt the most urgent of police interventions.'[19]

When Miller took the police to court, his barrister argued that Humberside Police's response had sought to 'dissuade [Miller] from expressing himself on such issues in the future' and had a 'substantial chilling effect' on his right to free speech. In February 2020, the High Court ruled that the force's response to Miller's tweets had been unlawful and a 'disproportionate interference' with his right to freedom of expression. Justice Julian Knowles said the effect of police turning up at Miller's place of work 'because of his political opinions must not be underestimated'. He added: 'To do so would be to undervalue a cardinal democratic freedom. In this country we have never had a Cheka, a Gestapo or a Stasi. We have never lived in an Orwellian society'.[20]

Despite finding in Miller's personal favour in February 2020, the High Court rejected his wider challenge to the College of Policing's guidance on non-crime hate incidents. Almost two years later, the Court of Appeal unanimously overturned the latter decision. But even this may not spell the end of non-crime hate incidents. The Court of Appeal ruling maintained that perception-based recording is not '*per se* unlawful', but that 'some additional safeguards should be put in place so that the incursion into freedom of expression is no more than is strictly necessary'.[21]

Hate-crime entrepreneurs

The policing of hate crimes and the recording of hate incidents has curtailed free thought and free speech. The fact that some groups now have legal protections not afforded to the general population politicises the law. And the focus on subjective perception allows for groups of hate-crime entrepreneurs to emerge. Ostensibly campaigners against racism or homophobia and for equal rights, these groups have a vested interest in recruiting victims and increasing the numbers of reported hate crimes and hate incidents against members of their community. In 2018, Stonewall claimed that 41 per cent of transgender people had experienced a hate crime in the past year, based on a survey.[22] Such claims generate publicity, portraying certain groups as particularly victimised and in need of public support, state funding and special legal protections.

The more broadly hate crime and hate incidents are defined, the more publicity that surrounds them, and the easier it becomes to report them, the more statistics rise. But given the subjective nature of these crimes and incidents, all that this data can confidently tell us is how many people perceive and are prepared to report acts of hatred. The weight of objective, comparative evidence suggests that society has changed considerably over the past half century. People have, for the most part, become a great deal more tolerant. Broader social and cultural change has led to changes in the behaviour and attitudes of individuals. And yet the preoccupation with policing hatred is more intense now than it has ever been.

Equality under the law was once a fundamental principle of civil-rights movements. Today, as the Law Commission notes, 'the law in England and Wales currently offers enhanced criminal protection, in different forms, to individuals and groups on the basis of race, religion, disability, sexual orientation and transgender identity'.[23] Within the legal system, the police and prison services, professional identity-based groups advocate for their members' interests. This increasingly means arguing for those in particular groups to receive special protections in order to compensate for historical disadvantage and discrimination.

The understanding that different identity groups deserve different levels of protection is now embedded in training for police and prison officers. Professional identity-based groups are supported by the College of Policing, an independent body that represents everyone working in the police service.[24] The National Black Police Association (NBPA), formally established in 1998, was the first such group. Its roots date back to a black police support network founded in 1990 as a joint initiative between black staff within the Metropolitan Police and a support unit specialising in community and race-relations training. It was particularly concerned with the high attrition rate of black officers. Today, the NBPA aims 'to improve the working environment of black staff by protecting the rights of those employed within the police service' and also 'to enhance racial harmony and the quality of service to the black community of the United Kingdom'.[25]

In the summer of 2020, after the murder of George Floyd in the US, the NBPA issued a statement:

> *At a time when we are grappling with the harsh reality that decades of structural and institutional racism has made us fodder not only to the disproportionate use of force in policing but also to Covid-19... now is the time for us to scramble to rid the world of the scourge of racism, structural and institutional, with the same intensity as shown to Covid-19...*
>
> *The time has come to accept that racism is clearly the public-health crisis, sadly shared by the US and the UK. It is imperative that both nations need to act now.[26]*

This statement presents the existence of structural and institutional racism as an indisputable fact and claims the role of NBPA members is to 'rid the world' of this 'scourge'. This moves policing away from enforcing the law and deterring acts of criminality and into the realm of politics; it moves this professional body away from protecting its members' interests and into a more activist role.

The National LGBT+ Police Network plays a similar role to the NBPA, in that it aims to both protect its members' interests and advocate for broader social and political change. It is explicit about its commitment to 'the inclusion of all lesbian, gay, bisexual and trans people, regardless of their background or characteristics'.[27] It has also worked closely with Stonewall. The network is listed as one of the partners for Stonewall's trans guidance for policing, which urges police forces to make a 'visible commitment' to members of the LGBTQ+ community both 'internally and externally'.[28]

A Stonewall booklet, entitled *Protecting lesbian, gay and bisexual people: A practical guide for police forces,* advises police to 'take targeted action to tackle homophobic hate in their force area, encourage reporting and enable gay people to live without fear of abuse and violence'.[29] Several police forces have registered as Stonewall Diversity Champions. A major focus of Stonewall's guidance for police is how officers can encourage reporting of homophobic and transphobic hate crimes and hate incidents.

Police powers were once seen by the left as potential incursions against individual liberty, the abuse of which must be guarded against at all times. Citizens were considered vulnerable in comparison to powerful state institutions, and left-wing activists argued that people needed protection from state overreach. Today, in stark contrast, campaigners argue that citizens are at risk from each other and that the state must intervene to stop hatred running amok. This turns an older conception of the relationship between the state and citizens, and the role of the legal system, on its head. It exposes the low opinion so-called progressives have of the general public and how woke ideas now bolster the authority of the state.

Bypassing democracy

The state, bolstered by the support of special-interest groups, increasingly has the power to define and to police what is offensive or hateful. The law is being used to promote woke values which are, in turn, reflected in judicial activism. Campaigners increasingly turn to lawyers and the civil service – rather than the people or their representatives – to bring about social change. The courts can appear to possess greater authority than the elected executive.

In practice, this means that while individual government ministers can rail against the excesses of woke thinking in the justice system, the balance of power has shifted towards state institutions and third-sector organisations and away from elected politicians (often, it must be noted, at politicians' own behest). The advantage of this for single-issue pressure groups is that they can circumvent the need to win public support. Woke values can come to dominate the most fundamental structures of our society without the electorate ever having been asked if they consent.

The criminal-justice system is increasingly shaped by special-interest groups that demand differential protections for their members. At the same time, the law has moved into far more subjective terrain and now involves itself in policing and punishing incorrect attitudes, beliefs and emotions. The combined effect of these changes is to overturn two fundamental and politically progressive principles: equality before the law and the presumption of innocence. Rather than equality or justice, the woke criminal-justice system is concerned with promoting the right values to sections of society assumed to be racist, sexist, homophobic and transphobic.

Just as with the cultural industry, schools and universities, the police have not been innocent victims of a cunning woke takeover. Woke protesters did not get together and decide that the best way to promote their worldview would be to train, en masse, to become police officers. Rather, we are witnessing yet another instance of an institution, confused about its purpose, latching on to woke values to provide some sense of meaning and direction. At the same time, it is increasingly common for new recruits to the police either to have a university degree or to be expected to study for a degree as part of their training. This means that, over the course of many years, police officers have come to take on board the values of the cultural elite. Individual officers are now more likely to identify as, and feel politically aligned with, members of the professional graduate class, especially those who secure promotion and work their way up the ranks.

Woke values have taken root in the police force gradually and organically, as the political concerns of the cultural elites have changed over time. But in some respects woke merely gives the police new methods to pursue old goals – to defend the interests of the ruling class and discipline ordinary people when they step out of line.

Endnotes

[1] This chapter draws extensively on work in *Policing Hate: Have we abandoned freedom and equality?*, published by Civitas in December 2020. It is reprinted here with permission

[2] Majority of women in prison have been victims of domestic abuse, Prison Reform Trust, 4 December 2017

[3] One in 50 prisoners identifies as transgender amid concerns inmates are attempting to secure prison perks, *Telegraph*, 9 July 2019

[4] Seven sex attacks in women's jails by transgender convicts, *The Times* (London), 11 May 2020

[5] The male rapist in a women's prison, *spiked*, 15 October 2018

[6] Quoted in: The court judgement that confirms women pay for trans rights, James Kirkup, *Spectator*, 2 July 2021

[7] Lisa Nandy reignites Labour trans rights row as leadership contender says male child rapists who transition to become women should be allowed to serve their sentences in female-only prisons if they 'choose' to, *Daily Mail*, 17 February 2020

[8] Rape suspects can choose to self-identify as female, *The Times* (London), 17 April 2021

[9] Rape, Sexual Offences Act 2003, Section 1

[10] Hate Crime, England and Wales, 2018/19, Home Office

[11] Report hate crime, Gov.uk

[12] What is hate crime?, Metropolitan Police

[13] Protected characteristics, Equality and Human Rights Commission

[14] *Hate crime laws: A consultation paper*, Law Commission, 23 September 2020

[15] Court of Appeal hate crime guidance ruling, College of Policing, 20 December 2021

[16] What is hate crime?, Metropolitan Police

[17] Rudd speech on foreign workers recorded as a hate incident, *The Times* (London), 12 January 2017

[18] 'Ecstatic and stunned': 'Colston Four' celebrate as jury acquits them of criminal damage over toppling statue of slave trader, *Evening Standard*, 5 January 2022

[19] Harry Miller, Fair Cop

[20] Harry Miller: Police probe into 'transphobic' tweets unlawful, BBC News, 14 February 2020

[21] Court of Appeal rules police 'hate incidents' guidance unlawful, *Law Society Gazette*, 20 December 2021

[22] Abuse of transgender people is endemic in UK with huge hate crime figures, report shows, *i*, 19 January 2018

[23] *Hate crime laws: A consultation paper*, Law Commission, 23 September 2020

[24] About Us, College of Policing

[25] About NBPA, National Black Police Association

[26] Statement on the death of George Floyd, Minneapolis, Minnesota USA, National Black Police Association, 31 May 2020

[27] National LGBT+ Police Value Statement, National LGBT+ Police Network, 5 January 2021

[28] *Trans Guidance for the Policing Sector: An Overview*, Stonewall, 2018

[29] *Protecting lesbian, gay and bisexual people: A practical guide for police forces*, Stonewall

7 Woke Capitalism

Even capitalism, and the pursuit of profit, is now woke. Gillette combines advertising razor blades with challenging toxic masculinity. Lynx deodorant once marketed itself as a surefire way for young men to attract sexy women – now it promotes gender inclusivity. Ben & Jerry's ice cream comes with messages of tolerance towards asylum seekers. Innocent Smoothies – owned by the Coca-Cola Company – is on a mission to save the planet. HSBC celebrates global community. Nike specialises in body positivity with a side order of feminism and support for Black Lives Matter.

Some adverts today are so intent on promoting particular values that they make barely any mention of the product being sold. Clothing retailer Mango's recent 'family portraits' campaign focused on the diverse and inclusive families featured, not on the clothes they were wearing. A commercial for Twix, designed to coincide with Halloween, showed a boy in a dress being teased by other children until his witch-like nanny made the bullies disappear. There was no mention of the chocolate-finger biscuit. Elsewhere, adverts trading in woke values have accidentally misled customers. A John Lewis home-insurance advert featured a boy in a dress tearing flamboyantly through his house, leaving a trail of destruction in his wake. It had to be pulled because John Lewis home insurance does not pay out for deliberate damage.[1]

Opponents might claim that businesses that 'get woke, go broke', but those in charge clearly disagree. Promoting woke ideas and chasing profits might appear like contradictory goals, but whether it's called 'stakeholder capitalism', 'corporate social responsibility', 'conscious' or 'caring' capitalism, or 'environmental, social and corporate governance', woke capitalism is not new. It is not an aberration or a minor blip before a swift return to business as usual. It is not simply a crafty disguise, with messages about anti-racism deliberately masking a capitalism that is still red in tooth and claw. Welcome to what author Vivek Ramaswamy calls 'the woke industrial complex'.[2]

Woke consumers

When George Floyd was killed in May 2020, businesses around the world felt they had to respond. Ben & Jerry's turned its website into a statement insisting 'We must dismantle white supremacy'. Under the headline 'Silence is NOT an option', these purveyors of posh ice cream declared: 'We have to stand together with the victims of murder, marginalisation, and repression because of their skin colour, and with those who seek justice through protests across our country. We have to say his name: George Floyd.'[3]

Many other global brands – including Nike, Adidas and Netflix – rushed to publicly endorse Black Lives Matter.[4] Nike inverted its usual tag line with a new slogan, 'Don't do it', and the plea: 'Don't sit back and be silent.' It followed this up by announcing a $40million commitment to support the black community in the US.[5] Google updated its logo with a black ribbon and tweeted the message: 'We stand in support of racial equality and all those who search for it.' PG Tips ran with #solidaritea. A year later, George Floyd's death was still at the forefront of marketers' concerns. Marks & Spencer announced that the Black Lives Matter protests had inspired its latest lingerie collection. It had apparently taken a 'global conversation on race, equality and unconscious bias' for someone to notice that the 'skin coloured' range at M&S was not, in fact, 'neutral' and did not match all skin tones.[6]

Some questioned the motives of these multinational corporations. 'Do companies really support the cause?', asked the BBC.[7] Others went further and railed against what they saw as big-brand hypocrisy.[8] It was generally conceded that, even if genuine, corporate support did not go far enough. Advertising, one critic said, still needed to be decolonised as 'it can and does support discriminatory thinking – thinking that often has its roots in the colonial era'.[9]

We should, of course, question the motives of companies that use adverts as an opportunity for moral grandstanding. But cynicism can get in the way of a far more straightforward understanding of what is going on here. Everyone who watched the video of Derek Chauvin's knee pressed on to George Floyd's neck was horrified. That's why Black Lives Matter protests were held across the world and celebrities and teenagers alike blacked out their social-media profiles for the day. Marketing managers and business leaders exist in the same cultural sphere as the rest of us and there is little reason to suspect their support for Black Lives Matter was not genuine. At the same time, they also realised that Black Lives Matter drew support from the very same section of the public they wished to attract as customers. Americus Reed, a marketing professor at the University of Pennsylvania, told the *New York Times* in 2020 that by aligning corporate values with customers' concerns, companies hoped to build a sense of loyalty and a deeper sense of personal connection. 'It's smart', he said. 'They're taking a stand, hopefully, because it's moral, but also because they understand the long-term economic game.'[10]

Companies began displaying woke values long before Black Lives Matter appeared on the scene. The Body Shop, Lush, Innocent Smoothies, Green and Black's chocolate and Ben & Jerry's ice cream are all hugely profitable brands that have been built around their 'corporate values'. Other brands, established in a different era, have tried to catch up. Pepsi's infamous protest advert, featuring Kendall Jenner single-handedly preventing police brutality with a can of fizzy pop, was roundly criticised for being tone deaf.[11] But other brands have negotiated this terrain with a little more success.

Gillette found itself embroiled in a culture war – with the bonus of primetime spots on TV talk shows and acres of press coverage – when its attempt at corporate wokeness sparked controversy. In 2019, its marketing department switched focus from razor blades to men. Gillette's decades-old slogan, 'The best a man can get', was changed to 'The best men can be'. Its #MeToo-inspired ad campaign ordered men to behave better and not join in with bullying or sexual harassment. For good measure, the company promised to distribute '$1million per year for the next three years to non-profit organisations executing the most interesting and impactful programmes designed to help men of all ages achieve their personal best'.[12]

Gillette was widely criticised for attacking its own customers by presenting men as boorish thugs. People were quick to point out that not all men harass women and that there are plenty of positive aspects to masculinity. Some on social media declared that they would boycott Gillette for having bought into feminist hectoring. Many assumed the campaign would backfire. Others welcomed Gillette's campaign and criticised the critics, labelling them 'snowflakes'.[13] They argued that men who don't fight, harass and abuse had nothing to fear from an advert. Clearly, Gillette's marketing managers wanted the brand to be associated with a new, gentler image. Whether they were pushing reluctant customers into accepting a more woke notion of masculinity or following the assumed concerns of a younger generation of consumers is debatable.

What's clear is that woke companies are so keen to demonstrate that they hold the correct values that they are prepared to risk offending their core customer base. Companies now aim to outdo their competitors on virtue. In trying to make sense of this, some argue that today's businesses are simply responding to a shift in consumer demand – that is, woke capitalism makes money from woke customers. And this certainly seems to be true to an extent. In 2018, Nike ran an advertising campaign featuring former NFL star Colin Kaepernick, who used to kneel to protest against police brutality at the start of games, long before Black Lives Matter protesters popularised the action. The Kaepernick campaign was followed by a big rise in Labor Day sales[14] and the company's market value soared by $6 billion in the year after it first ran.[15] This financial boost came despite the fact that some of Nike's customers took to social media to threaten a boycott in response to Kaepernick's hiring. Nike gambled that its woke star would go down well with customers – and it won.

Writing more than two decades ago, Naomi Klein argued in her bestselling book, *No Logo*, that multinational companies sold Western consumers an idealised lifestyle rather than the physical product on the shelf. This, she suggested, coincided with the emergence of a decadent middle class that could afford to shop for luxury beliefs.[16] In other words, when everyone can afford to buy a particular product, people reinforce their own social status by purchasing the one that they consider demonstrates the best values. Holding woke values, and purchasing the more expensive products associated with them, is today a status symbol.

In the pursuit of new and improved customers, companies are quick to acquiesce to complaints from activists. Indeed, groups have been set up specifically to exploit this corporate desire for woke publicity. Stop Funding Hate is a pressure group that targets businesses that advertise in media outlets it does not like. It rallies supporters on social media and directs them to boycott products until adverts are pulled from newspapers like the *Daily Mail* or the *Sun*. Following the launch of GB News in 2021, Stop Funding Hate went into overdrive, flagging up companies that advertised on the channel and using Twitter to call for consumer boycotts. Kopparberg cider, IKEA, Nivea, Octopus Energy, Grolsch and the Open University all acquiesced and suspended their adverts.[17]

But the proportion of the population with an active Twitter account is tiny and support for Stop Funding Hate is smaller still.[18] Neither can claim to be representative of the population as a whole. In capitulating to these boycott campaigns, companies are not responding to the concerns of a large number of consumers, but rather are focusing on the outrage of a small proportion of them: the proportion that just so happens to align most closely with those who work in advertising companies and marketing departments. It can often appear like a small group of people talking among themselves.

In May 2021, UK rail company LNER apologised to a 'non-binary passenger' for a 'ladies and gentlemen' train announcement. As is the way nowadays, both complaint and apology were made via Twitter, with LNER responding that 'our train managers should not be using language like this' and thanking the complainant for 'bringing it to my attention'. What's noteworthy is that the person making the complaint was not simply a member of the public. Laurence Coles is a train guard and the LGBT+ representative for the RMT, the railway workers' trade union. Coles' original tweet stated, 'as a non-binary person this announcement doesn't actually apply to me so I won't listen'. Coles was sat next to Charlotte Monroe, who is also a 'lifelong railway employee' and is the creator of the Progress Train, 'the UK's first-ever Pride train staffed by all-LGBT+ crew'.

The LNER social-media manager asked Coles to 'let me know which service you are on and I will ensure they remain as inclusive as we strive to be at LNER'. The train announcer who said 'ladies and gentlemen' presumably got a talking to, at least − all at the behest of a union representative. Coles and Monroe demonstrate a new, woke approach to politics. 'We (that is, railway staff in general) have a duty of care to all of our passengers', Monroe said on Twitter after the incident. Customer care, in this instance, has less to do with overseeing the safety of passengers and more to do with protecting the emotional wellbeing of some while re-educating others.[19]

Woke exploitation

Having staff members police and discipline each other is one example of the benefits of woke for business leaders. They may genuinely believe in social justice, but there's no hiding the fact that woke also serves them well. Promoting woke values as part of one area of a business, such as marketing, can sit comfortably alongside less ethically sound practices elsewhere, such as in the supply chain. In this way, woke values divert our attention from the uglier side of capitalism.

Nike may have partnered with Kaepernick and embraced Black Lives Matter. But the company itself is hardly a bastion of equality more broadly. Chief executive John Donahoe, a white man in his sixties, was reportedly paid $53million in 2020, more than 2,000 times what the firm's median employee takes home.[20] Beneath even Nike's lowest-paid US employees sit factory workers in China, particularly Uighur Muslims, working in Chinese factories that supply Nike. Despite Nike's claims to the contrary, reports of working conditions 'that strongly suggest forced labour' have surfaced.[21]

IKEA UK pulled its adverts from GB News in the same week IKEA France was fined €1million, and its former CEO was handed a two-year suspended prison sentence, after a French court found the company had spied on its employees for several years.[22] Nivea also responded to the Stop Funding Hate boycotters and withdrew its ads from GB News. It had previously come in for criticism for selling skin-whitening cream to women in Africa.[23]

Time and again, we see that a range of ethically dubious practices sit alongside corporate virtue-signalling. Indeed, the exploitation of workers who are paid less for their labour than the revenue they generate is not simply an immoral blunder – it is built into the very workings of capitalism. Woke business leaders want us to forget that, in its most basic principles, capitalism has changed little in two centuries. They hope that tweets about the evil of immigration controls will persuade us to look the other way.

The problem with woke capitalism is not that consumers are being conned into believing that corporations are moral exemplars. Rather, there is often no contradiction between displaying woke values in one arena while engaging in ethically dubious practices elsewhere. We have grown used to world leaders and business magnates preaching about the need to cut carbon emissions before boarding private jets. By the same token, Ben & Jerry's apparently sees no contradiction between tweeting about the need for open borders while buying from suppliers that underpay migrant workers. In August 2020, Ben & Jerry's issued a series of tweets calling on the British government to show more humanity towards migrants. Its UK-based social-media division argued that 'the real crisis is our lack of humanity for people fleeing war, climate change and torture'. Yet the Ben & Jerry's Vermont headquarters has previously been the target of protests because of the treatment of migrant labourers in its supply chain.[24] Workers have alleged that they sustained injuries when milk bottles exploded, and that they suffered with sleep deprivation due to midnight milking and long stretches of work without a day off. Workers also say they were housed in barns and unheated trailers despite the freezing cold Vermont winters.

Divide and rule in the workplace

Corporations don't just espouse woke values as a smokescreen for their exploitation of workers. Woke values are increasingly the means through which such exploitation is practised. One way this takes place is through diversity-training initiatives, where employees are encouraged to reveal their unconscious biases and taught how to be good allies to those who are less privileged. This has distinct advantages for the managerial class.

In 2020, the Behavioural Insights Team (aka the 'Nudge Unit') was commissioned by the UK's Government Equalities Office to analyse the effectiveness of unconscious-bias training. It found that there is 'currently no evidence that this training changes behaviour in the long term or improves workplace equality in terms of representation of women, ethnic minorities or other minority groups'.[25] The *Harvard Business Review* likewise notes that 'even when the training is beneficial, the effects may not last after the programme ends'.[26] Mounting evidence points to workplace diversity training actually having unintended negative consequences.

Yet increasing numbers of employers insist their staff undertake anti-racism training, with over 80 per cent of all UK-based companies reported to run training sessions specifically on unconscious bias.[27] Virtually all Fortune 500 companies offer some form of diversity training, too.[28] The diversity industry has become a global phenomenon, extending its reach to many millions of citizens in schools, universities and workplaces, with online courses targeting many more.

This massive rollout of diversity training is not only taking place without any evidence of its effectiveness – it is also happening at a time when, by all measures, race has never been less of a barrier to advancement in the workplace. Proponents of these programmes try desperately to square this circle. As Binna Kandola, author of *Racism at Work*, writes:

> *The racism in organisations today is not characterised by hostile abuse and threatening behaviour. It is not overt nor is it obvious. Today, racism is subtle and nuanced, detected mostly by the people on the receiving end, but ignored and possibly not even seen by perpetrators and bystanders. Racism today may be more refined, but it harms people's careers and lives in hugely significant ways.*

In other words, racism is so subtle people need training to perceive it, yet so devastating that it does irreparable damage to people's careers. It exists in indifference, in the things people do not say, and yet is apparently evident in every aspect of our daily lives.

Kandola's insistence that racism can be found within people who 'do not engage in expressing negative views about minority groups', those who 'believe in greater integration', and even those who 'may consistently support policies that promote diversity', comes directly from critical race theory. Legal equality may have been achieved, but the race experts insist that their services are needed now more than ever. It seems that they alone have the power to uncover a 'legacy of racist ideas, actions and imagery which lives on publicly in stereotypes – and privately in our unconscious minds'.[29]

The alleged importance of unconscious bias is fundamental to today's critical race theory-inspired diversity movement. Apparently, our minds quietly harbour all manner of prejudiced thoughts, put there by society and culture, our education and our upbringing. Proof of these bad thoughts supposedly appears through implicit-association tests (IAT), which track our response times when we match certain images, words or phrases with people of different characteristics.

Unsurprisingly, the idea that the content of the unconscious mind can be revealed through a rapid-fire computer test is highly contested. The American Psychological Association acknowledged over a decade ago that people's IAT scores vary from one test to another and are often context-dependent.[30] But still the testing continues. What's more, the preoccupation with unconscious bias implies there is a direct link between our implicit attitudes and our actions. Yet research has shown that test scores purporting to measure implicit attitudes do not effectively predict actual discriminatory behaviour.[31] Either the contents of our unconscious minds cannot be so easily measured, or people are able to exercise self-control and do not automatically act on their unconscious impulses.

If unconscious-bias and diversity training programmes were just ineffective then they could be written off as a harmless waste of time. But they are also deeply divisive. They push us to see each other as members of racial groups and, in their attempt to make us think twice about how we interact with one another, they risk preventing the spontaneity and informality that lead to genuine solidarity.

Often, unconscious-bias training is followed by instruction in how to avoid microaggressions, such as mispronouncing someone's name or asking where they are from. The diversity trainers tell us that it is our unconscious biases that lead us to mistreat people who are different to us. They tell us that the cumulative impact of these slights can have a devastating psychological impact on those on the receiving end. But the logic of this argument is that black people should be viewed – and perceive themselves – as especially vulnerable and sensitive to offence. In the workplace, this may lead colleagues to retreat from forging the informal connections with them that can lead to opportunities for promotion. It could also make managers less likely to offer the feedback that can lead to better performance. Not only does diversity training make little difference to social equality or workplace relations, it may also make things worse.[32]

Despite this, diversity training is a massive industry. Being an expert anti-racist is a highly lucrative business. Successful anti-racist authors and entrepreneurs, like Robin DiAngelo and Ibram X Kendi, earn vast sums of money through selling books and giving speeches. One investigation in 2020 claimed that DiAngelo 'has likely made over $2million from her book' *White Fragility*, but that 'the speaking circuit is where she is cleaning up... a 60-90 minute keynote would run $30,000, a two-hour workshop $35,000, and a half-day event $40,000'. The report also noted that Kendi 'charges $150 for tickets to public events and $25,000 for a one-hour presentation', and that 'former *Atlantic* writer Ta-Nehisi Coates has charged between $30,000 and $40,000 for public lectures'.[33] Sitting below these elite entrepreneurs are myriad academics, experts and workplace trainers who make money from race. For employers, the costs of diversity training go far beyond simply paying for a guest lecturer. They also include the wages of staff directed to spend time in workshops rather than focusing on generating revenue.

Businesses happily hand over money to the race experts. No doubt many well-meaning bosses genuinely believe diversity training will bring positive outcomes. Or they assume that in the wake of the Black Lives Matter protests they must be seen to be doing something. But the specific nature of critical race theory-inspired training, in bringing together identity politics and therapeutic practice, also holds significant benefits for employers. Elisabeth Lasch-Quinn argues that, from the emergence of workplace sensitivity training in the 1940s through to encounter groups in the 1960s, the ritualised practices that now epitomise the diversity industry 'cannot be understood apart from the culture of therapy'. She suggests that, in the 1960s, 'psychotherapeutic techniques became widely accepted as appropriate for an ever-broadening range of everyday issues or "life problems"', based on ideas that had been developed in the decades beforehand.[34] Race relations comprised one such life problem that was considered resolvable through therapeutic practices mediated by experts.

There is a particular therapeutic practice that forms the basis for most diversity training. As such, familiar patterns can be observed in these programmes, irrespective of the specific focus of the workshop. In order to take on board new ways of thinking and behaving towards others, people must first be made self-conscious about their existing relationships. Participants are taught to see themselves not as individuals, nor as friends and colleagues with interests in common, but as representatives of racial groups. Then, with spontaneity replaced by self-consciousness, attention is drawn to the differences between groups. Sometimes this process involves participants being asked to verbalise stereotypes they have encountered – even if they do not, nor ever have, accepted or reinforced those stereotypes themselves.

Next, participants are informed that there are racialised differences in the emotional responses people demonstrate when confronted with such stereotypes – namely, black anger and white guilt. And then, finally, trainers lead participants through a process of acceptance and validation of these emotional responses. Lasch-Quinn notes that in these sessions black anger and white guilt are validated on the assumption that no individual is responsible for their feelings. Rather, it is society that creates stereotypes and fuels prejudice. When it is accepted that stereotypes, not individuals, are responsible for racism, then the trainer can offer instruction in approved interracial etiquette that focuses on acknowledging and managing emotional responses in an acceptable way.

Expecting diversity training to reduce instances of racism may be to miss the point. The aim, it seems, is not a solution to racism but a reconciliation to its existence and a commitment to seeking it out wherever it is hidden. In turn, this exposes yet more problems to be resolved through more diversity training. Meanwhile, all criticisms of this process are dismissed as 'white fragility' and serve as evidence of the need for even more diversity training. The sole aim of the diversity industry thus appears to be its own self-perpetuation. Each new iteration provides additional moral weight and, of course, revenue for the professional anti-racists.

The benefits for employers of fuelling this industry are numerous. Diversity training breaks down any sense of solidarity between people. Individuals learn to be vigilant about their own behaviour, to appraise the actions of others and to report indiscretions to managers. As a result, HR departments take on a new lease of life in the woke workplace. Through unconscious-bias training, employers gain access not just to our labour, but also to our minds and emotions. The often mandatory nature of diversity training means the workplace is transformed into a place for the inculcation of a particular ideological approach. All of this divides workers according to identity, overriding social class and empowering employers to act as neutral, therapeutic arbiters in workplace conflicts.

He who pays the piper

Today's companies are led by people who have been educated in woke universities and business schools and socialised into a woke culture. Today's capitalists are certainly not averse to making money, but do not see it as an intrinsically good thing to do. In his 1976 book, *The Cultural Contradictions of Capitalism*, Daniel Bell explored the tensions between capitalism's inherent drive for economic growth and the elite's cultural hostility to such growth. This tendency for capitalism to undermine its own dynamism had previously been identified by Joseph Schumpeter in *Capitalism, Socialism and Democracy* (1942). Schumpeter wrote that capitalism undermines 'its own defences' because it 'creates a critical frame of mind which, after having destroyed the moral authority of so many other institutions, in the end turns against its own'.[35]

It was in response to internal insecurities as much as external attacks that a defensive capitalist class began, from the late 1960s onwards, repositioning itself as socially responsible. It hoped to resolve its inherent 'cultural contradictions' by making it possible to make a profit while also siding with the counterculture. This view was perhaps best summed up by R Edward Freeman. In his 1984 book, *Strategic Management: A Stakeholder Approach,* Freeman defined the task of executives as being to create as much value as possible for stakeholders without resorting to ethical or moral tradeoffs. He has argued that 'great companies endure because they manage to get stakeholder interests aligned in the same direction'. Today, arguing that boosting shareholders' wealth is the most fundamental objective of business is deeply unfashionable.

At the same time as this shift was taking place, ideas around activism began to shift, too. Consumption came to be seen not as separate from politics, but as a powerful political force. Organising boycotts and channelling consumer spending habits came to be seen as a means of instigating social change. A generation of consumers assumed that Apartheid in South Africa could be brought to an end if enough people stopped buying South African produce from their local supermarket. In the process, the impact of the protests and campaigns led by black South Africans was often overlooked when assessing the struggle for equal rights. But the myth of social change brought about through activist customers has persisted. And we now have a cohort of elite consumers and capitalists who are cut from the exact same cloth as the political activists – those who focus their attention not on persuading the public of their cause, but on changing society from the top down. It is no longer sufficient for private enterprise to make money for shareholders or to provide people with employment: it also assumes responsibility for resolving social and political problems.

In his book, *Woke, Inc,* Vivek Ramaswamy writes that 'woke consumerism is not nearly as big of a phenomenon as CEOs and investors claim'. He says the idea that 'consumers are demanding it and we're just giving them what they want' is 'often just a hollow excuse to justify top-down power-grabbing by influential executives and investors'.[36] This is undoubtedly true. What's most significant is that the power-grabbing is being done not in opposition to woke values, but in order to promote them. Capitalists and activists share the same set of values, and the same disdain for ordinary people. Both assume that the public need to be lectured and cajoled and have their choices limited.

Over the course of several decades, the boundaries between politics and private enterprise, between the political and business elites, have grown increasingly blurred. Just as members of the political class have business interests, so too are woke business executives happy to intervene in the sphere of politics over the heads of the people and their representatives. In April 2021, business leaders and lawyers in the US organised a campaign to defeat Republican state voting laws by withdrawing donations and refusing to move business or jobs to states that passed the proposed new laws. Corporations using their economic clout to influence the decisions of elected officials was presented as essential to the future of democracy.[37]

Time and again, the beneficiaries of woke capitalism are shown to be not the oppressed, but the social and economic elite. The business elite, with its money and power, gets to bypass democracy and intervene in politics to further its own interests and the interests of the political class. This could be seen most starkly in the decision of social-media companies to censor Donald Trump while he was still president. These anti-democratic and illiberal actions are cheered on by the rest of the cultural elite.

It is tempting to think of woke capitalism as a recent development, but it has its origins in the cracks that began to appear in the moral authority of capitalism almost a century ago. It is tempting to see it as a cynical smokescreen, but it is built on the genuinely held beliefs of the business elite. It is tempting to think that woke capitalism runs counter to making a profit, but it has become the way of doing business.

Woke capitalism is now one of the key ways through which the cultural elite consolidates power and brings about political change without the general public having a say. The biggest problem with it is not its hypocrisy, but the threat it poses to democracy.

In the remaining chapters of this book, we explore the ideas that underpin woke in more detail, looking at how important principles such as racial equality, social solidarity and individual freedom have come to be so devastatingly reimagined.

Endnotes

[1] John Lewis pulls controversial advert for being 'potentially misleading', *Guardian*, 27 October 2021

[2] *Woke, Inc: Inside the Social Justice Scam*, Vivek Ramaswamy, Swift Press (2021)

[3] We must dismantle white supremacy, Ben & Jerry's (2020)

[4] Nike, Adidas, Netflix, Ben & Jerry's and more show support for Black Lives Matter, *Campaign*, 1 June 2020

[5] NIKE, Inc Statement on Commitment to the Black Community, Nike News, 5 June 2020

[6] M&S claim new lingerie range was inspired by George Floyd's death, *Independent*, 23 June 2021

[7] Black Lives Matter: Do companies really support the cause?, BBC World Service, 13 June 2020

[8] These companies have the most hypocritical Black Lives Matter messaging, *Daily Beast*, 5 June 2020

[9] Brands may support Black Lives Matter, but advertising still needs to decolonise, Carl W Jones, *Conversation*, 24 June 2020

[10] Corporate voices get behind 'Black Lives Matter' cause, *New York Times*, 31 May 2020

[11] Kendall Jenner 'feels bad' after Pepsi Black Lives Matter advert controversy, BBC News, 2 October 2017

[12] #TheBestMenCanBe, Gillette, 2019

[13] People 'offended' by Gillette's ad about 'toxic masculinity' mocked as 'snowflakes', *Mirror*, 15 January 2019

[14] Nike sales surge 31% in days after Colin Kaepernick ad unveiled, analyst says, *Guardian*, 8 September 2018

[15] Nike's Colin Kaepernick ad sparked a boycott – and earned $6 billion for Nike, *Vox*, 24 September 2018

[16] *No Logo: Taking Aim at the Brand Bullies*, Naomi Klein, Knopf Canada (1999)

[17] Brands pull ads from GB News TV channel over content concerns, *Guardian*, 15 June 2021

[18] Twitter and Facebook are Not Representative of the General Population: Political Attitudes and Demographics of Social Media Users, Jonathan Mellon and Christopher Prosser, *SSRN Electronic Journal*, January 2016

[19] Railway firm apologises to non-binary passenger for 'ladies and gentlemen' announcement, *Pink News*, 14 May 2021

[20] Nike has spoken out about Uighur Muslim forced labour – it faces a choice between ethics and profits, Ian Birrell, *i*, 28 March 2021

[21] Uighur Muslims sent to work in Chinese factory that supplies Nike, report finds, *Independent*, 1 March 2020

[22] Ikea France fined €1m for snooping on staff, BBC News, 15 June 2021

[23] Nivea accused of racist advert after showing product lightening black skin, BBC News, 19 October 2017

[24] How migrant workers took on Ben & Jerry's – and won a historic agreement, *Guardian*, 25 February 2018

[25] Unconscious Bias Training: Statement from Cabinet Office, Julia Lopez MP, UK Parliament, 15 December 2020

[26] Does Diversity Training Work the Way It's Supposed To?, Edward H Chang et al, *Harvard Business Review*, 9 July 2019

[27] Unconscious bias training alone will not stop discrimination, say critics, *Guardian*, 2 March 2021

[28] Does Diversity Training Work the Way It's Supposed To?, Edward H Chang et al, *Harvard Business Review*, 9 July 2019

[29] *Racism at Work: The Danger of Indifference*, Binna Kandola, Pearn Kandola Publishing (2018)

[30] IAT: Fad or fabulous?, Beth Azar, *Monitor on Psychology*, July / August 2008

[31] Diversity-Related Training: What Is It Good For, Heterodox Academy, 16 September 2020

[32] Why Diversity Programmes Fail, Frank Dobbin and Alexandra Kalev, *Harvard Business Review*, July / August 2016

[33] The Wages of Woke, Charles Fain Lehman, *Washington Free Beacon*, 25 July 2020

[34] *Race Experts: How Racial Etiquette, Sensitivity Training, and New Age Therapy Hijacked the Civil-Rights Revolution*, Elisabeth Lasch-Quinn, Rowman and Littlefield (2001)

[35] *Capitalism, Socialism and Democracy*, Joseph Schumpeter, Start Publishing LLC (2012)

[36] *Woke, Inc: Inside the Social Justice Scam*, Vivek Ramaswamy, Swift Press (2021)

[37] The tyranny of woke capitalism, Frank Furedi, *spiked*, 25 June 2021

8 The New Racism

By almost all historical accounts and statistical measures, society today is less racist than at any point in the past century. This is rarely stated, let alone celebrated. This progress is not considered a reason to leave people to negotiate inter-cultural and interracial relationships for themselves. Instead, as legal discrimination and racist attacks have diminished, and overt displays of racism have become socially unacceptable, attempts to find and challenge racism have increased. The message from the media and bestselling books – as well as from an array of diversity workshops held in schools, universities and the workplace – is that racism continues to be endemic. Anti-racism is big business and, as we saw in the previous chapter, the most popular speakers and authors generate considerable revenue.

This woke anti-racism does little to improve outcomes for ethnic-minority people. Worse, it breathes new life back into racial thinking and emphasises differences between people that were only recently overcome. This chapter traces the development of woke anti-racism and argues that, in racialising society and perpetuating essentialist myths of white privilege and black victimhood, it is a regressive force that serves only the interests of the cultural elite.[1]

Black Lives Matter

The 2020 Black Lives Matter (BLM) protests that swept the globe in the wake of George Floyd's murder were remarkable. Neither police brutality towards black people nor mass demonstrations against racism were anything new. But rarely have people across so many countries, in cities with their own unique problems, turned out in such huge numbers to support the same cause. This wave of protests took place despite the fact that the world was in the grip of the coronavirus pandemic and, in most countries, legal restrictions limited the number of people able to gather together. BLM protests breached national lockdowns, and yet they often took place with minimal interference from law enforcement. In the UK, some police officers even chose to 'take the knee' before protesters.[2]

BLM was publicly endorsed by corporations, former members of the royal family and celebrities.[3] Following the initial wave of demonstrations, sports stars began kneeling prior to matches or competitions – a practice Premier League footballers have continued ever since. Never before has an anti-racist movement had such elite backing.[4]

The extent of this establishment support is surprising given the stated aims of BLM. The UK wing of BLM launched a public crowd-funding page that stated:

> *We're guided by a commitment to dismantle imperialism, capitalism, white supremacy, patriarchy and the state structures that disproportionately harm black people in Britain and around the world. We build deep relationships across the diaspora and strategise to challenge the rise of the authoritarian right-wing across the world, from Brazil to Britain.[5]*

Multinational corporations and wealthy individuals are apparently relaxed about dismantling capitalism. The UK page alone raised close to

£1.25million by the time it had closed in October 2020. The US-based Black Lives Matter Global Network Foundation raised $90million in 2020.[6] BLM also campaigns to abolish prisons, to defund the police, to remove national borders and to raise awareness of climate change.[7] As we have already explored in this book, many of these values align directly with those of the cultural elite.

The BLM movement was founded by three women – Alicia Garza, Patrisse Cullors and Opal Tometi – who met as community organisers and civil-rights activists. The phrase 'Black Lives Matter' was first used by Garza in a Facebook post she called 'a love letter to black people' following the acquittal of George Zimmerman in 2013 for the killing of Trayvon Martin.[8] Garza's Facebook post was shared on Twitter by Cullors, who tagged it with #BlackLivesMatter. The slogan migrated into a rallying cry for the street protests against police brutality that took place in 2014 in response to the killings of Michael Brown and Eric Garner. In 2016, Twitter reported that #BlackLivesMatter was the third most-used hashtag related to a social cause in the site's 10-year history.[9] The Pew Research Center notes that the organisers of BLM 'made social media – and specifically the hashtag #BlackLivesMatter – a centrepiece of their strategy. As a result, the growth of the movement offline was directly linked with the online conversation.'[10] As both a campaigning group and a social-media hashtag, Black Lives Matter exploded in the wake of Floyd's death.

But many of BLM's core claims, particularly about the scale of police brutality against black people, are deeply misleading. Data suggest that about 1,000 civilians are killed each year by law-enforcement officers in the US.[11] In the five years from 2015 to 2020, one victim in six was un-armed.[12] Although unarmed black people were three times as likely to be killed as white people, the total numbers are a tiny fraction of a national population of 330million citizens. We also need to acknowledge that, in 2019, 48 police officers were killed in the line of duty as a direct result of the actions of an offender.[13] This suggests that a significant proportion of police killings may have been acts of self-defence or attempts at stopping other serious crimes from being committed.

Roughly a quarter of those killed by the police each year are black – in other words, three quarters of all fatalities at the hands of police officers are *not* black people. Black Lives Matter points out that as black people make up only around 13 per cent of the US population, these figures show that they are disproportionately more likely to be killed than white people. According to one estimate, reported in the journal *Nature* and widely repeated elsewhere, black men are 2.5 times more likely than white men to be killed by police during the course of their lifetime.[14]

However, statistics like this make no adjustment for crime rates. If we assume that the police are more likely to kill people involved in crimes than random citizens, then we need to look at rates of fatalities in comparison to crime rates rather than general population size. In 2018, the rate of arrests for violent crime was 3.6 times higher for black people than white people. This would suggest that black people are proportionally less likely to become victims of police killings when the rate of police encounters is taken into account.[15] A 2016 study carried out by Roland Fryer for the National Bureau of Economic Research found that, while black men and women are treated differently by law-enforcement officers, there is no evidence of racial bias in police shootings.[16]

Author Wilfred Reilly argues that the portrayal of institutionalised racist brutality within the police force is a 'founding myth' of the BLM movement. He suggests 'an almost fact-free narrative of American black "genocide"... is sustained by selective dishonesty and plain old-fashioned censorship on the part of "allies" of the black community'.[17] The Manhattan Institute's Heather Mac Donald similarly rejects the perception that there is an 'epidemic of shooting unarmed black men and women, as we now hear daily'.[18]

In the summer of 2020, high-profile institutional support for

BLM continued, despite the fact that many of the protests that took place in the US in the weeks following Floyd's murder were far from peaceful and some descended into riots. As journalist Michael Tracey wrote at the time:

> From large metro areas like Chicago and Minneapolis / St Paul, to small and mid-sized cities like Fort Wayne, Indiana and Green Bay, Wisconsin, the number of boarded-up, damaged or destroyed buildings I have personally observed – commercial, civic and residential – is staggering… large swathes of a major American metropolis, Minneapolis / St Paul, still lie in rubble over a month after the riots.

Yet despite blanket global media coverage of the BLM protests, many outlets barely acknowledged that rioting had taken place. In fact, despite visual evidence to the contrary occurring even as they spoke to camera, reporters described the protests as 'mostly peaceful'. Tracey explains that 'media elites desperately do not want to undermine the moral legitimacy of a "movement" that they have cast as presumptively righteous'.[19]

There are many reasons why BLM became a lavishly funded global movement in receipt of high-profile backing and seemingly immune from establishment criticism. Few disagree that black lives matter. The official BLM website describes the movement's mission as being 'to eradicate white supremacy and build local power to intervene in violence inflicted on black communities by the state and vigilantes'. It is impossible to disagree with such a statement: the references to white supremacy and state-sanctioned violence are designed to garner support. But important questions need to be asked. How big a problem is 'white supremacy' and what form does it take nowadays? And who are the vigilantes?

BLM claims: 'By combatting and countering acts of violence, creating space for black imagination and innovation, and centring black joy, we are winning immediate improvements in our lives.'[20] These statements pose a stark contrast between, on the one hand, 'white supremacy', 'violence' and 'vigilantes' and, on the other, 'imagination', 'innovation' and 'joy'. The supposedly tremendous power of white supremacy today is assumed as fact, while the fight against racism is presented as a conflict between violence and joy. This rhetoric places BLM within a therapeutic sphere.

BLM also aims to 'fight against elected officials, be they Democrat or Republican, who don't share a vision that is radical and intersectional'. It is critical of previous black-liberation movements for having 'created room, space and leadership mostly for black heterosexual, cisgender men – leaving women, queer and transgender people, and others, either out of the movement or in the background to move the work forward with little or no recognition.'[21]

BLM's UK crowdfunder called for donations to 'support black life against institutional racism and enable radical reimagining / knowledge production from within our communities.'[22] Again, we see a sharp contrast between the rhetoric of 'fighting against elected officials' on the one hand and the goal of 'knowledge production' on the other. The radical language sits alongside a more individualised and therapeutic pursuit.

References to intersectionality – that is, the division and grouping of people according not just to race, but to sexuality and gender identity, too – firmly position BLM within the prism of identity politics in general and critical race theory (CRT) in particular. We have already discussed the influence of CRT in schools, universities and in the workplace. The elite backing of CRT suggests this is a form of anti-racism that resonates with, rather than challenges, the cultural elite's moral norms and economic practices. Far from challenging existing hierarchies, an individualised and therapeutic approach to tackling racism allows a social, political and corporate elite to gain a renewed sense of moral authority.

Anti-racism in the past

In the 19th and 20th centuries, imperialism, colonial exploitation and slavery were justified by a belief that white elites were physically, mentally and morally superior to the people they ruled over. This view, which has since come to be known as 'scientific racism', extended to the working class at home, who were portrayed as genetically distinct from and inferior to the upper class. This biological conception of race began to be called into question after the Second World War, although its legacy continued to play out in Apartheid South Africa, Jim Crow laws in the American South and discrimination in the UK.

WEB Du Bois, an American sociologist writing in the first few decades of the 20th century, argued that it was both society in the present and the historical legacy of differential treatment that prevented racial equality. He argued that black Americans experienced 'double-consciousness':

> [A] sense of always looking at one's self through the eyes of others, of measuring one's soul by the tape of a world that looks on in amused contempt and pity. One feels his two-ness, – an American, a Negro; two souls, two thoughts, two unreconciled strivings; two warring ideals in one dark body, whose dogged strength alone keeps it from being torn asunder.

Du Bois did not seek to eliminate this double-consciousness by disappearing into or separating off from white American society. Rather, he argued, the 'American Negro' desires a 'merging':

> He does not wish to Africanise America, for America has too much to teach the world and Africa; he does not wish to bleach his Negro blood in a flood of white Americanism, for he believes – foolishly, perhaps, but fervently – that Negro blood has yet a message for the

world. He simply wishes to make it possible for a man to be both a Negro and an American without being cursed and spit upon by his fellows, without losing the opportunity of self-development.[23]

Through self-development, Du Bois hoped that the black man could become 'a co-worker in the kingdom of culture'.

The desire for black citizens to be 'co-workers' in American life drove the civil-rights-era challenge to Jim Crow legislation, demands for legal equality and 'colour blind' policies. The concept of colour blindness was best summed up by Martin Luther King in his famous speech delivered at the Lincoln Memorial in Washington, DC in August 1963: 'I have a dream that my four little children will one day live in a nation where they will not be judged by the colour of their skin, but by the content of their character.'[24]

Colour blindness provided an important challenge to the legal segregation that operated in the US and the overt racism that existed in the UK. In both countries, formal and informal 'colour bars' kept black people out of jobs, housing and schools that were reserved exclusively for white people. Within this context, the demand that people not be judged by the colour of their skin was revolutionary. Sadly, many of the demands for colour-blind equality did not come to fruition. For example, after a long battle, in 1954 the US Supreme Court declared racial segregation in public schools to be unconstitutional, meaning that black and white children should learn alongside one another. However, in practice, most schools remained racially divided because of income inequality and segregated housing. Nonetheless, the demand for colour-blind equality led to significant progress and set a vitally important aspiration. Not reaching this standard exposed how far society still needed to progress.

Yet rather than continuing to struggle for a colour-blind society, the goal posts shifted in the post-civil-rights era. By the end of the

1960s, with both racism and poverty still major problems, many activists arrived at the conclusion that legal equality not only left social inequality intact, but also provided the context and justification for its continuation. To end racial inequality, they had to go further. For some, this meant a greater push for integration and assimilation. They continued to argue for universal human rights and championed initiatives such as 'integration busing' – the transportation of black children to schools in predominantly white neighbourhoods. At the same time, a new generation challenged the whole strategy of promoting black assimilation into an existing white-dominated culture and instead turned to black separatism or nationalism. As the authors of *Words That Wound*, a 1993 book on hate speech, put it:

> It became apparent to many who were active in the civil-rights movement that dominant conceptions of race, racism and equality were increasingly incapable of providing any meaningful quantum of racial justice.[25]

Only a few years after Martin Luther King spoke at the Lincoln Memorial, the Black Power movement was becoming increasingly influential. It drew inspiration from Malcolm X – formerly a spokesman for the Nation of Islam, a black-nationalist group – who critiqued King and argued instead for a more militant approach that would not appeal to white people to rescind power, or look for accommodations within existing structures, but rather would promote black self-sufficiency and complete social change.

This marked a significant shift. As Elisabeth Lasch-Quinn points out in *Race Experts*, the waning of the civil-rights movement overlapped with the psychotherapy boom, leading to a shift from civil-rights universalism to 'the black identity movement'. Black identity was something to be proud of – but in the process of celebration, racial difference was once more made real. Race may no longer have been considered a biological reality, but it rapidly became thought of as an identity created by society. Rather than challenging the basis for the formation of this identity, anti-racists instead focused on validating and empowering the socially constructed self. Race moved from people's bodies to their minds. By the mid-1960s, oppression was considered by some on the left to be as much a state of mind as it was a matter of economic exploitation or a denial of rights. This change in direction, from transcending racial divisions and creating a truly democratic society to a focus on black identity, would ultimately put an end to the most positive and forward-looking aims of the civil-rights movement.[26]

It was at this time that some anti-racist activists began to find a home within academia. According to the authors of *Words That Wound*:

> *[I]ndividual law teachers and students committed to racial justice began to meet, to talk, to write, and to engage in political action in an effort to confront and oppose dominant societal and institutional forces that maintained the structures of racism while professing the goal of dismantling racial discrimination.[27]*

This was the beginning of critical race theory.

The emergence of critical race theory

Critical race theory (CRT) began with academics committed to researching and changing attitudes to race and the interplay between racism and power. They merged scholarship from critical legal studies and radical feminism with work by philosophers and theorists associated with critical theory more broadly, such as Michel Foucault and Jacques Derrida. They embraced a psychological understanding of race and a therapeutic and behaviouristic approach to race relations that had emerged in the 1960s alongside the civil-rights movement.[28]

In their popular primer on CRT, Richard Delgado and Jean Stefancic note that when critical race theory first began to gain traction within academia, 'scholars questioned whether the much-vaunted system of civil-rights remedies ended up doing people of colour much good'. These academic activists, writing in *Words That Wound*, argued that 'majoritarian self-interest' was 'a critical factor in the ebb and flow of civil-rights doctrine'. In other words, a white-majority society would be unlikely to cede its power voluntarily.[29] A key text to come out of this period was Derrick Bell's *Race, Racism and American Law*, published in 1970. In it, Bell argued that white people only concede rights when it is in their interests to do so, a notion he labelled 'interest convergence'. As Delgado and Stefancic put it: 'Because racism advances the interests of both white elites (materially) and working-class whites (psychically), large segments of society have little incentive to eradicate it.'[30] Black scholars found common cause with professors engaged in critical legal studies who sought to formulate a radical, left-wing critique of the law. They drew from 'liberalism, Marxism, the law and society movement, critical legal studies, feminism, poststructuralism / postmodernism and neopragmatism'. A key aim was to examine 'the relationships between naming and reality, knowledge and power'.[31] This marked a distinct turn towards subjectivity and overlapped with work carried out by sensitivity-training counsellors who had been promoting therapeutic approaches to race relations in the workplace since the late 1940s. It led to racism being understood not just as legal and economic inequalities, but also as social and cultural practices and, above all else, a matter of psychology.

At this point, as the authors of *Words That Wound* put it, 'Scholars of colour within the left began to ask their white colleagues to examine their own racism and to develop oppositional critiques not just to dominant conceptions of race and racism but to the treatment of race within the left as well'. Their conclusions presented racism 'not as isolated instances of conscious bigoted decision-making or prejudiced practice, but as larger, systemic, structural and cultural, as deeply psychologically and socially ingrained'.[32] The focus on the 'vulnerable self' emphasised the emotional states of both black and white people, how feelings translated into behaviour, and how experts could help individuals better manage their emotions and behaviour in order to alleviate the consequences of racism across society.

Kimberlé Crenshaw has described the seminal protests at Harvard Law School in 1981, following Bell's departure. When the school refused to hire a black professor to teach Race, Racism and American Law, a course that had been regularly taught by Bell, students invited leading black academics and lawyers to lecture on a course aimed at 'developing a full account of the legal construction of race and racism'.[33] Bringing people together in this joint intellectual project crystallised the ideas underpinning CRT and many of the radical student organisers went on to become teachers themselves. By the end of the 1980s, Crenshaw's work led her to devise a framework she labelled 'intersectionality' to describe how multiple features of a person's identity can combine to create different modes of discrimination and privilege. Her 1991 essay, 'Mapping the Margins: Intersectionality, Identity Politics and Violence Against Women of Colour', has been highly influential.[34]

By the 1990s, a more identity-focused and postmodern understanding of race and racism, driven primarily by radical black feminists such as Crenshaw, Audre Lorde, bell hooks, Patricia Hill Collins and Angela Harris, was gaining ground. Black identity was assumed to be constructed through the collective experience of racism and made manifest through sometimes deeply repressed psychological wounds. This recast and re-established racial differences at the very point that their existence was being challenged most successfully.

Critical race theory today

Critical race theorists were not the first to point out that race is socially constructed – that it is not a naturally occurring phenomenon but rather is created and made meaningful by people collectively, over time and place. Few today disagree with this point. But whereas a previous generation of anti-racists challenged the notion of racial difference to argue that there was one race – the human race – and emphasised universal traits that create a common humanity irrespective of skin colour, critical race theorists argue that, once constructed, race becomes an incontestable fact. As Robin DiAngelo explains in *White Fragility*, 'While there is no biological race as we understand it, race as a social construct has profound significance and shapes every aspect of our lives'.[35] According to Ibram X Kendi, race is 'a power construct of blended difference that lives socially'. He explains: 'I still identify as black. Not because I believe blackness, or race, is a meaningful scientific category but because our societies, our policies, our ideas, our histories, and our cultures have rendered race and made it matter.'

This raises the question of who or what is responsible for constructing race. Kendi argues: 'Race creates new forms of power: the power to categorise and judge, elevate and downgrade, include and exclude. Race makers use that power to process distinct individuals, ethnicities and nationalities into monolithic races.'[36] Once, the 'race makers' were the white social and political elite who sought to justify slavery or colonialism. But today's race makers are woke.

DiAngelo, Kendi and others promote an inescapably circular argument, whereby race is constructed and made meaningful through racism. According to law professor Kendall Thomas: 'We are raced. We are acted upon and constructed by racist speech. The meaning of "black" or "white" is derived through a history of acted upon ideology.'[37] When race is socially constructed through racist attitudes, racism comes to be understood as systemic – that is, built into the very fabric of societies designed by white people, for the benefit of white people. Proponents of CRT argue that ideas of white superiority and black inferiority are intrinsic to our language, culture and interpretations of history. In this way, racial differences come to be seen as deeply psychologically entrenched. It is assumed that there are 'black ways of thinking' and 'white ways of thinking'. In order to challenge racism, it is no longer acceptable to argue for equality. Instead, it must be recognised that promoting equality is, in and of itself, symptomatic of a white frame of reference that, no matter how well intentioned, is ultimately hostile to black people.

When racism is seen in this way, arguing for improving the lives of black people through the exercise of individual autonomy, resilience and effort comes to be seen as promoting 'a racist myth',[38] because it reinforces stereotypically 'white' social attitudes. This traps everyone in what Lasch-Quinn refers to as a 'harangue-flagellation ritual', in which black people are put 'in the role of repressed, angry victims' and white people 'in the role of oppressors who need to expiate their guilt'. Whereas the civil-rights movement held out the prospect of overcoming racial differences, the psychologising of race ensures racial differences are never eradicated. The best we can strive for is healing and acceptance, performed through the correct etiquette and mediated by a burgeoning army of race experts. This way of thinking risks rehabilitating some incredibly regressive and racist ideas. Hard work, rationality, resilience and autonomy are not inherently 'white' values, and implying they are does black people no favours.

Today, race experts have taken the subjective, identitarian and psychological understanding of racism developed within universities and transformed it into a list of woke commandments. First, and most important, is the instruction to see race. Race is no longer considered a biological fact, but it is seen as structurally embedded within people's minds. As a consequence, today's race experts do not think that racism can be reduced by promoting equality or challenging individual instances of prejudice. Instead, their insistence on seeing race and recognising racism as systemic to white ways of thinking leads them to reject universal, Enlightenment-inspired values of objectivity, neutrality, equality and meritocracy. Personal, or 'lived', experience becomes all important, because people are assumed to be capable only of understanding the world from the standpoint of their own identity group. Next must come confessions of white culpability and guilt. The aim is not forgiveness, but perpetual penance.

Lived experience

Critical race theorists consider 'lived experience' to be the most significant factor in ascertaining the nature and extent of racism. The academic notion of 'lived experience' began as a methodological approach to qualitative research in disciplines such as sociology, but it is increasingly used by activists to refer to bringing their own perceptions, understandings and experiences to bear on a situation. The social meanings ascribed to different groups is said to create differences in people's lived experiences. In other words, it is because black people are treated differently to white people that they come to experience the world differently.

As the philosopher Kwame Anthony Appiah points out, when the phrase 'lived experience' first crossed from academia to activism it was used almost exclusively 'to designate firsthand experiences that were specific to women, minorities and other vulnerable groups'. However, it is now used far more liberally and is increasingly used to shut down debate. As Appiah notes: 'You can debate my sociopolitical analyses – those facts and interpretations are shared and public – but not my lived experience. Lived experience isn't something you argue, it's something you have.' This way of thinking now reaches all the way to the White House. Following the Democrats' 2020 presidential win, vice-president

Kamala Harris told a TV interviewer that she had promised President Joe Biden to always share with him her 'lived experience, as it relates to any issue that we confront'.[39]

As lived experience is only ever known to the individual concerned, it is incontestable. It is considered to be more true than mere objective measurement. But experience is never simply neutral. We interpret and relay our experiences according to our beliefs and prior understandings. Furthermore, no one person's experiences can truly be representative of a general phenomenon. We meet the world as individuals. Even though we may share ethnicity, class, sexuality or other features of our identity with others, we are no more a product of these features than we are a product of our biology. The assumption that there is a common female, black or queer experience risks falling back upon stereotypes.

David Goodhart describes lived experience as a type of knowledge, but one that is 'highly constrained and even misleading'. It is the unreliability of personal testimony that makes facts, data and objective knowledge so important in understanding the world. As Goodhart argues: 'We may then select the data based on our own interests or worldview – indeed it is almost impossible not to – but at least we are making some effort to use the apparatus of objectivity: logic and evidence.'[40] The lack of objectivity in lived experience makes it difficult to assess the extent of racism and therefore to make comparisons over time.

For critical race theorists, lived experience constitutes the basis for racism. Racially distinct experiences produce racially distinct understandings. White people are assumed to have a shared lived experience that determines how they make sense of the world, one that is fundamentally different from the lived experience of black people. As our actions are said to be determined by our knowledge and understanding, then prejudice, even unconscious prejudice, is assumed always to show up in our behaviour. This underpins an understanding of racism as something that can only be perceived by black people or those who have undertaken particular forms of anti-racism training.

This focus on the different lived experiences of black and white people, with only one group presented as having true insight into racism, confirms the rejection of colour blindness. Colour blindness is now criticised as essentially racist. Kendi tells us that, 'as with the "not racist", the colour-blind individual, by ostensibly failing to see race, fails to see racism and falls into racist passivity. The language of "colour blindness" – like the language of "not racist" – is a mask to hide racism.'[41] This stark accusation, that not seeing race is an example of racism and an illustration of white privilege, has become a key argument of woke anti-racists.

The problem of whiteness

In America, wealthy white women pay to be accused of white supremacy, racism and privilege. Race2Dinner, an anti-racism enterprise created by Regina Jackson, who is black, and Saira Rao, who is Indian American, charges $5,000 for dinners that promise a serving of guilt with every course. With their emphasis on systemic racism, white privilege, unconscious bias and microaggressions, Jackson and Rao teach their clients how to go beyond merely being 'not racist' to become fully trained-up woke anti-racists. In the process, they pander to a form of self-loathing that seems particularly prevalent among elite, white feminists.[42] All of this is designed to overcome the racism that allegedly lurks within nominally liberal white women, who can become defensive when accused of bigotry. Woke anti-racists argue that white women employ tears to avoid confronting the reality of their own racism.

Woke anti-racism demands that, having rejected colour blindness, people must see themselves and others as racialised beings within a system that constructs white people as privileged and black people as oppressed. DiAngelo argues that 'white people in North America live in a society that is deeply separate and unequal by race, and white people are the beneficiaries of that separation and inequality', because they are 'socialised into a deeply internalised sense of superiority'. From this perspective, even though individual white people may be against racism, they still benefit from a system that privileges whites as a group. White working-class people with no discernible privileges at all – people on low incomes, with few job prospects and poor-quality housing – also find themselves written off as the beneficiaries of white privilege.

Reni Eddo-Lodge, author of *Why I'm No Longer Talking to White People About Race*, argues that 'if you're white, your race will almost certainly positively impact your life's trajectory in some way. And you probably won't even notice it.'[43] This is because, according to the critical race theorists, whiteness is primarily a standpoint – that is, a set of cultural practices that benefits white people by positioning them as the norm and black people as a deviation from this norm. This standpoint supposedly exists in white people's unconscious minds. As DiAngelo puts it, 'whiteness has psychological advantages that translate into material returns'. For white children, the process of socialisation into a 'deeply internalised sense of superiority' is said to begin from the earliest days of infancy. 'I have a white frame of reference and a white worldview, and I move through the world with a white experience', DiAngelo writes.

Proponents of CRT argue that notions of objectivity and meritocracy allow white people to deny the privileges they are afforded by their skin colour. If white people become defensive or hostile after being confronted with their alleged privilege and racism they are said to demonstrate 'white fragility'. This is conceptualised by DiAngelo as 'a response or "condition" produced and reproduced by the continual social and material advantages of whiteness'. The focus on whiteness indicates another shift prompted by the psychologisation of race:

'whiteness', and not simply racism, is now seen as the problem, and as an immutable characteristic it is irresolvable and requires permanent acts of contrition. As DiAngelo puts it, 'a positive white identity is an impossible goal. White identity is inherently racist; white people do not exist outside the system of white supremacy.'[44]

More recently, there has been pushback not just against the idea of white privilege, but also against critical race theory more broadly, particularly its promotion in schools, universities and the workplace. CRT became a focal point of Virginia's gubernatorial election in November 2021. Republican Glenn Youngkin's victory over his Democratic rival, coming just a year after the state had backed President Biden, was widely interpreted as a rejection of CRT-inspired teaching and other progressive policies being enacted in Virginia's schools. A *Washington Post*-Schar School poll found that 24 per cent of voters said education was their top issue, up from 15 per cent in 2020. Youngkin called CRT 'toxic' and a 'poisonous left-wing doctrine' that is 'flagrant racism, plain and simple'.[45] In the UK, equalities minister Kemi Badenoch has said CRT should not be taught in schools as fact. Many parents instinctively recognise the divisive nature of the ideas being propagated. They do not want their children to be taught to see themselves and others through such a racialised lens. Black parents no more want their children to be told that they are victims than white parents want their children to internalise a sense of shame.

Woke activists try to have it both ways. They begin by denying that children are being taught CRT – disingenuously noting that pupils are not being given obscure lessons in academic legal theory. At the same time, they poke fun at parents unable to define CRT. They chastise critics of CRT for engaging in a culture war, while denying their own role in imposing top-down attempts at cultural change. They accuse parents who dislike the divisiveness of CRT of racism, and then argue that CRT is needed to tackle such racism.

Woke anti-racism enshrines the bogus idea of racial differences between groups of people. Whiteness comes to be conceived of as a form of original sin, with predominantly white societies permanently trapped in the legacy of their founding crimes. Black people, meanwhile, are cast as perpetual victims compelled to act out their psychological wounds. Dividing people along these lines is a deeply racist act that benefits no one other than a tiny proportion of elite race entrepreneurs – both black and white – who can command large sums of money for sharing their supposed insights. For members of the elite, contemporary anti-racism acts as a moral purification ritual, an opportunity for self-flagellation and an excuse to lay bare their sins.

Woke anti-racism not only entrenches racial divisions, it also speaks to a turn against the values of the Enlightenment. It rejects everything Western societies have traditionally stood for. It is true that, at various points in time, Western societies have failed to practise what they preach about universalism. But what is lost in all this self-loathing is any recognition of the positive role Enlightenment thinkers such as Kant, Locke and Voltaire played in sowing the intellectual seeds not just for individual liberty, but for racial and sexual equality, too. Through expressing their 'white guilt' elite anti-racists distance themselves from Western society and the Enlightenment values they have been taught to disdain.

Woke anti-racism does nothing to challenge racism. It rehabilitates racial differences, serves them up for mainstream consumption, and allows the elite to divide and rule. The population is divided by skin colour and then ranked according to hierarchies of oppression. Those with superior knowledge of concepts like white privilege, microaggressions and systemic racism are then empowered to manage and discipline the divided communities this racial thinking creates. The elite thus carves out a new permanent role for itself. It sows racial division and grievances and then positions its careful instruction as the only solution to these problems.

Endnotes

[1] This chapter draws extensively on work in *Rethinking Race: A critique of contemporary anti-racism programmes*, originally published by Civitas in April 2021. It is reprinted here with permission

[2] Police force warns officers who don't kneel at Black Lives Matter rallies that they may be targeted by protesters, *Sun*, 14 June 2020

[3] Harry and Meghan have also been supporting Black Lives Matter in Britain, *Vanity Fair*, 26 October 2020

[4] Here are the retailers going beyond solidarity for Black Lives Matter, *Retail Gazette*, 12 June 2020

[5] UKBLM Fund, GoFundMe

[6] The Black Lives Matter foundation raised $90million in 2020, and gave almost a quarter of it to local chapters and organisations, CNN, 25 February 2021

[7] Revealed: What 'Black Lives Matter' really stands for, Tom Goodenough, *Spectator*, 24 June 2020

[8] About, Black Lives Matter, 2020

[9] These 10 Twitter hashtags changed the way we talk about social issues, *Washington Post*, 21 March 2016

[10] History of the hashtag #BlackLivesMatter: Social activism on Twitter, Pew Research Center, 15 August 2016

[11] Police killed over 1,000 American civilians in 2019, *Forbes*, 1 July 2020

[12] Fatal police shootings of unarmed Black people in US more than 3 times as high as in Whites, *BMJ*, 27 October 2020

[13] FBI Releases 2019 Statistics on Law Enforcement Officers Killed in the Line of Duty, FBI, 4 May 2020

[14] What the data say about police brutality and racial bias – and which reforms might work, Lynne Peeples, *Nature*, 19 June 2020

[15] The statistical paradox of police killings, Aubrey Clayton, *Boston Globe*, 11 June 2020

[16] *An Empirical Analysis of Racial Differences in Police Use of Force*, Roland G Fryer Jr, National Bureau of Economic Research, July 2016

[17] Michael Brown: the founding myth of Black Lives Matter, Wilfred Reilly, *spiked*, 6 November 2020

[18] There is no epidemic of fatal police shootings against unarmed Black Americans, Heather Mac Donald, *USA Today*, 3 July 2020

[19] Stop pretending the BLM protests were peaceful, Michael Tracey, *UnHerd*, 16 July 2020

[20] About, Black Lives Matter, 2020

[21] Herstory, Black Lives Matter, accessed March 2021

[22] UKBLM Fund, GoFundMe

[23] Strivings of the Negro People, WE Burghardt Du Bois, *Atlantic*, August 1897

[24] Read Martin Luther King Jr's 'I Have a Dream' speech in its entirety, NPR, 14 January 2022

[25] *Words That Wound: Critical Race Theory, Assaultive Speech, and the First Amendment*, Mari J Matsuda et al, Routledge (1993)

[26] *Race Experts: How Racial Etiquette, Sensitivity Training, and New Age Therapy Hijacked the Civil-Rights Revolution*, Elisabeth Lasch-Quinn, Rowman and Littlefield (2001)

[27] *Words That Wound: Critical Race Theory, Assaultive Speech, and the First Amendment*, Mari J Matsuda et al, Routledge (1993)

[28] *Critical Race Theory: An Introduction*, Richard Delgado and Jean Stefancic, NYU Press (3rd edition, 2017)

[29] *Words That Wound: Critical Race Theory, Assaultive Speech, and the First Amendment*, Mari J Matsuda et al, Routledge (1993)

[30] *Critical Race Theory: An Introduction*, Richard Delgado and Jean Stefancic, NYU Press (3rd edition, 2017)

[31] *Words That Wound: Critical Race Theory, Assaultive Speech, and the First Amendment*, Mari J Matsuda et al, Routledge (1993)

[32] *Words That Wound: Critical Race Theory, Assaultive Speech, and the First Amendment*, Mari J Matsuda et al, Routledge (1993)

[33] *Words That Wound: Critical Race Theory, Assaultive Speech, and the First Amendment*, Mari J Matsuda et al, Routledge (1993)

[34] Mapping the Margins: Intersectionality, Identity Politics and Violence Against Women of Colour, Kimberlé Crenshaw, *Stanford Law Review*, July 1991

[35] *White Fragility: Why It's So Hard for White People to Talk About Racism*, Robin DiAngelo, Penguin Random House (2018)

[36] *How to Be an Antiracist*, Ibram X Kendi, Bodley Head (2019)

[37] *Words That Wound: Critical Race Theory, Assaultive Speech, and the First Amendment*, Mari J Matsuda et al, Routledge (1993)

[38] Is the anti-racism training industry just peddling white supremacy?, Jonathan Chait, *New York*, 16 July 2020

[39] Why are politicians suddenly talking about their 'lived experience'?, Kwame Anthony Appiah, *Guardian*, 14 November 2020

[40] The Left's obsession with subjectivity, David Goodhart, *UnHerd*, 23 November 2020

[41] *How to Be an Antiracist*, Ibram X Kendi, Bodley Head (2019)

[42] Ladies, your $5,000 'racism supper' is ready – don't choke on the guilt, *The Times* (London), 5 June 2021

[43] *Why I'm No Longer Talking to White People About Race*, Reni Eddo-Lodge, Bloomsbury (2017)

[44] *White Fragility: Why It's So Hard for White People to Talk About Racism*, Robin DiAngelo, Beacon Press (2018)

[45] How critical race theory turned the Virginia governor fight on its head, *Telegraph*, 3 November 2021

9 Choosing Gender

An obsession with gender is central to woke thinking. The idea that people have an innate sense of gender identity that is 'truer' than the arbitrary sex characteristics of their body has been taken up by activists, promoted within schools, and used as an organising principle for public institutions. This belief has serious consequences for how we socialise children and organise society; it calls into question sex-protected rights and freedom of association. Yet far from showing concern for women, or engaging in a free and open discussion about competing rights, transgender activists shut down debate and engage in acts of extreme intolerance towards those, such as author JK Rowling, who dare to challenge the mantra that 'transwomen are women'.

Gender ideology has become central to woke culture because it gets to the heart of who we are as people, what it means to live together in families and in society, and how we relate to the next generation. For those wishing to bring about social change, gender is a good place to start. In this chapter, we will focus on where the current thinking on gender came from, and why it has gripped society so intensely.

This chapter is concerned with transgenderism: a theory about individual identity that has broader social consequences. It is concerned with transgender activists: the people who promote transgenderism and campaign for changes to services and institutions based on their beliefs. Not all who advocate on behalf of the transgender community are transgender themselves and, by the same token, many transgender people simply want to lead a quiet life and do not seek to turn their identity into a political cause. This chapter is not, therefore, about individual transgender people. Instead, it focuses on the consequences of the relatively recent idea that gender identity should supersede biology as a primary means of organising society, and it asks why this cause has been taken on board with such alacrity by woke activists.[1]

The question 'What is your sex?' has appeared on every national census carried out in the UK since 1801. Before 2021 it had never been considered controversial or difficult for people to answer. The census of 2021 was the first time respondents were assumed to need guidance with this question. The Office for National Statistics (ONS) advised that those struggling to select their sex should use the sex recorded on an official document like a birth certificate or passport – even though passports are not a legal record of a person's sex at all, because gender on a passport can be changed with just a doctor's note.[2]

Following a legal challenge, brought by the group Fair Play for Women, the ONS was forced to return to a purely legal definition of sex.[3] But we need to ask why it ever even occurred to the census question compilers to alter the meaning of sex, a category that had previously been taken for granted. A clue appeared further into the census form, where there were new voluntary questions on sexual orientation and gender identity. In 2021, for the first time, respondents were asked: 'Is the gender you identify with the same as your sex registered at birth?' There followed a choice of two answers, yes or no. For those who answered no, there was a further instruction: 'Enter gender identity.' Unlike the binary choice presented in the answer to the question on sex, people whose gender identity differed from their birth sex were free to pick any label they preferred.

Transgender activists welcomed the inclusion of questions on gender identity as a 'good first step' – presumably a first step towards normalising the notion that everyone has a gender identity. Owen Hurcum, then mayor-elect of Bangor in Wales, told the BBC: 'I think it is great that we can finally put our real genders on the census.' Hurcum self-identifies as 'non-binary agender' and uses they / them pronouns. However, Hurcum added: 'As nice and as validating as that will feel for us to do, it really is only the tip of the iceberg for what the government can do.'[4] Such statements are revealing. Identifying as 'non-binary agender' – not being exclusively a man or a woman, having no particular gender – is a made-up concept. And the use of plural pronouns to refer to one person twists our collective language use.

Despite having created an identity that rejects both scientific fact and social convention, Hurcum wants validation from the census. Being unique, it seems, must now come with government approval and administrative validation. The purpose of the census has moved from being a straightforward population count to an instrument designed to affirm individuals' identities, while simultaneously producing statistics that will increase the visibility of certain groups. This shift has been hastened by the ONS involving charities and campaigning organisations like Stonewall in the design of the census.

From sex to gender

Throughout most of human history it was assumed that sex determined everything about a person. From the late 18th century onwards, thinkers such as Mary Wollstonecraft began to challenge the notion that women were naturally inferior to men. Wollstonecraft argued that it was society, most notably through differences in upbringing and education, that made males and females so different from one another.[5] A century and a half later, this view was developed by French philosopher Simone de Beauvoir, who wrote: 'One is not born, but rather becomes, a woman.'[6] Beauvoir's argument was not that people were born sex-less, but that the meaning given to sex, in particular to being female, is created within a particular context. People are born male or female, but the values and qualities attached to being a man or a woman are determined by the dominant culture.

The idea of being transgender arose through the confluence of two distinct schools of thought: academic and medical. At the time Beauvoir was writing, 'gender' was not used as a synonym for sex. The psychologist John Money was, in 1955, the first to use gender to draw a distinction between sex, or the physical and biological attributes that distinguish males and females, and the behaviour and attitudes people demonstrate. Money posited that sex bears little relationship to gender. He took particular interest in children born intersex – that is, with inde-terminate genitalia – and argued that it was children's socialisation that determined whether they grew up as a man or a woman, not whether they were born male or female. Taking this position to its logical con-clusion, Money suggested that a baby born with male genitalia who un-derwent surgery to alter these sex characteristics and was subsequently raised as a girl could go on to live successfully as a woman.

Indeed, Money not only proposed this as a theory, but also put it to the test with a baby boy, David Reimer, who had suffered surgical trauma to his penis.[7] His parents were instructed to go away and raise a girl: their son, David, became their daughter, Brenda. The results of this experiment were initially recorded as successful. However, many years later, as an adult, David de-transitioned and spoke out about the dis-tress the experiment had caused him. Tragically, he committed suicide aged just 38. Money's experiments reflect the emergence of transgender ideology within the medical profession. Surgery created the solution to a problem that barely existed. For the first time, it became possible to conceptualise 'gender identity' as dislocated from biological sex.

It was not until the 1970s that the word 'gender' began to enter mainstream vocabulary. It took off as the growing popularity of feminism prompted debate about the rigid and sharply distinct social expectations placed on men and women. Gender became a useful way to distinguish between the fact of being female and the performance of womanhood shaped by social stereotypes. As with Beauvoir before them, the feminists of the 1970s did not deny the existence of sex, that individuals born female become women while those born male become men. Rather, feminists like Germaine Greer sought to challenge the assumption that being female meant conforming to an invented and socially imposed set of gendered expectations.[8] The notion of gender allowed for a critique of masculine and feminine stereotypes; it did not lead automatically to the conclusion that some people were transgender.

Gender as performance

In the 1980s, feminism began to be shaped by ideas that emerged from inside universities as much as from broader political struggles. The influence of critical theory made it possible for a new generation of academic activists to convince themselves that changing language and images would have as profound an impact on society as, for example, campaigning for access to abortion services. These new ideas were applied to thinking about sex.

One assumption that soon emerged was that gender is a performance – that people 'act' in ways that are then perceived, by others, as masculine or feminine. What's more, these new theorists began to argue that if the connection between sex and gender is arbitrary, then sex is no more 'true' or 'real' than the performance of gender – that both are socially constructed. Judith Butler, author of the landmark *Gender Trouble*, argued not only that 'gender is performative', but also that there is no biological reality, no greater truth, underpinning the performance – that '"being" a sex or a gender is fundamentally impossible'. This means that rather than sex determining (or even just shaping) the nature of the performance, the performance itself comes to signify a person's sex. This belief leads activists to read history backwards and claim that women of a previous era who presented as men in order to join professions barred to women, or because they were lesbians, were actually transgender.

Butler – who is famed for her tangled academic phraseology – argues that it is our cultural and social views on gender that determine sex. 'What we take to be an internal essence [that we are male or female]', she writes, 'is actually manufactured through a sustained set of acts [that society dictates]'. She claims that 'gender is always a doing [an act], though not a doing by a subject [person] who might be said to pre-exist the deed'. Gender thus becomes a 'relational term' forged through interaction with others, and sex becomes a random label doled out by midwives or doctors at the moment of birth.[9]

Today, following on from Butler, sex has been rejected by many radical thinkers as an outdated concept that has no more basis in material reality than gender. The performance of gender is thought to float freely from biology: both are considered equally arbitrary. Gender can now be conceived as fluid and multiple. This is an attractive idea to the postmodern academic activists who are particularly keen to challenge and 'deconstruct' rigid binaries wherever they appear. Simone de Beauvoir established that patriarchy centres man and defines woman as 'the second sex'. Exploding the idea of there being only two sexes, argue academic activists, will therefore free members of the subordinate class from subjugation: without a male / female binary, there could be no subordinate woman. However, this 'freedom' comes at a high price: it involves denying that the subordinate class even exists in any clearly defined way. The logical consequences of this approach can be seen in the struggle many providers of services to women now have in using the word 'woman'. And while the notion of moving beyond binaries may sound liberating, its proponents often resort to crude gender stereotypes when it comes to explaining what it means to have a particular identity.

In the eyes of transgender activists, some people are socialised into accepting the arbitrary sex they are assigned at birth and dutifully perform the appropriate gender. For others, the conflict between this assignment and their interior sense of identity proves too much and they are unable to comply. These people are transgender, gender queer or genderfluid.

The importance of language

When the relationship between sex and gender is considered arbitrary, then it is the *perception* that someone is male or female that determines the gender that is then conferred upon them, rather than them actually *being* male or female. Primary and secondary sex characteristics are considered significant only in the sense that their presence (or absence) creates a perception that others respond to. And so gender becomes freed from biology only to be tied to public perception. When there is no biology underpinning gender, and there is no agent determining the performance, then the performance itself, and the interaction it compels, is all. This emphasis on perception goes some way towards explaining why leading figures in the transgender movement are so keen to compel people to use particular language and enshrine in law the rights of transgender women to access spaces and opportunities reserved exclusively for females.

In common with the new anti-racists, transgender activists share a particular concern with language. The practice of declaring your pronouns – perhaps in an email signature, a social-media biography or at the start of a speech – has rapidly taken off, even though it would have seemed utterly bizarre only a decade ago. Some embrace pronoun sharing enthusiastically, others are corralled into it in the workplace and do not want to stand out by dissenting. On top of this, activists have introduced new words into our vocabulary, such as 'cisgender', to indicate someone who identifies with their natal sex. The word 'cis' is useful to activists because – just like declaring pronouns – it implies that being female and therefore a woman is no more 'natural' or 'normal' than being female and identifying as a man. Both are equally arbitrary. At the same time, they campaign to have the word 'woman' replaced with cumbersome formulations such as 'cervix-haver', 'menstruator' or 'pregnant person'. Gender-critical campaigners have even sparked police investigations for distributing stickers bearing the dictionary definition of 'woman' – 'adult human female'.[10] The mantra 'transwomen are women' can make it seem as if the only people allowed to refer to themselves with the word woman nowadays are male.

Judith Butler argues that the language we use to describe people assigns them social roles to play. In other words, it is only the act of being called a woman or being referred to using feminine pronouns that makes someone a woman in the eyes of society. Using the wrong words – in particular, using the wrong pronouns or 'misgendering' someone – supposedly inflicts psychic harm upon individuals and, at the same time, invalidates the identity of an entire section of the population, even if that was never the speaker's intention. Clearly, this same logic does not also apply to women, who can be linguistically erased with impunity.

Transgender activists see words as a conduit of distress. In the 1990s, the definition of violence expanded – and the corresponding group of victims increased – with the idea that language can inflict not just psychic harm on people, but physical harm, too. The opening lines of *Words That Wound* explore the impact of what its authors describe as 'assaultive speech'. They describe how words are used 'as weapons to ambush, terrorise, wound, humiliate and degrade'. This 'assaultive speech' is supposedly not just psychologically damaging but also physically harmful. The authors argue that 'victims of vicious hate propaganda experience physiological symptoms and emotional distress ranging from fear in the gut to rapid pulse rate and difficulty in breathing, nightmares, post-traumatic stress disorder, hypertension, psychosis and suicide'.[11] Such alarmism trivialises real acts of physical violence. Arguably, it also creates the conditions for more violence. As we see with the abuse routinely dished out to feminists like Kathleen Stock or JK Rowling, transgender activists often issue death threats and sometimes use actual physical violence in an attempt to silence views they deem 'harmful'. Just as CRT rehabilitates racial thinking, so gender ideology allows for the rehabilitation of misogyny.

The rise of critical theory provides an explanation as to how we have arrived at this point, but it does not explain why transgender ideology has become so politically influential. In fact, out of all the woke issues the cultural elite is concerned about, gender identity and supporting transgender people seems to be No1. We cannot lay this at Judith Butler's feet. Looking for explanations solely in critical theory or in medicine does not help us answer the question of why this is happening. Academic theories can help us to understand where today's dominant ideas come from, but to understand why they have gained such traction we need to look beyond academia and at the broader political and cultural climate.

The core demand from transgender activists is twofold. First, they demand the freedom to name themselves and the world as they see fit, even if it means overriding social and linguistic conventions. Second, they insist that other people obey these decrees and use the language that they prescribe. By policing language, a relatively small group of activists is able to shape, to a considerable extent, what can be said, written and even, ultimately, thought about gender. To police language is to get to the very heart of spontaneous social interaction between people, and to begin to shape our perceptions and understandings of the world.

Adopting and enforcing a vocabulary sanctioned by the transgender movement serves a useful purpose in cohering group identity and asserting membership (or 'allyship') of that community. What's more, just as with the new anti-racism, this is an ever-changing language. It is hard to keep up. Words that were once politically correct, such as 'transsexual', are now considered outdated or even offensive. In this way, language is used to demarcate an in-group of acceptable people and an out-group considered to have transgressed the norms set out by activists. The insult TERF (trans-exclusionary radical feminist) is used to define the out-group: women who raise questions or challenge the impact of gender ideology upon women and children. This label legitimises abuse and even violent recriminations, just as the word 'transphobe' similarly closes down debate. Through controlling language, an elite group of influential transgender activists gets to shape our understandings of what it means to be human, curtail spontaneous interactions and readily demarcate those hostile to this project. This is a long way indeed from being tolerant of those who like to dress or act in non-stereotypical ways.

To woke activists, transgender people are the most oppressed group within capitalist society. The entire transgender experience is portrayed as being bound up in emotional, verbal and physical abuse. It is taken for granted that transgender people struggle when confronting an apparently heteronormative society divided along a rigid binary axis. If transgender women are 'successful' and 'pass' as female, then they are assumed to take on board all the oppression that feminists claim women routinely experience, in the form of misogyny, sexual harassment and the gender pay gap. If they are 'unsuccessful' in their quest, then they face the existential anguish of having their true self rejected.

Transgender-supporting charities like Stonewall and Mermaids often point to a greater incidence of suicide, self-harm and drug or alcohol misuse among trans people as evidence of the emotional and mental-health difficulties caused by daily experiences of discrimination and transphobia. Stonewall claims that 27 per cent of young transgender people and 48 per cent of trans people in Britain overall have attempted suicide. It offers this as proof that transphobia is widespread, induces trauma and leads to mental-health problems.[12] Such statistics have been challenged for drawing upon very small sample sizes of self-selecting respondents. They may also confuse cause and effect: the desire to transition may, in and of itself, suggest mental-health struggles. Suicidal thoughts may be a result of existing difficulties rather than a response to newly experienced transphobia.

Transgender author Shon Faye describes trans people as 'discriminated against, harassed and subjected to violence around the world because of deep prejudices'. Faye links this experience of abuse to economics. It is because of prejudice, discrimination and personal experiences of trauma, Faye argues, that transgender people do not compete as equals in the labour market.[13] Statistics would seem to support this point, with claims that 'half of transgender people are unemployed'. As there are difficulties in defining and counting transgender people, such surveys are hard to verify.[14] Nonetheless, claims of economic oppression and social discrimination lead activists to claim that trans politics is actually class politics.

Faye argues: 'The experience of being trans is shaped by social class. While there are middle-class trans people, the vast majority are working class – just as the vast majority of the total population is working class. Trans workers are often employed in lower-paid and more precarious jobs, with a high risk of discrimination and bullying in the workplace. As a result, trans political struggle is part of a wider class struggle.' It can seem that in their desperation to cling on to a perception of themselves as noble class warriors, today's middle-class activists will happily redefine working-class politics.

Transgender people stand out in the eyes of activists as having a unique experience of oppression. This makes them a special cadre of the working class, and fighting their cause comes to be seen as the purest and most effective form of class struggle. But this is not the only advantage gained by activists who throw themselves behind the cause of trans rights. Questioning the relationship between sex and gender throws open for debate the 'heteronormative' and 'cisgender' assumptions that activists assume underpin our attachment to family life. When we can no longer assume that girls grow up to be women and mothers, and boys to be men and fathers, then we can no longer take any of our assumptions about society for granted. When capitalism is thought to hinge upon the 'reproductive labour' of women and the heteronormative family, then challenging these positions is thought to threaten a racist, misogynistic, backward status quo. In the eyes of many transgender activists, pulling the rug out from under the relationship between sex and gender is to pull the rug out from under capitalism itself.

Bringing biology back in

More recently, there has been a shift in thinking about gender politics that heralds a renewed focus on biology. This is not a return to the idea that sex is inscribed in chromosomes, hormones and genitalia, but a shift towards understanding gender identity, an internal sense of being male or female, as being 'hardwired into the brain at birth'.[15] The problem here is that differences in the brain are, like height and weight, on a continuum rather than being marked by a clear distinction. This means that attempts to demarcate male and female brains rely upon averages. Just as some women may be taller than some men, likewise some women may have a larger-than-average amygdala and some men a larger-than-average hippocampus.

Activists are keen to prove the existence of a sexed brain so that they can show that some people are born with a biological disjuncture between brain and body. Just as an intersex person is born with mixed or indeterminate genitalia, or mixed or indeterminate chromosomes and phenotype, so it is argued a fetus may develop with a male brain and a female body or vice versa. If this happens then apparently an incongruence can exist between a person's internal sense of being male or female and their external anatomical sex characteristics. This would make transgender a special form of intersex located within the brain, rather than a sexual fetish or mental illness.

Transgender activists promote the idea that people are born with an internal sense of gender identity. They claim that transgender people have always existed and it is only now that there is greater awareness and acceptance that they can finally be their 'true selves'. The notion of the gendered brain also helps promote group identity. Biology-based groupings were once rejected by a previous generation of activists who sought to distance themselves from what they considered to be reductionist perceptions of who they were and what they could become. Once, campaigners urged people not to define others by reference to their genitalia, skin colour or group stereotypes. In contrast, as Terri Murray notes, 'today's transgender activists demand *recognition* of their allegedly innate difference, believing that membership in a biologically or essentially distinct group should entitle them to civil rights and legal recognition'.[16] For transgender activists, the concept of 'gender identity' trumps both social class as the basis of collective interests and individual self-determination.

Transgender children

Transgender children have come to be at the centre of much debate around transgender issues. To activists, they prove the claim that transgenderism is a naturally occurring and ever-present phenomenon.

The transgender child encompasses both the 'victim of nature' who was born in the wrong body, and the brave hero who will enlighten the rest of us about the true nature of transgender identity. But it is only relatively recently that the concept of the transgender child has come to be accepted outside of specialist and activist cliques.

The existence of children who experience a mismatch between their gendered essence and their anatomy has come to be taken for granted by many social workers, teachers, psychiatrists and health professionals. Current orthodoxy, promoted by advocates from the transgender community, is that the best approach to adopt towards children who identify as transgender is 'positive affirmation' – in other words, complete and uncritical acceptance that the child really is the gender he or she claims to be. It is argued that not affirming the child's new gender is psychologically damaging.

As we explored in Chapter Four, many schools go far beyond positively affirming individual transgender pupils and promote transgenderism to all their pupils. This serves to normalise the idea that brains and bodies do not always align and that gender identity is something that individuals must discover for themselves. Promoting these ideas gives schools and other public institutions that work with children a renewed moral mission. Only they have the expertise and special insight needed to deal with the victim / hero transgender child, or so these institutions come to believe.

Positive affirmation has been taken on board as the correct way to deal with transgender children by most institutions a child will encounter. But this approach is often not in keeping with the wishes of parents. Concerns and questions raised by the parents of children who identify as transgender are either overlooked or, worse, seen to run counter to the best interests of their own child. This can lead to parents being marginalised and excluded from discussions among social workers and clinicians as to the best course of intervention for their children. Promoting the expertise of a new woke professional class above the wisdom and traditional values of parents and grandparents undermines families.

It is worth reminding ourselves that parents ultimately have something to offer children that no amount of expertise can replace: love. Parents know instinctively that children and adolescents, in the process of growing up, change their mind about who they are and the type of adult they want, one day, to become. It may be the case that some children who come to see themselves as transgender are simply experimenting or going through a phase. A danger with positive affirmation is that it risks consolidating this new identity and thereby making it more difficult for the child to change his or her mind at a later date. Furthermore, positive affirmation rejects any questioning as to what might lie behind a child's declarations in relation to his or her gender identity.

Positive affirmation is often simply the first step in a process known as 'social transition', whereby children may adopt new names and come to be referred to using the pronouns in line with their chosen gender identities. They may also wear different clothes and expect to use certain toilets and changing rooms. The further children proceed along the path of social transition, the more difficult it becomes for them to revert to living as their original sex. To do so would involve not only an acknowledgement that they have made a mistake, but also an acknowledgement that they are not deserving of the praise that may have been heaped upon them.

Social transition often leads on to medical intervention, including puberty blockers and, for older teenagers, cross-sex hormones. Such hormone therapies are presented as 'life saving' for transgender children struggling to come to terms with their developing bodies. But it is, at best, highly simplistic and, at worst, dangerous to suggest that feeling suicidal is best treated through puberty blockers rather than psychotherapy and anti-depressants. Yet puberty blockers have been presented to young people as a straightforward solution to the apparent 'problem' of their changing body.

In 2020, a young woman named Keira Bell won a major victory in the High Court in London. As a child, Bell did not like being a girl and 'hated the idea of growing into a woman'. She thought this meant she wasn't actually female. When she sought medical advice, doctors did not sufficiently question her assumptions or her underlying feelings, but agreed that she was indeed male and set her on the path to transition. Aged just 16 and after only three appointments, Bell was prescribed puberty blockers. A year later, she was taking cross-sex hormones, and had a double mastectomy when she was 20. She says that she should have been challenged more by medical staff over her decision to transition to a male as a teenager. Bell says she was a tomboy as a child who decided to transition after being exposed to information online. As she went further down the medical route, 'one step led to another'.[17]

It was only after she had gone well down the route of medical transition that Bell began to realise her problems were not caused by her body. She took the clinic that treated her to court and three judges ruled that children under the age of 16 were 'unlikely to be able to give informed consent' to hormone 'treatments' because they were unable to 'understand and weigh the long-term risks and consequences of the administration of puberty blockers'.[18] Bell's victory was more than just a personal triumph; it provided important legal protections for vulnerable children. But, incredibly, this High Court ruling was appealed and the judgement was later overturned. The court ruled that it should be for clinicians and doctors to establish a child's competence to consent to medical interventions. It also ruled that puberty blockers are not an unlawful treatment.[19]

Unfortunately, some clinicians appear to be politically invested in the concept of the transgender child. A leading British publication, the *Journal of Medical Ethics*, published an article in 2021 by bioethicist Dr Maura Priest of Arizona State University on the topic of 'ongoing puberty suppression'.[20] Priest argues that medical practitioners should take LGBT 'testimony' seriously – concluding that this 'also means that parents should lose veto power over most transition-related paediatric care'. In other words, doctors should accept the beliefs and feelings of children who present as transgender and prescribe medication to suppress puberty, even if this goes against their parents' wishes. In this regard, we see that transgenderism has the capacity to challenge traditional family bonds.

Transgender children have become a key focus of activism because their existence appears to 'prove' that being transgender is a naturally occurring phenomenon. But woke activists know that it is also by targeting children that the ideas of the next generation can be changed. Sex-identification is a key part of socialising children. As adults, individuals may reject the expectations for their sex. But knowing that such expectations exist, knowing what they are, and knowing how you as an individual either fit into or reject them, is how communities cohere together in the present, and how they forge meaningful links with the past.

Promoting transgenderism to children is important to woke activists precisely because they are aware that notions of gender identity get to the very heart of what makes us human and what binds us into societies. Identifying with (or rejecting) the expectations for our sex provides us with templates for how to live meaningfully. Success for transgender activists means that all these certainties are taken away. We are left with a blank slate upon which they can inscribe their own ideas and shape the future of society. Gender ideology teaches children not to take anything for granted and to be wary of spontaneous interactions. Through children, transgender activists get to challenge the most basic tenets of human nature and undermine our instinctive trust in our families and communities.

Stonewall

The elite nature of transgender activism is increasingly being recognised. In the UK, gender-critical feminists question the influence on publicly funded institutions of organisations like Stonewall, a charity that campaigns for 'acceptance without exception' for lesbian, gay and transgender people, and Mermaids, a charity that supports transgender children and their families.

Stonewall was founded in 1989 by a group of lesbian and gay activists. They joined together to defend the rights of gay people at a time when they were under attack, and to challenge the continued legal inequalities facing gay people. The group took its name from the 1969 uprising that followed a police raid on the Stonewall Inn in New York City. Lesbian, gay and transgender people fought against police brutality over the course of three nights of unrest. The incident galvanised the gay-rights movement during a period when broader struggles for equality and the expansion of civil rights were taking place.

Stonewall was remarkably successful in achieving its goals and, with the legalisation of same-sex marriage in the UK in March 2014, the organisation seemed in search of a new mission. Advocating on behalf of transgender people provided a renewed sense of purpose (and source of funding). But this shift created confusions and tensions. As some Stonewall veterans have pointed out, the issues facing gay and transgender people are, in many respects, completely different. What's more, gender ideology, in effect, negates the idea of gay sexuality – for if there is no such thing as biological sex, then there is no such thing as same-sex attraction.

Following considerable efforts by gender-critical feminists and journalists to highlight the negative consequences of the charity's new direction for women, lesbians and gay people, Stonewall's influence on national institutions is currently being called into question. But the fact remains that it has been able to wield considerable influence over institutions including the police, the National Health Service, the Crown Prosecution Service and the Office for National Statistics, as well as within schools, universities, local councils and workplaces. In particular, Stonewall's Diversity Champions programme has given the charity remarkable sway over the practices and policies of companies and public-sector institutions.

Stonewall prefers to implement change from the top down, rather than having to go to the trouble of convincing ordinary people of its cause. Being open to public scrutiny risks exposing conflict between the rights of males who identify as women and the rights of females. Some feminists are rightly critical of what they see as the transgender lobby's 'hijacking' of institutions that are supposed to safeguard women's interests. Single-sex, female-only spaces such as prisons or domestic-violence refuges can no longer be said to exist if they are forced to accommodate biological males. But directives ordering exactly this to happen can easily be introduced, almost without much thought, when debate is bypassed.

Groups such as Stonewall and Mermaids have certainly taken advantage of opportunities to shape public policy and institutions, but we need to ask why these opportunities were made available to them in the first place. Why have so many organisations been ready and willing to give Stonewall representatives a seat at the boardroom table and allow them such influence? Stonewall clearly has an abundant supply of legal advisers and experienced lobbyists. But when it comes to shaping public policy, time and again Stonewall found itself pushing at an open door. From universities to the police, all manner of organisations sought out Stonewall, invited its representatives in, and voluntarily jumped through the hoops necessary to receive the Stonewall Diversity

Champions accreditation – a measure of compliance with Stonewall's suggestions that, for example, people declare their pronouns or toilets be made gender-neutral in workplaces.

It is the most elite institutions, the most exclusive schools and the highest-ranking universities that have taken gender ideology on board most enthusiastically. This tells us far more about a moral crisis within our institutions than it does about the alleged strategic brilliance of Stonewall's directors. Institutions that have lost faith in their core purpose are searching for a new mission. Our elite educational institutions are embarrassed about their exclusivity and their role in reinforcing social-class inequalities. Advocating for transgenderism provides them with an opportunity for moral rehabilitation.

Stonewall's success has been to capitalise on the end of class politics and to tap into identity politics, particularly notions of intersectionality, to promote the idea that transgender people are among the most victimised in society. Today, being a victim or acting on behalf of victims can justify almost any action. Victimhood is also an effective way to silence critics. Stonewall's influence stems, in part, from this new moral hierarchy, but it also stems from the cowardice of bystanders. The fear of being labelled transphobic or bigoted, or being seen to be on the wrong side of history, convinces many people who should know better to remain silent.

The expansion of transgender rights has gone hand in hand with an expansion of state and corporate regulation of speech and behaviour. This highlights a significant difference between today's transgender activists and the gay-rights movement of a previous era. Whereas the gay-rights movement demanded more freedom from the state, and for gay people to be free to go about their sex lives unconstrained by the law, the transgender movement demands the state's recognition and protection, often in the form of intervention to regulate the behaviour of the public.

Stonewall has been particularly keen to avoid debate about transgender issues. Simon Fanshawe, one of the co-founders of Stonewall, says some activists now prefer to smear their opponents rather than engage in debate. He has highlighted an instance in which Stonewall's current CEO, Nancy Kelley, used a BBC interview to attempt to shut down opposition by likening 'the view that people cannot change biological sex... to anti-Semitism'.[21] This reluctance to engage in debate is reflected in higher education, where gender-critical feminists are now most likely to fall foul of No Platforming campaigns led by censorious academics and students. Some activists say that to dissent from gender ideology is to 'erase' trans people. But no one disputes the fact that transgender people exist or, at the very least, that there are people who consider themselves to be transgender. Furthermore, no one other than transgender activists thinks that transgender people can simply be talked out of existence.

Preventing debate about the impact of gender self-identification has particularly angered campaigners for women's rights, and those seeking to protect children from being encouraged to transition before they are emotionally mature enough to understand the consequences of their decisions. It is precisely because so much is at stake that transgender activists seek to push through their woke agenda without scrutiny.

Sex is one of the most fundamental features of who we are. It is inscribed within our biological make-up at the moment of conception. Sex is also binary; with the exception of a minuscule number of intersex people, we are all either male or female. One simply cannot transition from one sex to the other, no matter how sophisticated the medical interventions. The fact that sex is so intrinsic to our sense of self and the structure of society means that getting people to question and reject sex brings advantages to the cultural elite far in excess of promoting other woke values.

Sex is biological, but how we perform gender is a product of the society we live in. This is not, of course, to say that the connection between the two is arbitrary. Female babies grow up to become adult women; male babies become men. But the belief that this relationship is arbitrary allows woke thinking to penetrate the most fundamental aspects of our lives. It requires us to challenge the very first certainties we come to learn about ourselves, our place in the world, our family and role models. It paves the way for the cultural elite to intervene in our most intimate thoughts and feelings. What's more, gender ideology requires such complete acquiescence to the cause that it demands we deny the reality we see before our eyes. 'Transwomen are women', we are expected to intone without question. We must all pretend that the emperor is not naked and does indeed have new clothes. In the fevered worldview of transgender activists, the concept of sex has come to be firmly associated with a heteronormative, racist, ableist Western world-view. They see pulling the rug out from under sex as crucial to bringing down the last vestiges of traditional values and an older social order.

Endnotes

[1] This chapter draws extensively on work in *The Corrosive Impact of Transgender Ideology*, originally published by Civitas in June 2020. It is reprinted here with permission

[2] Census 2021: Final guidance for the question 'What is your sex?', Office for National Statistics, 2021

[3] Fair Play for Women wins High Court challenge and judge orders sex must not be self-identified in the census, Fair Play for Women, 17 March 2021

[4] Census 2021: England and Wales gender question 'a good first step', BBC News, 14 February 2021

[5] *A Vindication of the Rights of Woman: With Strictures on Political and Moral Subjects*, Mary Wollstonecraft (1792)

[6] *The Second Sex*, Simone de Beauvoir (1949)

[7] David Reimer and John Money Gender Reassignment Controversy: The John / Joan Case, Phil Gaetano, Embryo Project Encyclopedia, 15 November 2017

[8] *The Female Eunuch*, Germaine Greer, MacGibbon & Kee (1970)

[9] *Gender Trouble: Feminism and the Subversion of Identity*, Judith Butler, Routledge Classics (2006)

[10] Police response to 'transphobic' stickers branded 'extraordinary', *Telegraph*, 14 October 2019

[11] *Words That Wound: Critical Race Theory, Assaultive Speech, and the First Amendment*, Mari J Matsuda et al, Routledge (1993)

[12] Trans key stats, Stonewall, accessed 15 October 2021

[13] *The Transgender Issue: An Argument for Justice*, Shon Faye, Penguin (2021)

[14] Half of transgender people are unemployed, *The Times* (London), 21 July 2016

[15] *The Remarkable Rise of Transgender Rights*, Donald P Haider-Markel, Daniel Clay Lewis and Jami Kathleen Taylor, University of Michigan Press (2018)

[16] *Identity, Islam and the Twilight of Liberal Values*, Terri Murray, Cambridge Scholars Publishing (2018)

[17] NHS gender clinic 'should have challenged me more' over transition, BBC News, 1 March 2020

[18] Puberty blockers: Under-16s 'unlikely to be able to give informed consent', BBC News, 1 December 2020

[19] Appeal court overturns UK puberty blockers ruling for under-16s, *Guardian*, 17 September 2021

[20] LGBT testimony and the limits of trust, Maura Priest, *Journal of Medical Ethics*, 8 June 2021

[21] Stonewall in Crisis: 'Why can't we have civil debates anymore?', Simon Fanshawe, *Telegraph*, 12 June 2021

10 From Class to Identity

To the woke, people are never simply individuals, each with our own life story, every one of us existing within a unique set of circumstances shaped by family, neighbourhood and work. But nor do they acknowledge common experiences of humanity, the challenges and emotions that make us part of the human race. Still less do the woke fully account for the role of social class, and the way that access to money and resources shapes people's lives and provides entire sections of the population with interests in common. The woke are primarily obsessed with just two characteristics: race and gender. Rather than seeing individuals or classes, they see identity groups that they label 'black', 'white', 'man', 'woman', 'cis' or 'trans'. They assume that everything that is worth knowing about a person can be determined from these labels.

The slightly more sophisticated among the woke allow for overlaps or 'intersections' between the identity groups, differentiating between 'black cisgender men' and 'white transwomen'. People are still put in boxes, but the boxes are just made smaller. As we explore in this chapter, arranging these smaller boxes into hierarchies of privilege and oppression provides the rationale behind woke thinking. It explains the shift in left-wing thinking away from a focus on social class and economic inequalities and towards identity politics – best understood as the employment of identity categories as the primary tool for understanding society and formulating political claims. In this chapter, we explore how the cultural elite's adoption of an identitarian outlook gave birth to the woke worldview.

Representation

It is not just young political campaigners who obsess over race and gender. Identitarianism reaches into the very heart of the political establishment. When President Biden addressed the nation on International Women's Day in 2021, he sought to celebrate key figures in his administration and in the military. We 'need to see and to recognise the barrier-breaking accomplishments of these women', he told the assembled press corps. 'We need little girls and boys both, who have grown up dreaming of serving for their country, to know this is what generals in the United States armed forces look like. This is what vice-presidents of the United States look like.'[1] The fact that International Women's Day is still marked at all is worth noting. Its existence is, in and of itself, a sign that identity politics is now the mainstream, establishment outlook. But Biden's particular words are revealing.

Biden asks us to recognise the accomplishments of women, but his explanation as to why these women should be applauded takes us away from anything they have *done* and focuses instead on what they *are*. What is important to Biden is what these women 'look like'. Rather than celebrating their achievements, we applaud their identity. Biden asks us to pay homage to characteristics people have little control over – sex and race – rather than the ways in which individuals have shaped the course of their own lives, or the ways in which groups of people have struggled in a collective endeavour to improve the lives of others.

Appearance matters to the woke. We saw this when the National Trust asked its guides to wear rainbow-coloured clothes, make-up, body paint or glitter in honour of Pride Month.[2] It was not enough for the organisation's mainly elderly volunteers to treat all visitors the same, irrespective of their sexuality. Nor was it enough for them to be tolerant of difference or support gay rights. Instead, they were expected to turn themselves into walking rainbow flags, parading woke values for all to see. The performance, and the act of submission to woke ideas it represents, is at least as important as beliefs to the identitarians.

This focus on appearance leads critics to argue that woke's proponents are far more concerned with 'virtue-signalling' or 'gesture politics' than they are with bringing about real social change. As we discussed in Chapter Seven, companies that display all the correct woke symbols, but still exploit their workers, damage the environment or have a gender pay gap, stand accused of hypocrisy or 'woke-washing'. But this line of criticism often misses the point. To the woke, performance and principle are often one and the same. Equality is no longer about anything as old-fashioned as disparities in income or access to resources. Instead, it has come to be much more concerned with diverse representation.

Arguing for greater – or more positive – visual representation for particular groups has a long history. The inVISIBLEwomen website notes that as far back as 1952 a correspondent wrote to *The Times* about the lack of women represented through statues.[3] In *The Feminine Mystique*, first published in 1963, Betty Friedan argued that the images of women in magazines and advertisements limited female ambition and presented 'young beauty', 'housewife' or 'mother' as the only socially acceptable female roles.[4] This issue was picked up by the women's liberation movement in the late 1960s. Second-wave feminists were concerned with bringing about practical changes in women's lives in areas such as employment, pay and reproductive rights. But they were also concerned with how women were portrayed. The 1970 protests at the Miss World beauty pageant in London and a focus on the representation of women in books, films, adverts and magazines morphed into a more coherent campaign against pornography in the latter half of the 1970s and into the 1980s.

In the 1980s, there was much discussion about the need for positive representation in children's literature. More books began to feature strong female characters as well as people of colour. Joan Drescher's *Your Family, My Family*, published in the US in 1980, was one of the first picture books to show a same-sex family.[5] More recently, we have grown used to calls for more diverse groups of people to be portrayed on statues, banknotes and in the pages of passports. Advertisers, publishers and film and television producers strive to show positive representations of women, black and LGBTQ people. Indeed, the UK's Advertising Standards Authority has banned 'harmful' gender stereotyping in adverts.[6]

The assumption underpinning many campaigns that focus on securing increased representation, made explicit in the popular 'you have to see it to be it' meme, is that unless we actually see diverse groups of people occupying certain roles, then only white men will ever take up those roles. It is only when women are seen to be playing sports, or black people are seen to be in leading roles in the military, that others come to believe that they can do these things, too. But this turns reality on its head. The fact is that someone always has to be first. If you really have to see it to be it, we would never have had female pilots, surgeons and prime ministers. On top of this, there are positions that no one has ever held before: if you have to see it to be it, we would never have had astronauts, nuclear physicists or computer programmers. And why should it be assumed that sex or race are the characteristics people most identify with? Seeing someone succeed from your hometown, or school, or with the same accent as you, may be more important in determining your aspirations.

The focus on representation also assumes that lack of vision or aspiration is the only thing holding people back from achieving their goals – not family income, levels of education or social class. Fixing representation is clearly easier than improving the education system or making the national economy more productive. Time and again, the importance of representation is returned to in discussions about equality. It is taken for granted that the images we see daily help construct – rather than simply reflect – our reality.

Identity politics

Critical theorists, initially associated with the Frankfurt School in the early decades of the 20th century, focused their attention on the role of culture in shaping the consciousness of the working class. Thinkers like Theodor Adorno, Herbert Marcuse and Walter Benjamin developed Antonio Gramsci's interpretation of Marxism. They were particularly interested in hegemony – or how a ruling elite makes ideas that appear to confirm their position as the dominant, commonsense view. After being closed down by the Nazis in 1933, the Frankfurt School's key members relocated to New York, where Max Horkheimer and Theodor Adorno wrote *Dialectic of Enlightenment*, one of the core texts of critical theory. They argued that culture plays a key role in legitimising existing social relations and that mass culture, in particular, had transformed the working class into willing accomplices in their own exploitation.

Increasingly disturbed by both Stalinism in Russia and the turn to fascism in Germany, Horkheimer and Adorno saw ideology as the primary determinant of social relations. They shifted their attention towards analysing the role that popular culture, in the form of advertising, music and the media, played in popularising ruling-class ideology. This new focus led them to see the working class as misguided and manipulated, less as positive agents of change and more as easily duped. As we will explore more below, it is this understanding of the working class – as easily swayed by mass culture and in need of re-education by an intellectual elite – that has influenced woke ideas. As such, woke represents a rejection of Marxism, rather than an extension or refashioning of it.

In the mid-20th century, a new generation of poststructuralist philosophers – people such as Jacques Derrida, Jean Baudrillard, Gilles Deleuze and Michel Foucault – gained influence both within the academy and as public intellectuals. They built on the work of an older generation of critical theorists associated with the Frankfurt School and, although their specific areas of research varied, they shared a common interest in exploring ideas about language, power, truth and knowledge. They began with the Swiss linguist Ferdinand de Saussure's insight that the relationship between words (signifiers) and reality (what is signified) was arbitrary. This led them to conclude that language had been created by people, over time, but with the most powerful people having most influence over the words we use. As such, our vocabulary comes with prejudices and assumptions built in – it reflects the dominant attitudes of people who have gone before us. What's more, they concluded, words do not simply reflect but actually shape the way we perceive reality. In this way, they argued, our knowledge of the world comes filtered through a lens that has already been fixed in place by the most powerful sections of society.

This new generation of poststructuralists argued that bringing about social change required a fundamental interrogation of discourse, the words and images we use, as it is through discourse that power is exercised. Because language appears natural and spontaneous, discourse also masks the power it contains. These assumptions about language and power called into question existing notions of truth. Truth was no longer understood as existing objectively, waiting to be discovered, but as dependent on context and determined by the situation and the status of the speaker. Individual poststructuralist philosophers, such as the frequently demonised Foucault, cannot be held personally responsible for woke thinking. Indeed, much of Foucault's writing actually challenges the contemporary logic of cancel culture and censorship. However, ideas that emerged from poststructuralism and critical theory more broadly have seeped into popular consciousness. The notion that language shapes our understanding of the world and that truth is not simply a measure of objective reality are important insights. But when transformed into a left-wing political project that is entirely separated from the real interests of working-class people, the result is a set of ideas that bears little relationship to the material circumstances and everyday concerns of most people's lives.

Helen Pluckrose and James Lindsay, writing in *Cynical Theories*, explore how critical theory came to dominate university humanities and social-science faculties across the Western world, and how this shifted postmodernism from a minority academic pursuit to an all-encompassing political framework. They identify two core principles of postmodernism: the 'knowledge principle' (the belief that there is no objective knowledge or truth about the world) and the 'political principle' (the belief that 'society is formed of systems of power and hierarchies'). These principles provide the foundation for four themes that run through every postmodern analysis, irrespective of the specific topic: the blurring of boundaries and the rejection of binaries, such as in relation to gender; the power of language to construct perceptions of reality, such as in advertising campaigns; a cultural relativism that forbids judgement; and the loss of the individual and the universal, replaced by the allotting of everyone into identity groups.

Pluckrose and Lindsay explain how what began as a reaction against grand narratives and totalising theories, which aimed to reduce everything to discourse before deconstructing and relativising it to the point of meaninglessness, began to be applied to real-world problems. It migrated off campus and emerged into the world as identity politics. They argue that in the process of being applied to real-world problems, the postmodern worldview actually comes to oppose some of the central tenets of the original proponents of poststructuralism. For instance, this process creates new and indisputable 'facts' about race, gender and identity.

This is perhaps most clearly illustrated in changing ideas about race. Pluckrose and Lindsay show that when power is separated from politics and the workings of institutions, and is relocated in language and knowledge itself, then racism can be identified everywhere: it supposedly exists within our unconscious mind and becomes real with our every utterance. The only solution is for people to submit to the superior insights of activist scholars who are apparently uniquely capable of revealing white privilege. In this way, a movement founded upon relativism and the idea that there is no truth comes to the conclusion that there is 'The Truth According to Social Justice' and that this is a truth that cannot, under any circumstances, be questioned. As Pluckrose and Lindsay explain: 'In the guise of Social Justice scholarship, postmodernism has become a grand, sweeping explanation for society – a metanarrative – of its own.'[7]

The notion that our perceptions of the world are constructed through our collective knowledge and beliefs is a valuable insight into the nature of human understanding. But when this is taken to an extreme position – that there is no objective reality – language and images become the focus for social change. The material conditions of people's lives become sidelined. From the 1960s onwards, a focus on culture was taken up by the New Left in the UK and across Europe. The left's political failure to convince the masses of its cause, and bring about fundamental social change, came to be reinterpreted as the fault of a working class all too happy to buy into consumer culture. For many around the New Left, this was an explanation that provided its own solution: popular culture must be interrogated and altered. For some, deconstructing the words and images used in advertising, children's books, pop music, films and television programmes was a more attractive proposition than standing on picket lines or canvassing for elections. It became an end in itself.

Cultural deconstruction became a key part of political agitation. The new social movements that emerged from the 1960s and 1970s onwards – for example, the women's and gay liberation movements – moved away from more traditional left-wing concerns with pay and working conditions because they focused on the identity of their members as much as, if not more than, their relationship to capital.

The successive political defeats experienced by the working class in the 1980s – as well as the collapse of what was seen as the only alternative to capitalism, the Soviet Union – hastened a move towards seeing the working class less as innocent victims of a dominant ruling class ideology and more as a barrier to progressive social change. To a new cohort of identitarian activists, the working class was seen as a problem for harbouring racist, sexist and homophobic attitudes. They spied a potential new constituency in a coalition of identity groups.

Stuart Hall, co-founder of the influential *New Left Review*, joined the Centre for Contemporary Cultural Studies at the University of Birmingham in 1964, before taking over as the centre's director in 1972. In a 1997 primer he co-edited, *Representation*, Hall argued that representation is 'one of the central practices that produces culture' (my emphasis).[8] Representation through language, he argued, is central to the way that meaning is produced. In turn, cultural meanings 'organise and regulate social practices, influence our conduct and consequently have real, practical effects'. Hall argued that the 'cultural turn' within the social sciences called into question traditional understandings about meaning and representation. Rather than meaning being 'found' within culture and then represented and reflected back to people as passive consumers, meaning is instead constructed through the process of representation. In this way, representation – the images, particularly of people, presented to us in advertisements, films and soap operas – took on a far greater significance. Those loosely associated with the New Left came to see representation as being as important to the process of shaping people and events as an economic or material 'base'.

This academic insight was taken on board by activists in what first came to be characterised as 'political correctness'. PC's obsession with children's books and television programmes, and with language use in schools and universities, spoke to a desire to change the way young people were taught to make sense of the world. Activists recognised that the language we are permitted to use can shape and limit the nature of our thoughts. At this same point in the mid-1990s, immigration had made society more diverse and women were entering the workplace in ever-greater numbers. These social changes meant that some of the casual sexism and racism that littered conversations, television sitcoms and song lyrics began to be questioned and frowned upon. Old stereotypes no longer sat comfortably with communities undergoing rapid change.

But we should not confuse political correctness with the organic, positive change to language and behaviour that came about as populations and personnel became more diverse. Academics and activists had little to do with that. Rather, PC was a deliberate attempt at shaping language and behaviour in order to bring about a new reality. Much of this linguistic social engineering was easy to ridicule. Attempts, possibly apocryphal, to remove the word 'black' from the nursery rhyme 'Baa, Baa, Black Sheep' or to edit fairy tales to switch the gender of the main characters found few defenders. But at the same time, a growing sense that words mattered and people's behaviour needed policing in the name of social justice came to dominate mainstream left-wing politics. On university campuses, the students' union policy of 'No Platform for Fascists' began to be extended to other groups, such as anti-abortion activists.

This emphasis on language leads critics of woke to assume a direct line between the woke ideology that dominates our cultural institutions today and the phenomenon of political correctness that began to take off in the late 1980s. It is certainly the case that woke activists promote the idea that the images we confront each day carve out, organise and construct reality. It is not just political radicals, but also teachers, healthcare workers and human-resource managers who assume that creating alternative signs, words and images can help shift people's understanding of reality and the meanings they draw from everyday life. This cultural turn is one reason why we see the UK tabloid press blamed for election or referendum results that don't go the establishment's way. It is why toppling historical statues and arguing over what should replace them have become major preoccupations. It is why new words and phrases like 'cis' or 'chestfeeding' have been introduced into our vocabulary, while older expressions, such as 'woman' or 'mother', are apparently now offensive.

But one problem with drawing a straight line from political correctness to woke is that we miss what is distinct about the current moment. Whereas yesteryear's PC focused on language and behaviour, woke's proponents go further and seek more fundamental change in our attitudes, beliefs and the nature of knowledge itself, as the previous chapters have shown. And whereas political correctness began as a fringe movement associated with left-wing activists, woke has become the dominant view of today's establishment, the new cultural elite. Recognising this helps us understand what is distinct about today's political landscape, while at the same time acknowledging that woke ideas have been a long time in the making.

In the decades following the civil-rights movement, with the loss of faith in the working class at home and the collapse of political alternatives abroad, left-wing activists looked to a coalition of identity groups for a new and readymade constituency. Writing in *The Diversity Delusion*, Heather Mac Donald outlines the set of beliefs that now dominates higher education: 'that human beings are defined by their skin colour, sex and sexual preference; that discrimination based on those characteristics has been the driving force in Western civilisation; and that America remains a profoundly bigoted place, where heterosexual white males continue to deny opportunity to everyone else'. These ideas now extend far beyond America and, indeed, far beyond university campuses. They are the guiding principles of the woke cultural elite.[9]

The turn to identity now dominates all political parties. As sociologist Heather Brunskell-Evans explains in relation to the demands made by transgender activists, 'politics has moved away from class politics and towards identity politics. This is not a left and right issue... Transgender typifies something much bigger going on in our culture; it is an attempt to reshape the world according to a particular ethic.' She continues: 'The trans movement comes from queer theory and postmodern theory and questioning the truths of binaries. In identity politics, power is located in the binary.'[10] In this way, as we noted in Chapter Nine, the very existence of transgender people becomes a radical political statement and a challenge to a seemingly outdated, binary, heteronormative order. Rather than left vs right, we have varying degrees of enthusiasm for, or acquiescence to, a woke outlook.

Not Marxism

A focus on culture more broadly, and imagery in particular, suits today's woke activists who are more concerned with gender, race and sexuality than social class. Kenneth McLaughlin, writing in *Surviving Identity*, explains that today social justice is often defined in cultural terms, with the problem of social injustice 'seen as one of cultural domination rather than of economic exploitation'.[11] If the working class is considered at all, it is as a regressive block on change or, at best, as one more oppressed identity among many. Rather than agitating for social change centred on the material priorities and political concerns of the working class, activists instead argue for better representation of different identity groups.

This approach to politics can be seen in the issues feminist and anti-racist campaigners choose to campaign on: for example, film and music award ceremonies that are dominated by white men; or children's books by authors like Dr Seuss or Enid Blyton that are said to promote outdated racial attitudes; or fashions or hairstyles worn by white women that are said to appropriate the culture of black women. In each case, the demand is for social justice through cultural change, rather than for economic justice through redistribution or changes to the labour market. Critics who insist that woke is simply Marxism in disguise are wide of the mark.

The equation of woke with Marxism has found favour with many on the political right. They assume that the resuscitation of a Cold War-era bogeyman will be sufficient to analyse the problem with woke ideas, sound the alarm and rally opposition. But this crude comparison demonstrates a misunderstanding of both Marxism and woke. It relies on blurring Marxism with critical theory, and then overstating the influence of obscure academic schools of thought on national political debates.

As we have already noted, members of the first generation of Frankfurt School critical theorists were certainly influenced by Marx and did indeed turn their attention to culture. But their work at this point was the product of their disillusionment with the working class. It represented less a continuation of Marxism and more a break with Marx. For a younger generation of critical theorists – scholars such as Foucault, Althusser and Derrida – Marxism itself, with its promotion of a 'grand narrative' of social relations, was worthy of critique. By the 1960s, these radical young scholars often found themselves pushing at an open door as an exhausted intellectual elite no longer had the confidence to defend Enlightenment values or traditional scholarly principles. Having already rejected both social class and grand narratives as the primary means of making sense of the world, academics turned to identity-based scholarship. What has emerged in the decades since this time is a hotchpotch of identity-based intellectual projects, from academic feminism to queer theory, from critical race theory to postcolonialism and even fat studies.

Critics argue that woke ideology deals in euphemism. Code words such as 'equity', 'social justice', 'diversity and inclusion' and 'culturally responsive teaching' are intended to sound non-threatening. They are chosen because they are easily confused with more readily accepted principles but hide an altogether different agenda. This point is well illustrated by a question in a compulsory induction module taken by incoming students at the University of St Andrews in Scotland. Students are asked: 'Does equality mean treating everyone the same?' If they answer yes, they are informed: 'That's not right, in fact equality may mean treating people differently and in a way that is appropriate to their needs.'[12]

A *New York Post* article warns readers to be wary of this new vocabulary, arguing that 'in contrast to equality, equity as defined and promoted by critical race theorists is little more than reformulated Marxism'.[13] There is an important point to be made about the changed meaning of certain words or the substitution of one set of words for another. But woke is not a conspiracy. There is no Trojan horse, red or otherwise, and there are no leaders disseminating code words from on high. Both sides of this debate promote a caricature of Marxism that seems to hinge upon the equal immiseration of all. This is a far cry indeed from Trotsky's vision of 'the distribution of life's goods, existing in continual abundance'.[14]

Critics of woke who focus their attention on academia assume that the intellectual power of critical theory was such that it readily convinced left-wing political parties to change direction. In reality, as we have noted, left-wing political movements were already giving up on the working class as a positive force for social change. It was not so much that academics convinced the labour movement to change tack, but that the left was in search of a purpose. Just as an earlier generation of professors abandoned traditional scholarly principles, leaving the door open for critical theory, so too did the left's abandonment of the working class leave the door open for identity politics. Left-wing parties that traditionally drew upon the working class for support readily shifted focus to this new constituency.

Marxism, most simplistically, offers an analysis of society that is grounded in social class. Marxism views social relations under capitalism in terms of the fundamental antagonism that exists between the mass of workers and the ruling elite that employs them for profit or oversees the system that legitimises their exploitation. Woke, by contrast, often fails to see social class at all. In its rush to affirm myriad identity groups, the woke cultural elite overlooks social class as a distinct social and political force, or it relativises it as just one more identity that people can try on for size. Meanwhile, it demonises the working class as backward, racist and nationalistic.

This disregard for social class in general, and loathing of the working class in particular, sets woke views in complete opposition to Marxism. Today, as Thomas Frank notes, would-be members of the elite are taught 'to deplore working-class movements for their bigotry, their refusal of modernity, and their borderline madness'.[15] It is now quite legitimate in many elite social circles to engage in open displays of prejudice towards white working-class men in particular. Insults like 'gammon' are casually thrown around. Those who fly St George flags or wear MAGA hats are easy targets. This illustrates the prevalence of anti-working-class sentiment among identitarians. It also reveals how identity politics elevates certain identities but denigrates others.

Comparing today's woke activists to Marxists flatters the identitarians and sends woke's opponents into combat with a straw man. And yet this is a game seemingly everyone is happy to play. In November 2020, a group of 28 Conservative politicians wrote to the *Daily Telegraph* to complain about 'a clique of powerful, privileged liberals' who, they argued, were attempting to 'rewrite our history in their image'. The letter described institutions like the National Trust as being 'coloured by cultural Marxist dogma, colloquially known as the "woke agenda"'.[16] This self-styled 'Common Sense Group' of parliamentarians was right to identify those powerful people who are trying if not to rewrite history then certainly to cultivate a sense of national shame. But these MPs are wrong to align this 'woke agenda' with Marxism, cultural or otherwise.

Despite all the talk of Marxism today, neither the woke nor the critics of woke are able to account for the role social class continues to play in determining people's life chances. Being born into a poor family increases a person's chances of suffering ill health and performing less well at school. It means you're less likely to go on to higher education, secure well-paid employment, or access good-quality housing. Despite all this, being working class does not make people objects of pity. These are the people whose daily labour enables the comfortably off cultural elite to go about its duties, managing, disciplining and pontificating about the masses. Woke does not simply ignore social class, its ideas are actually hostile to the best interests of the working class. Its practice of dividing society up into ever-smaller identity groups provides the managerial class with moral authority and a renewed sense of purpose.

The rehabilitation of bigotry

The working class, understood as an economic reality and not a cultural phenomenon, includes people of all identities. For this reason, it has a political power that far surpasses any one ethnic group, gender or sexuality. Understanding the world through the lens of social class asks people to consider what they have in common, not what divides them. It asks us to consider what makes us human. But woke ideology squarely rejects any notion of common humanity. This turns back the clock on the key gains of the civil-rights movement. Woke might co-opt the language and tactics of movements for social change that began in the US in the 1960s, but its insistence on dwelling upon rather than surpassing identity means its objectives are fundamentally at odds with those earlier, more progressive campaigns.

When Martin Luther King described his dream for America's future at the March on Washington in August 1963, his vision was one of a unified nation, where 'on the red hills of Georgia, the sons of former slaves and the sons of former slave owners will be able to sit down together at the table of brotherhood'. He argued that:

> When the architects of our republic wrote the magnificent words of the Constitution and the Declaration of Independence, they were signing a promissory note to which every American was to fall heir. This note was a promise that all men – yes, black men as well as white men – would be guaranteed the unalienable rights of life, liberty and the pursuit of happiness.[17]

The campaigners of the civil-rights movement wanted skin colour to become irrelevant, as black men and white men came to enjoy equal rights. In sharp contrast, as we explored in Chapter Eight, today's woke activists, inspired by critical race theory, see skin colour as the most important defining feature of a person and argue not for equal rights, but for differential treatment for black and white people. Racial division comes to be rehabilitated in woke garb.

In a similar vein, woke activists also rehabilitate misogyny. Women who want to take part in single-sex sports, use single-sex toilets or changing rooms, or seek refuge in a single-sex shelter, are told they need to make way for men who identify as women. Transwomen are almost feted as the best kind of women, whether it's Caitlyn Jenner being named *Glamour* magazine's woman of the year in 2015 or weightlifter Laurel Hubbard being named New Zealand's sportswoman of the year in 2021. Even the word 'woman' is now removed from medical materials discussing female anatomy. Instead of 'women' we must refer to 'bodies that menstruate' or 'cervix-havers'. Women who question why they are now, as a group, unmentionable and why they must make way for men are insulted, labelled TERFs and subjected to vile abuse, including rape and death threats.

Gender ideology has breathed new life into homophobia, too. As various writers have pointed out, some lesbians now feel under intense pressure to date and have sex with transwomen, even those still in possession of a penis. Lesbians who refuse risk being labelled bigots. Same-sex attraction is once again being presented as something weird and sinister.

This rehabilitation of racism, sexism and homophobia puts woke ideology at odds with the civil-rights movements of old. The civil-rights era brought equality to the fore through the universalism of campaigners' demands. Woke, in contrast, sets people against each other and divides communities into ever-smaller groups with competing interests. Whereas the leaders of the civil-rights movement recognised the importance of free speech in giving the least powerful sections of the population a voice, today's woke activists think they should decide who has the right to speak. They think censorship, not free speech, is fundamental to allowing the oppressed to speak. And whereas the demands of the civil-rights movement posed a threat to the status quo and, in particular, the ways in which capitalist societies organised labour at the time, woke ideas pose no such threat, as we see with the rise of woke capitalism.

Since the 1960s, the focus of debates about inequality has shifted from disparities in income to disparities in representation. Better representation is something capitalists can readily accommodate.

In fact, it is to their benefit, as boosting representation necessitates the further concentration of power in the hands of the professional-managerial class. Campaigners focus relentlessly on the number of women or black people on boards of directors, or working in the science and technology sector, in senior leadership positions or other high-profile, public-facing roles. Activists agitate for equal representation for different groups of people in elite institutions, often through the setting of targets or the imposition of quotas.

Representation has long been an important political demand. 'No taxation without representation' is one of the most enduring political slogans. From the Chartists to the Suffragettes, campaigns for the vote were concerned with representation: citizens wanted their views to be represented, for a person of their choosing to represent them in parliament. But under this older definition of representation, parliamentary representatives were elected specifically to relay the views of their constituents; it mattered little whether or not they looked anything like the people they purported to represent. Today, by contrast, representation is all about appearances, and an obsession with it has spread well beyond the political arena. As Ben Cobley explains in *The Tribe*, 'the role of favoured group members in positions of power is to represent, or rather to appear as representative'.[18]

To feminist campaigners, having women in powerful positions – in the media, universities, the professions and sport – is more than just a personal achievement for the women concerned. It is seen as a victory for women everywhere. All women can take satisfaction from the triumph of a few, or so the argument goes, because their success is indicative of a culture that values all women. For this reason, when highly paid BBC presenters win equal-pay cases and gain even higher salaries, this is considered a cause for celebration – all women are thought to be empowered by this greater 'equality'. That the women who work for the BBC as cooks, cleaners, secretaries and make-up artists will still only receive a tiny fraction of the salaries of these highly paid stars is apparently irrelevant. Likewise, preventing women from working as grid girls at Formula 1 races is considered a feminist victory, because even though the individual women concerned may lose money, the overall representation of women is said to be improved.

Intersectionality

Once it has been established that society can be divided into different identity groups, then the path is cleared for the subsequent positioning of each group within an intersectional framework. As we touched on in Chapter Eight, Kimberlé Crenshaw, a feminist, academic and critical race theorist, coined the label 'intersectionality' and set out what she meant by it in her now famous 1991 essay, 'Mapping the Margins: Intersectionality, Identity Politics and Violence Against Women of Colour'.[19] Crenshaw explored the experience of overlapping discrimination – of being, say, a black woman. Not only do such individuals suffer from prejudice because of their identity, they also find that legislation or campaigning organisations designed to protect people from discrimination do not apply to their specific situation. For example, the black woman denied a job at a car plant can't appeal under race-equality laws if black men are employed on the factory floor, and she can't appeal under sex-discrimination laws if white women are employed in secretarial positions. Her unique experience of discrimination falls between the intersections.

At first glance, intersectionality may appear to resolve the inability of identity politics to account for more nuanced personal experiences. But by putting people into ever-smaller categories, it leads us to a dead end. People are positioned according to hierarchies of privilege, often based upon historical legacy rather than individual circumstances. White men, the first to benefit from legal rights and those historically most likely to benefit from social conventions, are positioned at the top. Black women, discriminated against on account of both their race and their gender, come much lower down. This hierarchy is thought to hold true even when the black woman is a wealthy, well-educated lawyer and the white man has no qualifications and is unemployed. Woke activists see their role as to amplify the voices of those considered to be at the bottom of the pyramid. This is why they will always look to champion black women above white men, irrespective of income, social class or geography. Those supposedly at the bottom, such as Muslims or transgender people, must also be shielded from all criticism, even criticism that stops far short of attacking individuals. For this reason, transgender people must never be questioned about their identity and Islamist terror attacks must be hushed over to prevent aspersions being cast on members of the Muslim community more broadly. In this way, as Christopher Lasch argued, 'diversity turns out to legitimise a new dogmatism, in which rival minorities take shelter behind a set of beliefs impervious to rational discussion'.[20]

Today, many government officials, university admissions officers and workplace human-resource managers see getting people of colour, disabled or trans people into public positions, top jobs and university places as their primary goal. In the process, people stop being individuals with their own strengths, weaknesses and complex life histories and are reduced to their biology. Each 'diverse' person recruited and retained is a box ticked, a target reached and another nail in the coffin of what is perceived to be an oppressive white, male, heteronormative, cisgender society. By the same token, statistical disparities between men and women or between white and black people are presented as a problem, with prejudice and discrimination the only possible explanations for them.

Securing more diverse representation comes to be seen as a legitimate means of correcting historical injustices and instigating broader social change. But representation soon becomes an end in itself. As a consequence of this, as Ben Cobley suggests, institutions end up 'passing favour not just outside of themselves but within, so the institution itself comes to reproduce itself by identity-based preferentiality. Their focus therefore turns more on to themselves and their own composition, and away from any other purposes they might have had.'[21]

Diverse representation creates an appearance of equality, but it is a performance and can exist in the absence of meaningful social change. For example, having more women professors or more BAME film directors does not, in and of itself, challenge class inequality. Indeed, it may well entrench class divisions further; a purely meritocratic approach to allocating roles allows for at least the possibility of social mobility. Just as when higher education first began to expand in the 1960s and places began to go to doctors' daughters as well as their sons, so too can a checklist approach to diversity create more opportunities for those who are already economically privileged. It is possible to achieve equal representation without shifting the balance of power in society. Indeed, this focus on representation gives elite institutions an opportunity to rebrand themselves with a diverse new image.

The emphasis on representation might appear radical, but the shift from class to identity robs it of any progressive potential. Whereas social change instigated by and benefitting the working class would threaten the status of the cultural elite, demanding elite representation for myriad minority groups does not. Top roles will be filled largely by middle-class, highly educated women and minorities. More to the point, the existing cultural and political elite will remain intact to manage this new diversity and confer recognition on those previously underrepresented.

Identity politics and intersectionality also come with the insidious assumption that all members of a particular group think alike. Opinions come to be seen as an extension of a person's race, gender or sexuality rather than a carefully considered perspective. In reality, our views are no more determined by our genitalia than they are by our pigmentation. Our identity may shape our experiences of the world, but the suggestion that this determines what we think is, as David Swift puts it, 'both highly essentialist and reductionist'. Swift goes on to note that an assumed link between race and opinions 'holds little appeal for actual ethnic-minority voters. It is largely the creation of self-appointed "community leaders", acting in concert with crank academics and guilty white people. It misses the crucial fact that most of the concerns of women, BME people and gays are the same as those of straight white men.'[22]

Under the rule of woke, individuals who do not espouse the views that have been assigned to their particular identity group come in for severe criticism. Black British politician Kemi Badenoch, for example, is targeted for abuse because she does not believe that to be black is to be a victim of systemic and structural racism. This linking of opinions to race and sex returns us to the racist and sexist thinking of a long-dead era. As Kwame Anthony Appiah puts it, this starts from the assumption that 'there will be proper ways of being black and gay, there will be expectations to be met, demands will be made'. Appiah continues: 'It is at this point that someone who takes autonomy seriously will ask whether we have not replaced one tyranny with another.'[23]

With the working class viewed as a politically backward, spent force, identity-based groups have provided a new focus for the social-justice left. But while activists might pose as speaking for the downtrodden, they only reflect the outlook and concerns of the intellectual elite. The left's frustration with the working class led it to retreat into universities for refuge. Disillusioned political activists found it far easier to persuade middle-class students and university lecturers of their cause. They are far more comfortable arguing that womanhood is a social construct than they are engaging with women who work as cleaners or carers.

'You have to see it to be it' might make for a snappy slogan, but it is inaccurate as well as incredibly limiting. The woke preoccupation with representation completely ignores social class and prompts us to see ourselves as entirely determined by group membership. It tells kids to invest in the success of a privileged Californian duchess like Meghan Markle if they happen to share one or more arbitrary characteristics with her. Then, as adults, they must pay homage to an elite that manages diversity in order to maintain power.

Endnotes

[1] Remarks by President Biden on International Women's Day, The White House, 8 March 2021

[2] National Trust asks volunteers to wear rainbow face paint and glitter for Pride, *Telegraph*, 14 June 2021

[3] What they have been saying, inVISIBLEwomen, accessed 15 June 2021

[4] *The Feminine Mystique*, Betty Friedan, Penguin Modern Classics (2010)

[5] The representation of LGBT families in children's picture books, Janie Lynn Johnson, *Queer Culture Collection*, 29 April 2015

[6] Ban on harmful gender stereotypes in ads comes into force, Advertising Standards Authority, 14 June 2019

[7] *Cynical Theories: How Activist Scholarship Made Everything About Race, Gender, and Identity – and Why This Harms Everybody*, Helen Pluckrose and James Lindsay, Swift Press (2020)

[8] *Representation: Cultural Representations and Signifying Practices*, Stuart Hall et al, Sage Publications (2013)

[9] *The Diversity Delusion: How Race and Gender Pandering Corrupt the University and Undermine Our Culture*, Heather Mac Donald, St Martin's Press (2018)

[10] Interview with author, recorded in *The Corrosive Impact of Transgender Ideology*, Joanna Williams, Civitas (2020)

[11] *Surviving Identity: Vulnerability and the Psychology of Recognition*, Kenneth McLaughlin, Routledge (2011)

[12] Purity tests damage students and universities, Clare Foges, *The Times* (London), 4 October 2021

[13] What critical race theory is really about, Christopher F Rufo, *New York Post*, 6 May 2021

[14] *The Revolution Betrayed: What is the Soviet Union and Where is it Going?*, Leon Trotsky (1936)

[15] *The People, No: A Brief History of Anti-Populism*, Thomas Frank, Metropolitan (2020)

[16] Letter to the *Telegraph*, Sir Edward Leigh MP, 11 November 2020

[17] Read Martin Luther King Jr's 'I Have a Dream' speech in its entirety, NPR, 14 January 2022

[18] *The Tribe: The Liberal-Left and the System of Diversity*, Ben Cobley, Societas (2018)

[19] Mapping the Margins: Intersectionality, Identity Politics and Violence Against Women of Colour, Kimberlé Crenshaw, *Stanford Law Review*, July 1991

[20] *The Revolt of the Elites and the Betrayal of Democracy*, Christopher Lasch, WW Norton & Company (1996)

[21] *The Tribe: The Liberal-Left and the System of Diversity*, Ben Cobley, Societas (2018)

[22] *A Left for Itself: Left-wing Hobbyists and Performative Radicalism*, David Swift, John Hunt Publishing (2019)

[23] Cited in: *The Tribe: The Liberal-Left and the System of Diversity*, Ben Cobley, Societas (2018)

11   The Weaponisation of Victimhood

The shift from class to identity, as discussed in the previous chapter, offers a partial explanation for the cultural elite's turn to woke values. But in order for identity-based claims to gain traction, they must also carry the moral authority that is assumed to come with victimhood. The very real disadvantages experienced by some communities lend legitimacy to woke activists and, where disadvantages cannot be found, psychological problems, often premised on historical oppression, are created and promoted. Here, we explore the emergence of a victimhood culture and consider how entire identity groups have been constructed as victims and then had their status weaponised, often for the benefit of others.

Woke has arisen in the context of a culture that valorises individual fragility and is contemptuous of personal or collective strength. We have to go back a long way to find a time when values such as stoicism, courage, resilience, duty, sacrifice and self-control were widely celebrated as positive attributes and consciously nurtured in children through schools, literature and parenting. For example, in 1908 Lord Baden-Powell published *Scouting for Boys*, which launched the scouting movement. The aim was to cultivate chivalry, bravery and a sense of duty and national pride in boys. Today, these values seem old-fashioned. They are more likely to be considered problematic than worthy of inculcation. Those who hold them are often thought to have repressed their emotions. Not acknowledging that you experience mental-health difficulties is today considered *prima facie* evidence that you are struggling with mental-health difficulties.

We are encouraged to be open about our vulnerabilities and let others know about our emotional fragility. Individuals who step back from success in order to protect their mental health, people like world-beating gymnast Simone Biles or tennis champion Naomi Osaka, are held up as role models with important lessons for us all. Prince Harry wins more praise for speaking out about his mental-health struggles than he ever did for serving in the armed forces. People who openly display their suffering are lauded for their bravery and honesty.

The message coming from all areas of public life today is that aspiring to be stoic and courageous is cause for suspicion. At best, this may signify a misguided bravado. At worst, it may be a sign of a more generalised toxic masculinity. Feminists and men's rights activists alike argue that traditionally masculine values can lead to pent-up aggression or even suicidal thoughts among men.

It is often assumed that mental-health problems are on a spectrum, with everyone suffering from stress, anxiety or depression to some degree. For this reason, mental-health support is no longer the preserve of professionally trained psychologists, but has become the responsibility of everyone. Institutions such as schools, universities and prisons are now more likely to relate to students or inmates through a therapeutic lens. Techniques that might once have been associated with therapy, like positively affirming a person's feelings or encouraging meditation or breathing exercises, are now routinely practised within schools, where children imbibe a message that feeling stressed or anxious from time to time is a condition that requires special help.

Just as there is no longer any sense of shame attached to discussing feelings of anxiety or depression, so too is therapy no longer considered a specialist form of help. Rather, it is seen as an essential component of 'self-care'. We talk of retail therapy, aromatherapy and pets as therapy. Baking cakes, taking a bubble bath or curling up with a good book are no longer just nice things to do, they are psychologically essential. Ironically, all this openness and therapy has not led people to feel more positive about life and better able to cope, but the exact opposite. We continually reinforce our perception of ourselves as unable to cope with the stresses and strains of everyday life. Our vulnerabilities and mental-health difficulties come to define us as people and become intrinsic to our sense of who we are. This affirmation of vulnerability is taking place across society, reflecting a shift towards what has been labelled a 'victimhood culture'.

The idea of 'victimhood' was first subjected to academic scrutiny in the 1960s. Over the course of the following two decades there was a growing awareness of problems caused by harassment and abuse at home, school, work and in all areas of life. News investigations into sexual abuse, child abuse, Satanic ritual abuse, domestic violence and sexual harassment proliferated. In his 1979 book, *The Culture of Narcissism*, Christopher Lasch identified this new vulnerable self.[1] At this point, new medical conditions and syndromes were being discovered and recognised. For example, post-traumatic stress disorder (PTSD) was first added to the American Psychiatric Association's *Diagnostic and Statistical Manual of Mental Disorders* in 1980. Experiences that had previously been thought of as personal or social problems came to be reconsidered as medical or psychological conditions. Far more people than ever before found that, whether they liked it or not, the label 'victim' had been applied to them.

Since this time, the idea that people are vulnerable has become so widely accepted that it is assumed to be simple common sense. Two changes have occurred in parallel: people are perceived to be more fragile and susceptible to harm and, at the same time, definitions of harm have expanded to encompass not just the physical, but also the emotional and psychological. This means that safety is threatened not just by people or actions that may inflict physical injury, but also by those who may use words to inflict emotional distress. Indeed, this emotional distress is often considered more damaging than physical injury, because wounds will heal over time but psychological pain may remain indefinitely. The claim that words wound justifies not only calls for censorship, but also, ironically, physical violence: for when speech is considered violence then violence becomes a legitimate response to speech.

In their 2018 book, *The Coddling of the American Mind*, Greg Lukianoff and Jonathan Haidt identify a range of factors that encourage young people to see themselves as vulnerable, such as trends in parenting and schooling. They argue that, having been treated as if they are fragile by parents and teachers, today's young adults are more likely than previous generations to arrive at university believing that they are vulnerable. Significantly, this view extends beyond the self and is projected on to others: 'Even those who are not fragile themselves often believe that *others* are in danger and therefore need protection.'[2] In the context of identity politics, this morphs into a focus on the fragile self that must be protected from offence and continually affirmed through public acts of recognition.

Within a culture that celebrates victimhood, people are rewarded for proclaiming their suffering and their struggles. In *The Rise of Victimhood Culture*, sociologists Bradley Campbell and Jason Manning argue that people today are incentivised to identify as victims in return for recognition, support and protection, observing that 'victimhood is in fact a social resource – a form of status'.[3]

Woke activists and writers learn to use victimhood as a resource to good effect. At times, their claims are so distanced from reality as to be fantastical. *Guardian* journalist Nesrine Malik writes: 'To be a woman is akin to being a prisoner with something to trade – cigarettes, alcohol, sexual favours, anything you have at your disposal to earn you that extra half hour to stretch your legs in the exercise yard or save you from a beating.' Perhaps unsurprisingly, Malik is scathing of arguments put forward by free-speech advocates: 'They overwhelmingly [want] to exercise their freedom of speech in order to agitate against minorities, women, immigrants and Muslims.'[4]

Campbell and Manning contrast victimhood culture to its predecessors – namely, a far older 'culture of honour', which attached status to reputation and its defence through acts of physical bravery and violent retaliation directed towards challengers; and a 'culture of dignity', which afforded people an inherent sense of self-worth and was manifested in the exercise of restraint and toleration.[5] As Campbell and Manning suggest, perceptions of victimhood today extend beyond mental-health problems to encompass basic facts about a person's identity, such as their race, sex, sexuality, gender identity and sometimes even social class. There is an assumption that such characteristics completely determine how we relate to the world. Being white, male, heterosexual and cisgender is to embody privileges inaccessible to others. Alternatively, being a transgender woman of colour means you are generally oppressed and victimised – no matter your wealth or social class.

Free speech is one of the casualties of victimhood culture. In the civil-rights era, fighting for free speech was considered key to political success. People were assumed to be innately equal despite an unequal distribution of resources and power. The right to free speech was thought to allow the best arguments to win out. However, in a victimhood culture, people are assumed to be innately unequal not simply because of material differences, but also because of features intrinsic to their identity. According to this way of thinking, free speech simply allows the already privileged – heterosexual white men – to have their voices amplified. In order to 'truly' have free speech, the argument goes, we must first level the playing field by enhancing the speech rights of the oppressed and telling the privileged to shut up and listen. This reifies a sense of difference between groups, and it assumes the existence of neutral arbiters to decree who has speech rights and who does not in any given situation.

Organisations representing so-called oppressed groups often adopt a policy of not engaging with critics. Those acting on behalf of transgender people, for example, frequently assert that any challenge to trans ideology is putting 'trans lives' up for debate – that is, invalidating the identity of an entire group of people. Shon Faye writes: 'Trans people have been dehumanised, reduced to a talking point or conceptual problem: an "issue" to be discussed and debated endlessly. It turns out that when the media want to talk about trans issues, it means they want to talk about their issues with us, not the challenges facing us.' This could be seen to suggest that if a debate is not conducted on their terms, trans activists will refuse to participate.[6]

This same argument is increasingly made by a cohort of activists who refuse to debate critical race theory. Unfortunately for these campaigners, there are inherent conflicts in both contemporary anti-racism and transgenderism – between single-sex spaces and gender self-identification, between class and race. Refusing to participate in discussion about these issues doesn't make them disappear. It simply swaps rational discourse for a highly charged, emotive and seemingly interminable struggle. This is of little benefit to anyone, least of all to trans people who simply want the freedom to live undisturbed.

Ironically, as Campbell and Manning note, a victimhood culture is 'most likely to arise precisely in settings that already have relatively high degrees of equality'.[7] On many university campuses, for example, students are – to a large extent – equal. Clearly, some may be in the fortunate position of having wealthy parents who provide generous allowances. But in terms of educational resources and the material benefits that accrue from being a student – such as favourable access to loans, accommodation, leisure activities, education and future employment prospects – there is far more equality between students at a university than there is among people in society as a whole. It is within this context that new sources of oppression are actively sought out and concepts like 'microaggressions' are invented. Students quickly realise that being wealthy, educated and privileged is not enough to stake a claim to authority. They must also garner experience (or experience by proxy) of suffering.

Historical oppression

A key way that identity groups lay claim to a collective experience of suffering is to turn to the past. History provides plentiful examples of minorities being exploited, oppressed, brutalised and killed. It is too easy to argue that things were done differently then and that the past should not be judged by the standards of the present. Clearly, atrocities have been committed that will forever be a stain on humanity, and from which we can only hope to learn and not repeat. But the degree to which the past reverberates and shapes people's lives in the present must be subject to debate. To what extent can people be held responsible for the actions of long-dead ancestors? And, by the same token, to what extent are historical injustices to blame for inequalities in the present? As always, our answers to these questions are shaped by the social and political culture in which we find ourselves. In the context of identity politics and a victimhood culture, we are inclined to view history as apportioning privilege and oppression and shaping people's lives in the present. This means that, as Lasch put it, minorities become entitled to respect not by virtue of their achievements, but by virtue of their sufferings in the past.[8]

This mining of history to substantiate accusations of privilege or claims to victimhood in the present is incentivised in a victimhood culture. We see this play out with Oxford students who argue that the statue of colonialist Cecil Rhodes must be taken down because having to walk past it on their way to class is traumatic. It can be seen in the Bristol students who claim that having to sit in the Wills Memorial Building induces racial trauma, due to the Wills family's alleged links to slavery. Being a victim affords people social status and the past provides a useful source of suffering. However, this short-term increase in status comes at a high psychological cost. Communities that see themselves as oppressed may be given concessions and privileges, but they will struggle to be considered truly equal.

The cultural shift towards validating experiences of suffering can be traced within the history of feminism. In its first and second waves, feminism primarily focused on overturning legal inequalities. For women, winning the right to receive an education, vote, open a bank account, own property, initiate divorce proceedings, receive equal pay for equal work and secure access to abortion services, contraception and childcare represented a huge step towards the achievement of sexual equality. Such demands were not premised on claims of female victimhood, but the precise opposite: they were grounded in the assumption that women were equal to men and only legal and social structures stood in the way of their liberation and equality being realised.

Today, this view has been turned on its head. Too many feminists are invested in a narrative that presents women as eternal victims of sexism and misogyny. Material inequalities are reinvented as intractable psychological states. Such problems cannot then be solved by legal equality or even by special treatment: they become an intrinsic part of what it means to be a woman. The upshot is a permanent need for feminism to turn up new forms of female victimhood. A previous generation of women may have laughed at the suggestion that winking, whistling or overhearing lewd jokes were the biggest problems they faced, but feminists today count such incidents as sexual harassment and demand that offenders be investigated by the police for committing misogynistic hate crimes. In exaggerating women's disadvantages and pinpointing male behaviour as the cause, victim feminism imbues young women with a false and degraded sense of their own position in society. Women are encouraged to see themselves as passive objects, unable to stand up for themselves or to exercise control over their own lives.

Victimhood even colours the feminist pushback against gender ideology. The main feminist challenge to allowing transwomen (that is, biological males) into female-only spaces is to present women as either bigger victims than transwomen or as at risk from transwomen. In an open letter to protest against the inclusion of transgender author Torrey Peters in the long list for an all-women literary prize, a group of female authors argued that in the UK men are 'hunting us like prey in the streets'.[9] This hysterical exaggeration detracts from a more principled case for freedom of association, and pitches women against transwomen in an unedifying competition to see which group is the more victimised.

Many of the claims made about apparently oppressed groups can be challenged. Women are not more likely to be attacked in public than men, nor are women routinely paid less than men for doing the exact same work. By the same token, black school leavers are not less likely to go on to university than their white peers. But such facts are rarely welcomed and frequently dismissed because they challenge a dominant narrative of oppression. They do not, we are told, correspond with people's 'lived experience'. When the UK government's Commission on Race and Ethnic Disparities produced its report in 2021, arguing that 'we no longer see a Britain where the system is deliberately rigged against ethnic minorities',[10] it was met by outrage and claims that the commissioners deliberately ignored black people's lived experience of racism. Identity groups accustomed to the status that comes with claiming to be oppressed find it difficult to let it go. Rather than challenging claims to victimhood, different identity groups compete for state protections and special treatment in recognition of their suffering. Claims of suffering are, in turn, amplified by an array of activists, politicians and journalists who readily align themselves with those perceived to be victims.

The struggles experienced by members of apparently oppressed groups take on a more collective and powerful force in the context of a victimhood culture, where experience of suffering brings with it a morally elevated status. Transwomen are celebrated for their suffering, and transgender children are praised for their bravery. As psychoanalyst Lisa Marchiano writes: 'Numerous glowing media reports about brave trans kids and their heroically supportive families offer celebrity status to both.'[11]

This model of the brave-but-suffering victim stands in stark contrast to the way that activists saw themselves in previous eras. In generations gone by, political change was instigated by people coming together in acts of solidarity and displays of strength. Whether it was striking workers or marching protesters, people brought about change when they got together, in sufficient numbers, to show that they were angry, not that they were downtrodden. As Lasch argued: 'It was the strength of the civil-rights movement, which can be understood as part of the populist tradition, that it consistently refused to claim a privileged moral position for the victims of oppression.'[12] Today's activists, in contrast, demonstrate not their strength, but their weakness. They do not ask to be taken seriously as equals, but to be treated with pity and handed special protections.

For Nesrine Malik, it is in the very act of expressing victimhood that people demonstrate their agency: 'It takes agency to be a victim; it takes grit, determination, confidence and honesty to stop running away from pain and perceived humiliation, to assert that you have been compromised professionally or physically for being a woman and reject the blame for that. Gritting teeth and moving on is not displaying agency.'[13] But this form of agency-as-victimhood is fundamentally at odds with demands for equality. Whereas equality is about freedom *from* state interference and discrimination, recognition premised on suffering is a demand *for* the state and society to compel respect. Victim status is an insistence that others act on your behalf: you have a voice, but you can only talk of your suffering.

In this way, today's identity-driven campaigners look to the police, the judiciary, government ministers or university managers to act on their behalf. Writing in the *American Conservative*, Jason Morgan argues: 'Natural rights have yielded to state-granted ones, letters of marque issued by central government authorities that entitle the bearer to do some particular thing that others do not get to do.'[14] This allows people in positions of power to assume the moral authority that comes with acting on behalf of victims.

Desperately seeking purpose

Today, we have people in positions of power who lack moral authority. They head up institutions that lack moral legitimacy. This situation has come about slowly, over the course of several decades. One cause is that many institutions no longer have a sense of the importance of their core purpose. Many teachers, for example, no longer see the subjects they teach as being valuable in and of themselves and so they look for an extrinsic purpose to justify their role. They might convince themselves that education improves social mobility or that reading the right books in English classes can make children more tolerant. Local councils order zebra crossings to be repainted in rainbow stripes and for traffic lights to show gender-neutral characters. Neither comedy nor soap operas can just be entertaining these days, there must always be a lesson as well. In various cases, it seems that an organisation's primary purpose no longer provides sufficient justification for it. Moral authority must be drawn from elsewhere.

Even the law is looking for a new sense of purpose and source of legitimacy. Historically, the law has stood above the feelings of victims and the opinions of offenders. A crime was a crime, irrespective of how either party felt about it. Over recent decades, this has changed. Victim-impact statements are now heard in court. Hate-crime legislation has introduced subjective definitions of harm, in which the perception and feelings of the victim form the basis of a criminal offence. The legal system has begun to play a role that is both therapeutic and political, intervening in citizens' interpersonal relationships and arbitrating competing claims to victimhood. The recording of 'non-crime hate incidents' in recent years has served a didactic function, re-educating individual offenders and sending a message to the wider community about acceptable language and attitudes.

As we have seen, authority today often comes from acting on be-half of people cast as victims. One attraction of this is that victims make few demands of us. They simply ask to be recognised and believed. As Campbell and Manning put it, for those of us who are not members of a particular victim group, 'believing certain claims of victimisation is upheld as a kind of moral duty'.[15] The victim is placed on a pedestal – a heroine, blameless. To believe her is to affirm her identity as a victim. The assumption of blamelessness, however, is at best a hollow victory. To be blameless is to have lacked all ability to control your own destiny. It leads to demands for protection, not equality. Through expressions of victimhood, people gain recognition and affirmation, but at the expense of having to present themselves as vulnerable. Through this process, many come to internalise vulnerability as a part of their identity.

Those who have been encouraged to see themselves as vulnerable find even everyday interactions carry the risk of psychological harm. They are left unable to shake off perceived slights or 'microaggressions'.

Instead, they seek out professionals in positions of authority to intervene, remove the source of offence and reprimand the sinner. Diversity training in the workplace or consent classes in universities insist that people must be taught the 'correct' way to interact with one another. This justifies a vast administrative apparatus, 'the diversity bureaucrats', who are paid to promote and manage a culture of victimhood and grievance.[16] As Morgan notes: 'As the transgender movement comes ever more fully into its own, we find that it is not its own after all. It is the state's, and the state is using it to erase freedom – both positive and negative – for all of us.'[17]

The rise of victimhood culture puts members of apparently oppressed groups in a bind: they can never relinquish claims to victimhood. No matter how much they achieve or earn, no matter the titles or influence they accrue, they are bound by the fact that their status is entirely dependent upon them – or those they represent – being recognised for the suffering they have endured. Evidence that calls into question the alleged suffering of people because of their sex, sexuality or skin colour poses a challenge to the claims made by today's woke activists. It threatens the position of people whose identity, income, social status and source of influence and power is premised upon claims of victimhood. For this reason, professional anti-racist activists can never be successful in defeating racism, and woke campaigns against transphobia can never reach a point of acceptance for transgender people. Were this ever to happen, the activists would no longer have a purpose – or an income.

A new authoritarianism

Woke activists often portray the people they claim to represent as victims of prejudice, discrimination, abuse, or circumstances and life events they have no control over. If those they speak for are seen to have any agency themselves, it lies only in the power to name their own particular trauma. This leads to a pervasive insecurity which, in turn, compels increasingly authoritarian action. Although transgender rights are promoted in the name of tolerance, their enforcement is often extremely intolerant. Oppressive measures – for example, policing speech or eroding sex-based rights – can be justified if they are carried out in the name of protecting victims or offering affirmation to the vulnerable.

Such is the authority gained from acting on behalf of victims that it appears to excuse otherwise morally reprehensible behaviour. The label TERF – applied to gender-critical feminists by transgender activists – seems to legitimise the most atrocious treatment. On university campuses, gender-critical academics routinely put up with being No Platformed. Some have had death threats, had their office doors drenched in urine, or need security guards to accompany them to lectures. Similarly, no insults are considered too gross or racist that they cannot be hurled at people of colour who do not promote a narrative of black victimhood.

Elevating the moral status of members of victim groups has far-reaching social consequences. As David Green argues: 'Group victimhood is not compatible with our heritage of liberal democracy in three particular ways: it is inconsistent with the moral equality that underpins liberalism; it weakens our democratic culture; and it undermines legal equality.'[18] A culture of victimhood suggests some groups are more deserving of moral authority and legal protections than others, and that the majority's rights to freedom of speech, freedom of association and freedom of conscience must be curtailed in order to protect minorities.

Some of those who purport to speak on behalf of the transgender community are as explicit about their hostility towards democracy as they are about their disdain for free speech. Academics argue that 'direct democracy may endanger transgender rights'.[19] This is because both democracy and free speech raise the prospect of scrutiny from the general public. 'Sunlight is the best disinfectant', goes the old saying, uttered by US Supreme Court justice Louis Brandeis. Sadly, it seems that many woke activists fight shy of sunlight.

Challenging woke ideas can be incredibly difficult, especially within particular institutions. The notion of challenging what is considered best for victims marks an individual out as perversely selfish and morally bankrupt. No one wants to be that person. As Ben Cobley puts it: 'Conformity to the system has become a matter of self-interest as much as political commitment. The carrot of favour and inclusion draws us in to conform while the stick of disfavour and exclusion draws us away from any doubts we might have.'[20]

A culture of victimhood provides the moral justification for enacting woke values. But the cultural elite, having adopted an outlook shaped by identity politics, still requires a rationale for action. A relationship therefore develops between the cultural elite and political activists. Activists learn that cowardly managers are likely to accept their claims to victimhood at face value and act on their demands. In turn, the cultural elite nurtures and encourages claims of victimhood to bolster its moral authority. But this 'compassion' degrades the supposed victims, who are reduced to objects of pity rather than treated as fellow citizens. As Lasch argued, compassion can readily become the human face of contempt.[21]

Claiming to represent the interests of the oppressed enables those in positions of power to foist their worldview on society. Wokeness, with its veneer of egalitarianism and moral righteousness, lends credence to what are often deeply authoritarian and divisive policies. Those interested in genuinely progressive social change need to push back against the elitist, censorious and anti-democratic instincts of the woke outlook. How this might happen is the subject of our final chapter.

Endnotes

[1] *The Culture of Narcissism: American Life in an Age of Diminishing Expectations*, Christopher Lasch, WW Norton & Company (1979)

[2] *The Coddling of the American Mind: How Good Intentions and Bad Ideas Are Setting Up a Generation for Failure*, Greg Lukianoff and Jonathan Haidt, Penguin (2018)

[3] *The Rise of Victimhood Culture: Microaggressions, Safe Spaces and the New Culture Wars*, Bradley Campbell and Jason Manning, Palgrave Macmillan (2018)

[4] *We Need New Stories: Challenging the Toxic Myths Behind Our Age of Discontent*, Nesrine Malik, Orion (2019)

[5] *The Rise of Victimhood Culture: Microaggressions, Safe Spaces and the New Culture Wars*, Bradley Campbell and Jason Manning, Palgrave Macmillan (2018)

[6] *The Transgender Issue: An Argument for Justice*, Shon Faye, Penguin (2021)

[7] *The Rise of Victimhood Culture: Microaggressions, Safe Spaces and the New Culture Wars*, Bradley Campbell and Jason Manning, Palgrave Macmillan (2018)

[8] *The Revolt of the Elites and the Betrayal of Democracy*, Christopher Lasch, WW Norton & Company (1996)

[9] Open letter to the women's prize, Wild Woman Writing Club, 6 April 2021

[10] Independent report: Foreword, introduction and full recommendations, Commission on Race and Ethnic Disparities, 28 April 2021

[11] Transgender Children: the making of a modern hysteria, Lisa Marchiano, in *Inventing Transgender Children and Young People*, Michele Moore and Heather Brunskell-Evans (eds), Cambridge Scholars Publishing (2019)

[12] *The Revolt of the Elites and the Betrayal of Democracy*, Christopher Lasch, WW Norton & Company (1996)

[13] *We Need New Stories: Challenging the Toxic Myths Behind Our Age of Discontent*, Nesrine Malik, Orion (2019)

[14] The left unleashes the new furies of unfreedom, Jason Morgan, *American Conservative*, 8 January 2020

[15] *The Rise of Victimhood Culture: Microaggressions, Safe Spaces and the New Culture Wars*, Bradley Campbell and Jason Manning, Palgrave Macmillan (2018)

[16] *The Diversity Delusion: How Race and Gender Pandering Corrupt the University and Undermine Our Culture*, Heather Mac Donald, St Martin's Press (2018)

[17] The left unleashes the new furies of unfreedom, Jason Morgan, *American Conservative*, 8 January 2020

[18] *We're (Nearly) All Victims Now!: How Political Correctness is Undermining Our Liberal Culture*, David Green, Civitas (2006)

[19] *The Remarkable Rise of Transgender Rights*, Donald P Haider-Markel, Daniel Clay Lewis and Jami Kathleen Taylor, University of Michigan Press (2018)

[20] *The Tribe: The Liberal-Left and the System of Diversity*, Ben Cobley, Societas (2018)
[21] *The Revolt of the Elites and the Betrayal of Democracy*, Christopher Lasch, WW Norton & Company (1996)

Conclusion – Is the Future Woke?

Woke has won. It has won because its fundamental assumptions have become so widely accepted among the cultural elite that they are considered not just uncontroversial but common sense. Woke has won because its values have been adopted by members of the professional-managerial class, who have allowed woke thinking to take root within public institutions and to shape policies, practices and laws. Woke has won because it has become embedded in schools and universities. Teachers and lecturers cultivate woke attitudes in children and young adults who take for granted that what they are taught is factually accurate and morally correct. After graduation, they carry the lessons imbibed back out into the world.

Woke has won because its leading advocates appropriated the rhetoric of the civil-rights-era struggles for equality. The overwhelming majority of people who are not racist, sexist or homophobic have gone along with campaigns claiming to promote tolerance, diversity, equality or inclusion. Yet they find that these words no longer mean what they once did. At the same time, woke has allowed many in the cultural elite to cultivate a distorted sense of their own victimhood. They have then weaponised this status, and the compassion it inspires in others, to bolster their own moral authority.

In truth, as this book has shown, woke is not compassionate, kind or politically neutral. Woke divides people according to race, gender and sexuality and, in the process, rehabilitates outdated prejudices. But woke still serves a purpose. It gives the cultural elite a sense of mission and allows it to intervene in the lives of others and manage society as it sees fit. Woke provides the elite with a sense of moral superiority that rationalises its own privileged position, and with a source of authority that justifies managing and disciplining everyone else. As an added bonus, the language of woke allows members of the cultural elite to identify one another and differentiate themselves from the politically incorrect masses. Critics, meanwhile, learn to self-censor. Those who fall short suffer social ostracism, public humiliation, loss of platforms or livelihoods, and potentially find themselves with a police record.

For all these reasons, challenging woke policies and practices is not an easy task. For a start, many of woke's leading proponents resist public accountability and avoid debate. Transgender activists, in particular, are notoriously hostile to discussion. Any attempt at rational engagement is met with the retort that 'my identity is not up for discussion' and the argument that debate is a form of 'erasure'. Facts and statistics are brushed off with the trump card of lived experience. And in the woke worldview, the lived experience of some counts for considerably more than that of others. Social-class inequalities, once the primary concern of left-wing political parties, are now crowded out.

Woke has won. But challenging it remains essential – and its victory in the long term is far from assured.

Challenging woke

On occasion, woke collapses under its own weight and needs very little challenge at all. Its internal inconsistencies and competing claims are sometimes sufficient for it to crumble of its own accord. Activists rapidly find that, however woke they might claim to be, there will always be others who are woker still. By the same logic, organisations can never claim to have fully achieved goals of equality, diversity or inclusivity, as there will always be one group that remains underrepresented. And to claim success is to claim you have nothing else to learn – itself an anti-woke position. But while it might be fun to watch woke eat itself on occasion, there are no guarantees that it will bring itself down for good.

Unfortunately, we can't rely on our existing politicians to mount a challenge to woke. The UK's current Conservative government, led by Boris Johnson, makes occasional noises about resisting woke when the most extreme examples of it come to light. But its attempts to safeguard free speech on campus, remind schools that critical race theory should not be taught as fact and ban woke speakers from addressing the civil service have not so far been successful.

There are two problems here. Elected representatives can pass legislation and introduce policies but are not the ones who put them into practice. Whatever the views of MPs or government ministers, civil servants and heads of public institutions are free to espouse woke values away from the glare of democratic accountability. More significantly, many Conservative MPs buy into woke values and practices themselves. Even Boris Johnson defaults to woke. He told a gathering of world leaders in 2021 that the world needs to be 'more feminine'.[1] A few months later at Conservative Party conference, Johnson's wife, Carrie, pledged further legal changes to support transgender people, despite the conference having made headlines for hosting the LGB Alliance, a group that defends the rights of same-sex-attracted people and pushes back against gender ideology.[2]

Government challenges to wokeness are often performative. When they are sincere, their failure exposes ministers' lack of power. In any case, banning woke speakers or the dissemination of woke ideas, be it in the civil service or in schools, would be illiberal and destined to fail. To do so would represent a clampdown on intellectual freedom and institutional autonomy that could, before too long, end up being exploited by the very same groups such bans would be intended to curtail. In the meantime, an air of martyrdom would be lent to woke activists. For all these reasons, we can't resort to bans or legal edicts to stop the spread of woke thinking.

By far the biggest threat to woke rule comes not from government ministers or woke's internal inconsistencies, but from the vast majority of people who do not identify with the goals and aspirations of the cultural elite. The professional-managerial class prefers an acquiescent population. They need people to agree with their instructions or shut up. A lot of people keep quiet for fear of being labelled a bigot, being disciplined by their employer, or even losing their livelihood. But when pushed most people just do not agree with woke values.

Woke is not popular. A May 2021 YouGov survey suggested that just 41 per cent of Brits understand what the word 'woke' means, but of those who do most think it's a bad thing. Among those who say they know what woke is, just 29 per cent see themselves as woke, while 56 per cent do not.[3] It seems that the more people come to understand woke, the less they agree with it. Perhaps this is because woke's insistence on dividing people up according to identity groups proves suffocating for those not personally invested in a particular identity. Or perhaps it is down to the insistence on labelling people as oppressor or oppressed, which leaves no room for self-creation, while the perception of people as victims holds out little aspirational promise. The bottom line is: people are not stupid. They spot the hypocrisy of policies that purport to challenge racism yet emphasise race and the differences between people, boxing some in as victims and others as inherently guilty.

Woke values are certainly more prevalent among younger people, who have been socialised through school and higher education into accepting a particular way of thinking about society. But, even then, not all young people are woke. A 2021 survey conducted in the US reported that 55 per cent of 13- to 24-year-olds ('Generation Z') view cancel culture negatively. A majority (61 per cent) are either unsure or neutral on the topic of critical race theory, with 19 per cent expressing negative feelings towards its ideas.[4]

The unpopularity of woke means that, despite how things might seem to individuals being asked to wear pronoun badges at work or to attend mandatory diversity workshops, critics of woke policies and practices are rarely lone voices. It may not always seem like it, but there will always be others who feel the same way. The unpopularity of woke should make it possible to challenge policies and practices from within existing institutions.

We have seen some examples of pushback recently. In December 2020, academics at the University of Cambridge overwhelmingly rejected guidelines requiring them to be 'respectful' of the opinions and identities of others. Revised guidelines protected the rights of speakers to express 'controversial or unpopular opinions within the law' and stated that staff, students and visitors should be 'tolerant of the differing opinions of others'.[5] Elsewhere, it is at least in part down to the exposure of Stonewall's activities by journalists within the BBC that the broadcaster withdrew from the Stonewall Diversity Champions programme in 2021.[6]

More people must have their voices heard and their views represented, both within and outside of institutions. Publicly funded organisations – from the taxpayer-funded health service and education system to charities that depend on public donations to the licence-fee-funded BBC – need to be made more accountable to, and representative of, the society they serve. This requires more than just issuing reports or commissioning opinion polls. There needs to be a cultural shift towards recognising and valuing the contribution made by a far greater proportion of citizens.

Some institutions have been so colonised by woke values that the possibility of change coming from within is minimal. Fortunately, new organisations are being set up to challenge woke thinking from the outside. The Free Speech Union was founded in the UK by Toby Young in 2020 and regularly defends people at risk of losing their jobs for having expressed an unorthodox opinion. Counterweight and Don't Divide Us are other organisations that show solidarity with and provide support for people who fall foul of woke speech codes. Such groups point to an important way forward in challenging woke's grip on society.

The growing popularity of online publications like *spiked* and new media outlets like GB News challenges the political consensus that emerges from the *New York Times*, the *Guardian* and the BBC. Journalists like Bari Weiss who have resigned from legacy publications have found it possible to thrive independently using platforms like Substack. The previously mentioned LGB Alliance has also become a notable challenger to Stonewall's authority, and Restore Trust has recently been established to hold the leadership of the National Trust to account.

One exciting new development in higher education is the University of Austin. Committed to 'the fearless pursuit of truth', this Texas-based project is upfront in its commitment to academic freedom, unfettered intellectual inquiry and knowledge-based higher education. Founding member Bari Weiss says the 'anti-cancel culture' university will back 'witches who refuse to burn'. Led by Pano Kanelos, formerly president of St John's College in Annapolis, the university is driven by a clear analysis of what has gone wrong in higher education and a principled commitment to scholarly values. Kanelos criticises the world's leading universities for maintaining ancient commitments to truth and intellectual freedom while, in practice, failing to live up to even a shadow of such noble intentions. 'We can't wait for universities to fix themselves', he argues, 'so we're starting a new one'.[7]

Democracy

It is in the privacy of the voting booth that people express their rejection of woke most clearly. Democracy has been shown to defeat woke time and again. Democratic accountability is the best way to challenge the woke practices of the cultural elite. Perhaps more than anything else, the election of Donald Trump in 2016 – and his still impressive vote count in his 2020 defeat – spoke to the rejection of woke values in America. In the UK, we see that when Keir Starmer and other Labour Party higher-ups are unable to say that only women have a cervix, they stop being taken seriously by voters. In a May 2021 by-election, Labour lost Hartlepool, a constituency in the north-east of England that the party had held since the seat was first created. Soon afterwards, former Labour leader Tony Blair said his party was, essentially, too woke to win elections.

The gubernatorial election in Virginia in November 2021 represented yet another ballot-box defeat for woke values. Parents furious about critical race theory in schools helped swing it for the Republicans, almost a year to the day after Biden had easily won the state. But it's not just in Virginia. All across the US – and increasingly in the UK, too – parents unhappy about CRT-inspired teaching practices in their children's schools have begun to organise on Facebook and in their communities.

Even on single issues, such as toppling statues, votes do not always go the way that woke activists want. Denbigh in Wales has a statue of the explorer Sir Henry Morton Stanley, best known for tracking down Dr David Livingstone in what is now Tanzania in 1871. The BLM movement sparked a debate in the town about Stanley's role in the colonisation of Africa. Campaigners called for the statue's removal, but local council officers decided to put Stanley's fate to a public vote. By a clear majority, residents backed keeping the statue.[8] Likewise, in Sheffield, the local authority launched a public consultation on whether street names and public art that were alleged to perpetuate racist or outdated messages should be removed. A majority of respondents did not want to see any changes. A council spokesperson said: 'We acknowledge this strong feeling and are not currently intending to change any of the existing street names or remove any statues.'[9] Such acts of local democracy could provide a useful model for resolving similar disputes elsewhere.

But we can go further. At present, the electoral register could be used to recruit people to sit on any number of local or even national decision-making bodies, just like people are appointed to undertake jury service. Citizens' parliaments could be set up to help shape policy in a whole range of areas, from transport to health provision. The one proviso would have to be that people are genuinely left to decide issues for themselves, rather than guided towards predetermined conclusions by expert supervisors. A further benefit of these citizens' parliaments is that they would require greater mixing between people of all different social classes. In the past, churches and parish councils brought the political class into contact with the public. Today, these institutions need reinventing.

Clearly, letting the public have more of a voice only works if it goes hand in hand with a rigorous defence of free speech. Rather than engaging in hollow posturing against woke, the UK's Conservative government would be better off not pushing through legislation such as the Online Safety Bill, which would further restrict what people can say online. Defending free speech means pushing back not just against censorious government legislation, but also employee codes of conduct that punish staff for utterances made away from the workplace, and Big Tech censorship that limits what can be expressed in the modern public square.

Ultimately, woke is a defensive stance from an elite that has lost its authority. Woke ideas provide a moral and political justification for an attack on the lives of working-class people. That left-wing 'progressives' have so readily adopted this way of thinking is shameful. Woke has much bluster, but it offers little in the way of substance and next to nothing to improve the lives of ordinary people. For this reason, woke will never gain ground among citizens who recognise that people have far more in common than the cultural elite would have us believe. It is only through coming together that we can hope to forge a freer, more democratic and truly egalitarian future.

The UK's Brexit vote showed us that when individuals demand that their voices be listened to, major change can occur. This is a call to courage everywhere. The first step in challenging woke is for people to speak out and join up with others who feel the same way. Woke may have won, but only for now.

Endnotes

[1] Boris Johnson: Post-Covid world needs to be 'more feminine', *Evening Standard*, 15 June 2021

[2] Carrie Johnson urges Tories to back transgender rights, *Guardian*, 5 October 2021

[3] What does 'woke' mean to Britons?, Matthew Smith, YouGov, 18 May 2021

[4] More Gen Zers have negative views about capitalism than of critical race theory, Morning Consult, 8 July 2021

[5] Cambridge University votes to safeguard free speech, BBC News, 9 December 2020

[6] BBC withdraws from Stonewall LGBT diversity scheme after Nolan investigation, *Belfast Telegraph*, 10 November 2021

[7] We can't wait for universities to fix themselves. So we're starting a new one, Pano Kanelos, *Common Sense*, 8 November 2021

[8] Africa explorer HM Stanley statue to stay in Denbigh, BBC News, 27 October 2021

[9] Sheffield's racist street names 'will not change', council says, BBC News, 29 November 2021

Index

About sp!ked

spiked is the magazine that wants to change the world as well as report on it. Edited by Tom Slater, and launched in 2001, it is irreverent where others conform, questioning where others wallow in received wisdom, and radical where others cling to the status quo.

At a time when it is fashionable to cancel 'problematic' people, to sideline voters when they give the 'wrong' answer, and to treat human beings as a drain on the planet, we put the case for human endeavour, the expansion of democracy, and freedom of speech with no ifs or buts.

Our motto is 'question everything' – or as the *New York Times* put it, we are 'the often-biting British publication fond of puncturing all manner of ideological balloons'. Read us every day at spiked-online.com